Understanding
The Tempest

The Greenwood Press "Literature in Context" Series
Student Casebooks to Issues, Sources, and Historical Documents

Understanding
The Tempest

A STUDENT CASEBOOK TO ISSUES, SOURCES, AND HISTORICAL DOCUMENTS

Faith Nostbakken

The Greenwood Press
"Literature in Context" Series
Claudia Durst Johnson, Series Editor

Westport, Connecticut • London

For Rick Bowers,
for his insight, enthusiasm, and generosity

Contents

Contents

Acknowledgments

I wish to thank and recognize Greenwood Press for offering me yet another opportunity to add to their "Literature in Context" series. I also gratefully acknowledge Rick Bowers, who has been my first respondent on all four books that I've contributed to this series. His enthusiasm and critical eye have been invaluable in the preparation of each manuscript for publication. Thanks also go to my longtime friend, Kim McLean-Fiander, for completing some vital research in England when I could not do the work myself. Pam Farvolden and Arlette Zinck listened patiently to some of the early ideas that eventually came to life in various chapters. These supports added greatly to my own work as I faced the challenges and encountered the delights of Shakespeare's magical "last" play.

Introduction: For Students and Teachers

The Tempest is a play written in Shakespeare's maturity. Apart from two collaborations, it is the last play he wrote and has often been seen as his swan song, his final artistic effort for the stage. It is difficult to categorize, having been termed a comedy, a tragicomedy, and a romance by various editors and commentators through the centuries. What makes it other than tragedy is the celebration of life and renewal through repentance and forgiveness. What makes it other than comedy is the series of political plots involving attempted murder and usurpation. What marks the play as romance is not only the love relationship between Miranda and Ferdinand, but the marvelous sense of wonder and enchantment that spills out over the whole play through Prospero's magical spells and the spectacles of extravagance he devises for one cause or another. This is a play about Art, many would say, and Prospero is the artist who controls the medium and reveals just how fantastical and powerful the limits of Art can be.

The following study is written under the rubrics of a series titled "Literature in Context." The first chapter focuses on the question of genre categories and the dramatic and poetic elements of the play—looking at the Art within the art. The four chapters that follow it attempt to shed some light on the historical issues and concerns that created the "context" for the play when it was written, likely in 1610 or 1611 during the reign of King James I. Chapter 2 identifies the "New World" as one of the contexts for *The Tempest*. Shakespeare makes several references that allow one to consider what was happening in the New World of the Americas and the West Indies, particularly what was known about a shipwrecked group of colonials headed for America but stranded for a year on a deserted West Indies island. Shakespeare's play invites a sense of otherworldliness where the island seems both enchanted and haunted at the same time, a place that causes Gonzalo to muse about the perfect Golden Age and Caliban to curse about contemporary tormenting spirits. Chapter 3 gives the word "magic" to the haunting and the enchanting elements of the play and explores the history of magic up to and including the early seventeenth century, providing Prospero's art a context within the mystical practices of astrology and alchemy. The intersection and tension between religion and science play an important role in perceptions about magic and its relative influence in political as well as intellectual spheres in the European Renaissance. Chapter 4 focuses more specifically on the political aspects of the play, tracing legitimate and illegitimate uses of power in England and on the continent that add weight and significance to the many treasonous plots occurring within *The Tempest* or providing the background for its interactions. Chapter 5 looks at social issues connected to the play, particularly the import of the betrothal between Miranda and Ferdinand. As celebratory as this event appears to be for Milan and Naples, it too has political ramifications and draws our attention to both the familial and court aspects of royal marriages and celebrations in King James's time. That *The Tempest* was played at the wedding of King James's daughter Elizabeth to a European prince in 1613 allows a variety of contextual insights to be offered.

Shakespeare's plays are always about "performance in context" as well as "literature in context." Consequently, chapter 6 examines how *The Tempest* has been received, adapted, interpreted, and appropriated through the centuries to the present. Changing social and political expectations and attitudes, as well as artistic perspectives, have influenced responses to this play. Of significance is an acutely intentional effort to appropriate—that is, to adopt or make use of—the characters Prospero and Caliban in the opposition between power holders and power servers, especially in the context of colonial powers subjugating and exploiting indigenous or aboriginal peoples. From this angle art becomes politics and sometimes simply forgets to be art because of the significance of politics in culture. This is part of the unfolding story of *The Tempest* as both performance and literature are constantly being given new birth and new life in new forms for each culture that emerges from the past.

The final chapter in this study attempts to focus on today's emerging cultures and looks at ways in which aspects of *The Tempest* connect with contemporary concerns in recent times around the globe. Two political topics are considered in light of the popular politicization of Prospero and Caliban. The first is the postcolonial endeavor of the government in Zimbabwe to redistribute land to landless blacks from the minority whites who have dominated the farming economy for almost a century since the British came and settled in that central South African country and claimed it as their own. The second is the protest movement of anticorporate globalization that recognizes the burgeoning power of transnational companies at the expense of national governments and civil societies, as well as the efforts to raise awareness and heighten consciousness about this emerging power struggle. The last two sections explore the more traditional comedic and romantic rhythms suggested by the play, looking at paranormal phenomena as a modern parallel to the "magic" of Prospero's wand and at the genre of fantasy as a current fashion in literature that celebrates some of the same enchantment that Shakespeare presents in his play.

A variety of documents excerpted throughout the book invite direct involvement in the historical and current topics being presented. The range of materials includes the following:

a letter from a shipwrecked Englishman
a treatise on witchcraft and demonology
a letter of defense written by a Renaissance magician
passages from plays about magic
an account of an English traitor's execution
a king's treatise of advice to his son
a king's speech to parliament
a counselor's advice to a reigning prince
a sonnet
Elizabethan marriage conduct books
an account of a royal wedding
words from a director, an actor, and a stage observer
a newspaper article about Zimbabwe
the voices of anti-globalization activists
passages from *The Lord of the Rings* and the Harry Potter series

At the end of each chapter or subsection, a series of "Topics for Written and Oral Discussion" offer a wide range of ways to respond to the material. Some questions address specific issues in the documents themselves to encourage comprehension of the ideas, facts, and thoughts being presented. Other questions are much broader, suggesting connections between the documents and Shakespeare's play or between material from different chapters. The responses elicited range from formal essays to classroom debates, from dramatic presentations to drawing and musical assignments, from invented diary entries for various characters to scripted imaginary encounters between fictional and historical figures. It is hoped that the broad scope from specific questions to more complex inquiries, from formal answers to informal activities, will stimulate young minds and imaginations, providing alternative approaches to choose from in engaging with Shakespeare's play.

This study aims to cultivate an interdisciplinary approach to *The Tempest* by examining many diverse contexts including historical, cultural, social, political, and philosophical perspectives. The variety of angles presented as well as the conflicts or controversy shown to sometimes exist between viewpoints within any one discipline, such as the attitudes toward magic in Shakespeare's time, encourage readings of the play that move beyond simplistic generalizations to a more informed understanding of the complexities woven into the drama. Interpretation is a skill and an art that matures out of practice and critical exchange. For those approaching the play for the first time and for those coming to it with a broader or deeper awareness of the issues, *Understanding The Tempest* attempts to provide the tools for critical exchange that can enrich appreciation of Shakespeare's dramatic art as a whole, and the wonders and challenges that this play in particular continue to present to today's audiences and readers.

The Tempest has traveled well through time.

NOTES

All quotations from *The Tempest* throughout this book come from the Signet Classic version: William Shakespeare, *The Tempest*, Ed. Robert Langbaum (1964; New York: Penguin Books, 1998).

Spelling and punctuation have been regularized and modernized for clarity where necessary in excerpted documents included in the four historical chapters (2 through 6) of this study.

1 _____

Dramatic Analysis

This first chapter begins by placing *The Tempest* in the context of its dramatic tradition, tracing the characteristics of genre from tragedy and comedy to romance, identifying some of the key patterns that link *The Tempest* to other plays before and after it, and looking at nondramatic influences on this theatrical romance. Following that overview, discussion will focus more directly on literary and dramatic elements within the play that give it shape and meaning.

ROMANCE AND THE DRAMATIC TRADITION

Although probably written in 1611, Shakespeare's *The Tempest* did not appear in print until it was published in the First Folio, the first collection of Shakespeare's plays printed in 1623, seven years after Shakespeare's death. The First Folio divided the plays into three categories, comedies, tragedies, and histories. *The Tempest* was listed as a comedy and appeared as the first play in the edition, although it is thought to be the last play written by Shakespeare alone. No one knows exactly why *The Tempest* appears first in the 1623 collection, but many see it as Shakespeare's intentional conclusion to his life as a playwright. Therefore many critics read Prospero's dominance in the play employing his magical "Art" (always capitalized) as a representative of Shakespeare himself exercising his dramatic art for the last time. Observers surmise that such a self-conscious act of stagecraft deserved a place of prominence at the beginning of the First Folio, as a drama about how to read and appreciate plays.

Equally as interesting is the fact that the First Folio editors labeled *The Tempest* a comedy. The following discussion about genre can help us understand the tradition out of which *The Tempest* was written, what characterized its comic status, and why in modern times it has been relegated to a separate category altogether, that of romance.

Genre Categories and Tragicomedy

Genre categories in Shakespeare's time were somewhat loose to begin with partly because secular playwriting in England was a comparatively new literary and social act. Although drama had its seeds in church liturgy of the medieval period when early plays began to enact the Christian salvation story from pageant wagons in village streets every year on the feast day of Corpus Christi, drama as a relatively stable secular public performance really began in earnest—or perhaps more in deliberate "playfulness"—with the construction of the first London playhouse, the Theatre, built in 1576. Shakespeare began writing the first of his 38 plays a decade later and charted new ground in many of his works as he played with the boundaries of known forms, writing comedies such as *Measure for Measure* later termed "problem plays" because their disturbing qualities make them difficult to accept as "comic" or lighthearted productions. For that matter, two history plays, *Richard II* and *Richard III,* have as their protagonists men who display tragic aspects, although both plays in "historical" fashion focus on the social and political angle of the plot over and above the protagonist's plight. Contrariwise, several plays listed as tragedies, including *Julius Caesar,* can be considered "historical" because of their focus on ancient Roman history. Categories, in other words, were never meant to constrain or limit drama but rather to provide a model or framework to allow the playwright a structure for his or her creativity. Shakespeare even makes some fun of the distinctions through the words of Polonius in *Hamlet* who indicates in his long-winded, pretentious fashion the various permutations of dramatic form one might behold, including "tragedy, comedy, history, pastoral, pastoral-comical, historical-pastoral, [tragical-historical, tragical-comical-historical-pastoral]" (*Hamlet* 2.2.396–399). Such a mouthful of words is amusing as it ridicules both Polonius for his seeming sophistication and the art form itself for its endless possibilities of transformation.

It is perhaps useful, however, to highlight the main features of tragedy and comedy as they oppose one another in order to see how *The Tempest,* initially identified as a comedy but sometimes later termed a tragicomedy, comes up the middle between the two genres and takes on new characterizing features. An influence on playwrights in Shakespeare's time, Greek philosopher Aristotle (384–322 B.C.) distinguished the two genres by suggesting that tragedy began quietly but ended in horror while comedy began with conflict but ended in peace. This distinction sets up other expectations for the two genres. In tragedy, an individual character is central, while in comedy, the community is the prime focus. In Shakespearean tragedy, suffering accompanies a serious struggle that usually concludes with the protagonist's death while lighter struggles of comedy move toward life's celebration in which regeneration and communal resolution are more important than individual characters. Tragedies such as *Hamlet* or *Macbeth* closely follow the actions of the central hero to sustain the emotional intensity of his struggle which revolves around public or political responsibility. Comedies—more loosely developed—often involve subplots or simultaneous overlapping plots because of their focus on community. If death is the predictable ending of tragedy, marriage is the typical resolution of comedy with its plot often revolving around lovers and romance.

John Fletcher, the collaborator on Shakespeare's last two plays, wrote his own plays independently, as well, and was interested in the ways tragedy and comedy might come together. In defining tragicomedy, he suggested that this mixed genre did not simply combine "mirth and killing" but that it lacked death although it brought some characters near enough to it as to be not considered comedy. That *The Tempest* should sometimes be regarded as a tragicomedy makes sense according to this definition. The play is not typical romantic comedy with love and marriage as the sole focus of the plot, even though the match between Miranda and Ferdinand is an important element in Prospero's larger plan. Moreover, the play is not filled with mirth, even if the buffoonery of the drunken trio, Caliban, Stephano, and Trinculo, offers some potentially amusing moments. There is, in fact, a very serious situation unfolding both in Prospero's narration of his past and in the plot itself. That situation involves treason and murder. Prospero was cast out to sea and left to the mercy of the elements when his brother Antonio persuaded Alonso, the king of Naples, to assist him in overthrowing Prospero and taking his dukedom of Milan. After years on a Mediterranean island where Prospero explains how he and Miranda landed safely by the aid of providence, the pattern of treachery and intended murder repeats itself as Antonio convinces Sebastian to assist him in murdering the sleeping king of Naples and his companion Gonzalo and so become the new king of Naples. In a similar plot, Caliban persuades Stephano and Trinculo to help him murder Prospero and thus take over the island. Only Ariel's intervention in the first scheme and Prospero's interruption of the second one prevent serious harm from occurring. The play, as John Fletcher would suggest, lacks death but not danger, bringing some characters close enough to destruction so as not to be a typical comedy. And yet the potential deaths never quite engage us emotionally as an audience and the comic element prevails in the conclusion, with the celebration of Miranda and

Ferdinand's betrothal and an emphasis on communal resolution as characters are reunited, pardoned, and promised a safe return home.

Romance

If *The Tempest* can be seen as a blended genre—tragicomedy—which was identified and recognized in its own time, it has more often been described in recent times as a romance than a tragicomedy. The word "romance" was first used for plays such as *The Tempest* by literary scholar Edward Dowden in 1877, more than 250 years after Shakespeare wrote his final plays. Scholars began to see Shakespeare's last four independent plays written between 1607 and 1613 as sharing common qualities or characteristics that set them apart from other so-called comedies and tragedies. Thus, a new category emerged for *Pericles, Cymbeline, The Winter's Tale,* and *The Tempest.* But "romance" was by no means a new term, being based on a tradition of romantic literature that existed as far back as in ancient Greece.

Greek romances from the second and third centuries unfolded tales in which love suffers abnormal trials, such as jealous intrigues and conflicts between male friendships and romantic love (Boyce 555). Lovers might be parted more than once and often grief arises over a dead body mistakenly believed to be one of the lovers (Wells 70). There are oracles and dreams, and fantastic journeys to exotic places. Knights appear demonstrating displays of chivalry, while the heroine's virginity is valued and emphasized. The main characters belong to royal or noble classes, and although the plot is compelling, the characters' motives seldom appear realistic. More emphasis is geared toward action than to character development. The element of the supernatural is introduced through appearances of monsters, other nonhuman beings, and pagan gods. As the epic plot develops, many improbabilities, absurdities, coincidences, and mistaken identities are introduced, but the story ultimately moves toward reunion, reconciliation, and a happy conclusion to the love affair. This was escapist literature, designed to be fantastic and meant solely for pleasure rather than instruction or moral purpose. Such romances were popular in Shakespeare's time, having been revived from antiquity and used as a model by more contemporary writers. The genre was especially popular in King James's reign when Shakespeare wrote his four late plays subsequently to be labeled "romances" (Boyce 555).

"Romance," applied to these four plays, refers to recurrent patterns and attitudes toward the subject matter rather than rigid structures or formal characteristics. Some of the patterns reflect the interests of Greek romances: a "love story," noble or court characters, supernatural elements, fantastic or exotic places and other unrealistic elements, and a resolution focused on reconciliation. Thus, in *The Tempest,* there is the sudden love interest between Miranda and Ferdinand, and the supernatural world of spirits, witches, devils, and magicians, with the main plot of Prospero's relationship to Ariel and Caliban and Caliban's identification as the son of a witch and the devil. The setting is an enchanted island, and most of the plot is based on improbable or incredible occurrences brought about by Prospero's magic, from the initial sea storm to the meeting between Miranda and Ferdinand, to the many ways that Prospero causes other characters to fall asleep at particular times, immobilized from action or vexed with visions or spirits. Ultimately, the play ends in harmony with the announcement of Ferdinand and Miranda's betrothal, the reunion of lost characters assumed to be dead, and the return of Prospero's dukedom after 12 years spent in exile.

Along with these Greek-derived patterns in the plot, romances emphasize other qualities that are less apparent in either traditional tragedy or comedy. These include special attention not only to lovers' relationships but also to the family unit, with close ties between parent and child demonstrated in the connection, as, for example, between Prospero and Miranda, or with children lost to their parents and then restored, as Ferdinand is to Alonso. Included with the supernatural elements are other visual spectacles, such as the storm in act 1 of *The Tempest,* the visions that Prospero conjures up of the banquet table that suddenly disappears, or the show of mythical spirits who entertain Ferdinand and Miranda, with one of the goddesses descending on them from above. Music adds to the visual impression as well, and is not simply ornamental but crucial to the action of the plot in *The Tempest* as characters are led here and there on the island by the sound of Ariel's pipe and tabor. All these elements together foster a strong sense of wonder, which is made all the more apparent by Ferdinand's response to Miranda, "My prime request, / Which I do last pronounce, is (O you wonder!) / If you be maid or no?" (1.2.426–428), and by Miranda's response to the human world she has never known before until she meets the shipwrecked party at the end of the play, and says,

> O, wonder!
> How many goodly creatures are there here!
> How beauteous mankind is! O brave new world
> That has such people in't! (5.1.181–184)

Even Miranda's name means "wonderful," as she represents in her own reactions and in the reactions she elicits from others the wonder, the awe, the admiration, and the astonishment that pervade the entire enchanted play.

Finally, what characterizes the romances as a special category of Shakespeare's drama is the strong attitude of forgiveness central to the reconciliation and

harmony at the close of the play. In fact, although the audience remains unaware of it until late in the plot, Prospero's intention seems to be first to chas-
ten the guilty parties but then to bring them together so that grace can
transform the patterns of error, revenge, and hatred that have been manifest
among characters both prior to the play's action and in the conspiracies bred
on the island after the shipwreck occurs. As Prospero says, "The rarer action
is / In virtue than in vengeance" (5.1.27–28). Prospero offers mercy, unde-
served pardon, rather than demonstrating a need to keep score and repay
wrongs. The play moves from suffering—Prospero's that began 12 years before the shipwreck, and the others' from their loss and isolation on the island—
to deliverance for all. Even Antonio and Sebastian, who exhibit no signs of
remorse or repentance, share in the bounty of Prospero's pardon. And so there
is a sense of rebirth not only as those presumed dead appear again in living
flesh, but as those separated by hostilities are reunited and given a chance to
rectify the past and begin life anew. This is romance: the possibility of the
miraculous, the celebration of renewal.

Sources and Traditions

Most of Shakespeare's plays have as a source for their plots other previously
written stories or portions of history that Shakespeare borrows from another
author. Typically, Shakespeare reshapes the material he borrows according to
stage expectations and refashions them according to his own imagination. *The
Tempest* is one of very few plays in which Shakespeare's plot does not derive
from another existing source. It appears to be a drama of Shakespeare's own
invention. However, there are some stories and traditions that provide parallels or echoes in Shakespeare's characterization or the development of his plot.
The influence from Greek romance has already been discussed. Two other
more specific influences or suggestions also come from classical myth and legend.

The first is Virgil's Latin epic poem, *Aeneid* (c. 30 B.C.), about Aeneas, a Tro-
jan who fled the city of Troy when it fell and experienced many adventures before he came to be known as the founder of the great empire of Rome. In *The
Tempest,* the argument between Gonzalo, Antonio, and Sebastian about the
Widow Dido and the association of the African city of Tunis with the legendary city of Carthage (2.1.77–106) invite a connection between Shakespeare's plot and the adventures of Aeneas. Dido was the founder of Carthage,
a city very close to or perhaps even identified with the North African city of
Tunis in Shakespeare's time. In Virgil's account, Aeneas and Dido fall in love
with one another after Aeneas and his mariners have been shipwrecked on a
Mediterranean island in a storm raised by the goddess Juno. Dido had previously been married but her husband had been murdered. Sebastian and An-

tonio mock Gonzalo's reference to "widow Dido" because although she had been widowed, her amorous relationship with Aeneas causes her reputation to shift from faithful "widow" to erotic lover. When Aeneas receives strong counsel to leave Carthage and continue on his journey to found Rome, he leaves Dido and she kills herself in a passion at his departure. Although the story is by no means a source for *The Tempest*, the shipwreck on a Mediterranean island after a storm caused by supernatural powers is similar in both plots, and Alonso and Ferdinand's journey from Tunis in Africa to Italy via the island is a movement comparable to Aeneas's travels. Aeneas also encountered a banquet at which harpies, like Ariel, appeared. These connections highlight a heroic element to Shakespeare's plot and heighten concerns Prospero raises about Ferdinand's appropriate treatment of Miranda, for if Ferdinand in any way resembles the heroic Aeneas, Prospero ought to be concerned about his daughter's virginity and safety in Ferdinand's presence as well as in Caliban's.

The second specific classical reference in *The Tempest* is to Medea, an enchantress or witch who became known for her vengefulness, violence, jealousy, and sorcery. Caliban's mother, the witch Sycorax, perhaps raises a possible parallel, but oddly enough Shakespeare draws the direct connection not between Medea and Sycorax but between Medea and Prospero. Prospero's significant soliloquy in act 5, scene 1 in which he announces his intention to "abjure" his "rough magic" clearly echoes the very words of one of Medea's speeches in the collection of tales, *Metamorphoses*, by Roman poet Ovid (43 B.C.–17 A.D.). Prospero's speech begins, "Ye elves of hills, brooks, standing lakes, and groves" (5.1.33); Medea's speech, with very similar words, includes the following lines:

> Ye Ayres and winds: ye Elves of Hills, of Brookes, of Woods alone,
> Of standing Lakes, and of the Night approach ye everyone.
> Through help of whom (the crooked banks much wondering at the thing)
> I have compelled streams to run clean backward to their spring.
> By charms I make the calm Seas rough, and make the rough Seas plain,
> And cover all the Sky with Clouds, and chase them thence again.
> By charms I raise and lay the winds, and burst the Viper's jaw,
> And from the bowels of the Earth both stones and trees do draw.
> Whole woods and Forests I remove: I make the Mountains shake,
> And even the Earth itself to groan and fearfully to quake.
> I call up dead men from their graves: and thee O lightsome Moon
> I darken oft, though beaten brass abate thy peril soon.
> Our Sorcery dims the Morning fair, and darks the Sun at Noon.
> —Ovid, *Metamorphoses*. Trans. Arthur Golding (1567),
> The Seventh Book, p. 83v, ll. 265–77

The relationship Shakespeare draws between Prospero and Medea is particularly interesting in terms of the portrayal of Prospero's magical art. If Prospero is a white magician, then what is he doing echoing the practices of an evil sorcerer? This issue receives much more attention in chapter 3 on Magic: Religion, Art, and Science, but is of significance here because it indicates how allusions or references to other literature can enrich the meanings or possible understanding of the play without necessarily being a direct source for the plot.

Two final influences on Shakespeare's romance are worth noting. These are the court masque and a series of documents about a shipwreck on an island in Bermuda in 1610, the year before the first recorded performance of *The Tempest*. A masque was a type of entertainment performed for court audiences. It was like drama without having a strong story line but involving music, dance, spectacle, magic, and mythological characters. Masques were performed as early as Henry VIII's reign in England but became especially popular during the monarchy of James I. *The Tempest* includes a mini-masque that Prospero arranges for Ferdinand and Miranda's entertainment at their betrothal. It involves three mythological figures, the goddesses, Ceres, Iris, and Juno, as well as a number of nymphs who dance. Apart from this performance within the play, the importance of music throughout *The Tempest,* the dependence on magic for the plot, and numerous visual spectacles all contribute to masquelike effects. More will be said about the play's masquelike elements in chapter 5 on Society: Marriage and the Court.

The second contemporary influence on the plot derived from information found in letters about a shipwreck that Shakespeare clearly knew about in which a single ship in a fleet on its way to a British colony in Virginia was destroyed in a storm, its survivors landing on a deserted island from which they later departed, and to the surprise of the other colonists, arrived safely in Virginia. This story will be given attention in chapter 2 about The New World: The Discoverer and the Discovered. Here it is simply important to note that while Shakespeare did not borrow from a single existing plot, he did rely on a series of materials and traditions to shape the details of his drama, influence its atmosphere, and enrich the interaction among his characters. The play as tragicomedy, as romance, as celebration of art, has its roots in Shakespeare's Renaissance surroundings and in literary patterns from his past.

POETIC AND DRAMATIC PATTERNS

As a text for performance, *The Tempest* involves language and gesture together to engage the audience by creating the illusion of an invented reality on stage. But the play text is also a literary work that includes patterns of language, plot, image, and characterization that may not be immediately obvious to spectators watching a stage production. These patterns become apparent in a close reading of the text, although they can also unconsciously—even if not consciously—add to an audience's psychological, emotional, and intellectual response to a performance. Spending time with the words on the page can, therefore, create a greater appreciation of Shakespeare's role as both poet and dramatist, allowing for a more conscious awareness of the connection and tension between the various elements of language, imagery, character, and theme, thus contributing to the experience of readers and spectators alike.

Language

Language in *The Tempest* is rich and full of variety, helping to establish the context of the action and set the scene, as well as characterize the different groups on stage. Unlike most of Shakespeare's plays, the action in *The Tempest* takes place in one location—the island, though at various points on it—and occurs during the same time frame that it takes for a three-hour performance of the plot. In other words, there are no long periods of time between scenes that have to be explained or sudden changes of setting that need clarification. The experience is focused and compressed. The story, however, has significant background material, marked by Antonio's seizure of Prospero's dukedom 12 years before the play's action begins. The way Shakespeare incorporates important details of that background into the plot is through narration in act 1, scene 2 in which Prospero explains to Miranda where they have come from and how they came to be on the island. Although narration is one way to use language, it is not dramatic; it is what one expects in a novel rather than a play. Shakespeare helps to keep it interesting partly by the very dramatic opening scene of the storm which piques our interest to want to know more about what is happening, and partly by turning the narration into a dialogue between Prospero and Miranda in which we identify with Miranda as being ignorant of the circumstances and echo her interjections as she responds with shock and wonder to the news she receives. Still, this is an unusual style for Shakespeare, to have his characters talk more than act; it is a unique characteristic of *The Tempest* that action is often secondary to the language of explanation and that what action does occur is orchestrated by the magical powers of the main character, Prospero. In fact, he speaks more than a quarter of the lines in the play, and no other character comes close to matching his dominance by line-count alone.

Language is used not only to establish the significance of the past but also to set the scene for *The Tempest*, especially describing the climate and appearance of the island. Considering that theater sets were quite simple in Shakespeare's time, description is an essential aid to the imagination in entering the world of the play. Adrian and Gonzalo offer their observations as they land on the island after the storm. Adrian notes that "It must needs be of subtle, tender, and delicate temperance.... The air breathes upon us here most sweetly"

(2.1.45–49), and Gonzalo remarks that "Here is everything advantageous to life.... How lush and lusty the grass looks! How green!" (2.1.52–55). Ironically, however, the monstrous, churlish character Caliban provides one of the most poetic and wistful descriptions of the island's atmosphere as he explains to Stephano and Trinculo the significance of the sounds they hear:

> Be not afeard; the isle is full of noises,
> Sounds and sweet airs that give delight and hurt not.
> Sometimes a thousand twangling instruments
> Will hum about mine ears; and sometimes voices
> That, if I then had waked after long sleep,
> Will make me sleep again; and then, in dreaming,
> The clouds methought would open and show riches
> Ready to drop upon me, that, when I waked,
> I cried to dream again. (3.2.140–148)

Caliban's dreamy description helps to establish the enchanted quality of the island which even he, in his coarsened nature, seems to appreciate.

Language and Character

Along with narrating the past and setting the scene, the play's language is used to distinguish groups and individualize characters. The main form of Shakespeare's poetry in his drama is blank verse: unrhymed lines with 10 syllables in which the stress or accent falls on every second syllable. This form is called iambic pentameter, in which "iambic" refers to the pattern of an unstressed syllable followed by a stressed syllable and in which "pentameter" refers to the number of accented or stressed syllables—five—in the line. Blank verse closely approximates the natural rhythm of the speaking voice, thus drawing together the sound and sense of prose and poetry.

Typically, Shakespeare reserves blank verse for his upper-class or noble characters or for serious and dignified speeches. Prose characterizes lower-class figures and humorous conversations. It is easy to identify lines of poetry because each new line begins with a capital letter while the prose speeches run on with no break from one line to the next. Often, however, one line of blank verse is split between two or three characters, the pattern being identified by the indentation of the second—and possibly the third—line all adding up to 10 syllables. Throughout *The Tempest,* Prospero, Miranda, and the other court characters speak in blank verse. In the second scene, for example, Miranda begins, "If by your art, my dearest father, you have / Put the wild waters in this roar, allay them" (1.2.1–2), and Prospero's later response follows the same unrhymed poetic pattern: "I should inform thee farther. Lend thy hand / And pluck my magic garment from me. So." (1.2.23–24). By contrast, the social inferiors, who also provide some of the play's humor, Stephano and Trinculo, speak always in prose. This simple linguistic distinction marks the stature of the characters and differentiates the serious from the comic elements throughout the play.

However, such patterns are not rigid, and some significant exceptions are worth noting. The first scene, for example, is characterized almost entirely by prose, even when court characters such as Gonzalo speak. This is a deliberate departure from convention to suggest that the storm is a social leveler treating everyone equally, from the common boatswain to the royal characters who travel with him. As the boatswain acknowledges with his ill-mannered question to Gonzalo, "What cares these roarers for the name of king?" (1.1.16–17), the stormy sea makes no distinction between men with royal authority and sailors hard at work: all face potential death. By simple attention to language, Shakespeare enhances the meaning of these lines.

Two other characters interesting for the variety of their language are Ariel and Caliban. Ariel is a spirit who does not fit into the two contrasting categories of noble and lower-class characters. When he addresses Prospero, he adopts the language of the court, speaking in blank verse. But when he wanders the island, he makes music, sometimes playing the rough songs of Stephano, Trinculo, and Caliban or barking like a dog, and sometimes singing in short rhyming lyric lines of poetry, such as his song to Ferdinand that begins, "Full fathom five thy father lies; / Of his bones are coral made" (1.2.397–398). The rhyme and the shortness of the verse contribute to a light atmosphere that suggests Ariel's airy quality as a spirit, while his ability to join in with the music of the three drunkards indicates his adaptability as a character who is not human.

Caliban is a rough and monstrous creature who is not white, European, and civilized. His language reflects the complexity of his character. He is capable of speaking in blank verse when he converses with Prospero or even when he describes the mysterious beauty of the island to his drunken companions in the lines quoted above (3.2.140–148), but sometimes he speaks prose along with Stephano and Trinculo. More provocatively, Caliban admits to Prospero, "You taught me language, and my profit on't / Is, I know how to curse" (1.2.363–364). If Ariel as an unconventional figure is a singer of songs, Caliban is master of curses. Even in the poetic language of blank verse, his words are foul and filled with hate: "All the infections that the sun sucks up / From bogs, fens, flats, on Prospero fall, and make him / By inchmeal a disease!" (2.2.1–3). Caliban is a fishlike, doglike "mooncalf" or human monster of unusual, even bizarre appearance who combines the poetry he learned from an exiled duke with the curses he learned from his witch-mother, Sycorax. Both he and Ariel are developed as characters by their language, by what they say and the way they say it. Shakespeare's deliberate use of language serves a variety of functions from relaying the past in narration to setting the scene by description, to conveying qualities that breathe life into his characters and distinguish them, one from another.

Imagery

Language can be shaped into images with a visual or sensual appeal that adds to the overall effect of the drama. Throughout *The Tempest,* for example, images circulate that refer to the four elements thought in Renaissance times to be the foundation of all matter in the universe: earth, air, water, and fire. The sea serves as a prominent image especially immediately after the storm. Francisco, one of the lords, describes how Ferdinand embarked from the damaged ship:

> I saw him beat the surges under him
> And ride upon their backs. He trod the water,
> Whose enmity he flung aside, and breasted
> The surge most swol'n that met him. (2.1.119–122)

Such imagery magnifies the experience of the first scene, also identifying it with Prospero and Miranda's fortune as they, too, were cast out on the water to live or die. Prospero offers a picture of the stormy violence they encountered:

> There they hoist us,
> To cry to th' sea that roared to us; to sigh
> To th' winds, whose pity, sighing back again,
> Did us but loving wrong. (1.2.148–151)

Ariel, whose spirit's nature allows him to move freely and transform himself, describes to Prospero his own adaptability to the elements:

> Grave sir, hail! I come
> To answer thy best pleasure; be't to fly,
> To swim, to dive into the fire, to ride
> On the curled clouds. To thy strong bidding task
> Ariel and all his quality. (1.2.189–193)

Caliban is more closely associated with the earth than the air as he says,

> And I with my long nails will dig thee pignuts,
> Show thee a jay's nest, and instruct thee how
> To snare the nimble marmoset. (2.2.176–178)

With so many references to the elements, weather even becomes a metaphor that Gonzalo uses to describe Alonso's mood: "It is foul weather in us all, good sir, / When you are cloudy" (2.1.146–147). Imagery about the raw elements of nature is appropriate in a play in which all the characters are vulnerable to the wildness beyond civilization, where a magician can control the effects of the wind and the sea, and where spirits, monsters, and people of various social circumstances interact.

Another set of images revolves around the shifting level of consciousness between waking, sleeping, and dreaming. Prospero exercises his supernatural powers directly or through Ariel to put other characters to sleep temporarily, to rob them of their natural physical strength to yield a sword, and to wake them up again. Throughout the play this pattern breeds images of sleepiness or wakefulness that contribute to questions about illusion and reality. Caliban, in describing the sweet noises of the island characterizes them as if part of a dream so beautiful that he comments, "when I waked, / I cried to dream again" (3.2.147–148). After the vision of mythological goddesses that come to bless Miranda and Ferdinand vanishes, Prospero muses about the illusory quality of life itself: "We are such stuff / As dreams are made on, and our little life / Is rounded with a sleep" (4.1.156–158). Vanishing visions, sudden sleepiness, and strange awakenings all add to the tone of wonder and enchantment that prevails throughout *The Tempest*.

A third recurring image pattern focuses on the importance of garments and clothing as signs of the miraculous, symbols of power, and signifiers of status. Gonzalo repeatedly notes that the garments of the shipwrecked party "are now as fresh as when [they] put them on first in Afric" (2.1.72–73) and sees this occurrence as a sign of their miraculous survival. Prospero's power as a magician depends upon not only his books and staff, but also his robe. He takes it off to speak to Miranda and puts it on again to engage in his supernatural art. His rich ducal garments serve as a temptation to Stephano and Trinculo, drawing them away from their intention to murder him, portraying them as common people who hope to be transformed by what they wear. Finally, in the last scene, Prospero changes from his magician's gown to his ducal attire, for his fellow Italians do not recognize who he is apart from the clothing he wears. From beginning to end, garments reveal the importance of survival and transformation as topics central to the plot.

Irony

Another literary technique that adds meaning to the play is irony. Although there are different kinds of irony, in its dramatic form it depends primarily on the difference between appearance and reality or knowing and not knowing. Shakespeare creates irony in the gap or discrepancy between what the audience knows and what some of the characters know. Prospero plays an almost godlike role in *The Tempest,* knowing everything because he has special powers of vision and because he orchestrates the action of the other characters. As audience members, even we are not always allowed to know what Prospero intends to do next until it happens. But sometimes we are given an insider's view on his purposes and consequently watch the other characters with a greater understanding of their plight than they have. While we do not know what causes the storm in act 1, scene 1 when we first see it, we do learn from the conversations between Prospero and Miranda and Prospero and Ariel that the storm was created by magic and that everyone survives the shipwreck. Thus, when the court characters appear on the shore of the island and converse, we know more than they do about their circumstances and watch their arguments and amusements, their amazement and gloominess with insight that rises above their moods, distances us from their feelings, and prevents their exchanges from appearing too serious. We know before Stephano crawls under Caliban's cloak for protection that things are not as they seem, and our awareness contributes to the humor when Trinculo appears and mistakes the other two for a four-legged monster. We know before Stephano and Trinculo become distracted by Prospero's rich garments that the clothing has been placed before them as a trap to entice them and thus we engage in the anticipation of a plot that will end without danger. We also know when Ferdinand and Alonso speak of each other as dead that both of them still live. This ironic perspective throughout the play adds both to the moments of humor and to the sense of ambiguity between illusion and reality that Prospero engages in creating. Our level of knowledge as the audience, falling somewhere between Prospero's omniscience and the other characters' naive vulnerability, also contributes to the quality of the play as a romance, in which serious action happens and death threatens but the comic or delightful tone prevails because we remain sufficiently informed to be distanced from the characters' responses and therefore sense no need to fear for their safety.

Stage Conventions

Dramatic irony is related to stage conventions which are aspects of the stage activity that, though unrealistic, are accepted by the audience and actors alike as part of the play's dramatic illusion. A chief stage convention arises from the various forms of speech that occur, from dialogue to asides, to soliloquies. Dialogue happens between two or more characters on stage, an aside occurs when one character speaks while the others on stage appear not to hear, and a soliloquy is spoken by one person alone on stage seeming to think out loud so that the audience can know what is evolving. Prospero's dominance in the play is partly established by asides and soliloquies that inform the audience of what he is planning and preparing. In act 1, scene 2 when Miranda and Ferdinand first meet, for example, Prospero watches the interaction and comments in asides about how the encounter suits his expectations. He says as the attraction between the two others evolves, "It goes on, I see, / As my soul prompts it" (1.2.420–421), "They are both in either's pow'rs. But this swift business / I must uneasy make, lest too light winning / Make the prize light (1.2.451–453), and "It works" (1.2.494). At each stage of the sudden love between Miranda and Ferdinand, we are allowed to hear Prospero's intentions and his deliberate interference to control the outcome of the relationship he so desires. Asides are also a chief means of contact between Prospero and his essential helpmate, Ariel. Early in the play, Prospero commands Ariel to become invisible, being "subject / To no sight but thine and mine" (1.2.301–302) and from then on, unless they appear alone on stage, they speak in asides that no one else can hear, engaged in a private dialogue that no one else can see. In an important soliloquy in 5.1.33–57, Prospero recounts his magical powers only to announce his intention to give up his "rough magic" once all his plans are fulfilled; in an equally significant speech, Prospero turns to the audience at the end of the play when all the characters have departed, seeking liberty through applause to draw the drama to its completion. As audience members we must suspend our disbelief and accept the conventions of speech that involve us directly or indirectly in order to participate in the entertainment of Shakespeare's art.

Character Development

Most characters in Shakespeare's romances tend not to be well-rounded or complex. Prospero is the most dominant character in *The Tempest* and yet most of his speeches reveal his plans and intentions rather than his thoughts, feelings, doubts, or personal struggles. In this respect, romance leans more toward comedy with flat, undeveloped characters than tragedy with rich, fully rounded individuals. What Shakespeare does offer involves groups of characters and patterns between individuals or groups that contribute to the overall movement and meaning of the play.

As the discussion on language has already suggested, characters can be grouped into three loose categories: court characters such as Alonso and Antonio, common characters such as Stephano and Trinculo, and nonhuman characters including Ariel and other spirits attending Prospero. Contrasts and similarities between individuals within these categories create the play's balance and symmetries. A clear balance exists, for example, between the machinations of Antonio and Sebastian who conspire to take Alonso's life, and Stephano, Trinculo, and Caliban who likewise scheme to take Prospero's life. Both unsuccessful intrigues reflect on the successful treason of Antonio years earlier in taking Prospero's dukedom and casting him out to sea. The various treacherous ambitions establish a pattern of threes that not only enhances the thematic development within the plot but indicates a commonality amongst characters who would otherwise seem distinct. They may speak differently, but the court characters, the commoners, and the monstrous figure of Caliban are equally tainted by the corruption that breeds in their hearts.

Other interesting connections arise among the three individual characters with close relationships to Prospero: Miranda, Ariel, and Caliban. Miranda is a daughter whom Prospero treats with care and attention, having tutored her well in their solitary years on the island. Ariel is a kind of servant who addresses Prospero as "master" and whom Prospero has freed from Sycorax's imprisonment only to demand his services while promising a future freedom. Caliban, the basest of the three characters, Prospero refers to as "slave," treating him with harshness and cruelty, even as Caliban responds with surliness and vindictiveness in return. Each of these relationships develops some aspect of Prospero's character, suggesting a range of possibilities that define his powerful presence as both benevolent and mean-spirited, raising questions about how an audience might understand and relate to him. These questions are reinforced by a mirrorlike reflection between Prospero's relationship to daughter, servant, and slave and the witch Sycorax's relationship to her son Caliban and the spirit, Ariel. Like Prospero, Sycorax was once ruler over the island and could exercise supernatural powers. She clearly had an influence on Caliban's coarseness through his upbringing that even Prospero cannot educate out of him. She used Ariel as a servant just as Prospero does, and for disobedience bound Ariel within a tree, an act that Prospero also threatens to do. These common relationships establish both a contrast and a curious parallel between Prospero and Sycorax, in which the magician may seem nobler than the witch but is equally imposing or even more so in his exercise of power.

Caliban also sets off a parallel with Ferdinand. Again their correspondence is established by their relationship to Prospero, as well as Miranda. Caliban had been attracted to Miranda and attempted to rape her; for this transgression he was cast out of the cave in which Prospero and Miranda live. Ferdinand is also attracted to Miranda, an outcome that pleases Prospero, although he pretends otherwise and charges Ferdinand with the same slavish task that he demands of Caliban, to collect and carry wood for Prospero's fire. For Ferdinand, the labor is light work because it allows him the presence of Miranda, but even though Prospero eventually admits his approval of the match between the prince and his daughter he cautions them to use discretion before their marriage. While Caliban is monstrous and Ferdinand is civilized and of noble birth, Prospero evinces a similarly protective father's concern for his daughter's safety and virginity in the presence of both "slaves."

Another correspondence, already mentioned under the heading of "Language and Character" exists between Ariel and Caliban, one suprahuman and the other subhuman, one working closely with Prospero to bring about his plans and the other striving to end Prospero's power. Ariel is faithful; Caliban is a traitor. Ariel relishes freedom; Caliban seems only to understand subservience, exchanging his slavery to Prospero for an equally submissive role to Stephano. Both ultimately achieve their freedom since Prospero intends to leave the island with everyone else. But Ariel anticipates his freedom with a little, airy song, "Where the bee sucks, there suck I" (5.1.88), while Caliban slouches off, muttering about his folly, "I'll be wise hereafter, / And seek for grace" (5.1.295–296). One senses that Caliban, the earthbound, witch-bred creature, never really receives true freedom because his very nature is beneath it or because he has been systematically repressed, while Ariel, lighter than air itself, drifts off to liberty once he is released from human restraints.

Finally, there is an obvious correspondence between Alonso and Prospero, as sovereigns over their states, Naples and Milan, and as shipwrecked rulers with single children whom they seem to "lose." Alonso temporarily loses his son Ferdinand, thinking him dead in the storm. Prospero recognizes that he has lost his sole relationship with Miranda when her love to Ferdinand divides her loyalties. In the final scene, this identification between Alonso, king of Naples, and Prospero, reinstated duke of Milan, becomes part of the pattern of regeneration and rebirth that defines the conclusion of romance. While both rulers are ensured of a safe journey back to their places of authority, their real power is being transferred to a new generation of leaders, Ferdinand and Miranda, who promise a healthy relationship between the two Italian states in place of the toxic relationship based on Antonio's usurpation. In the younger couple, there is a sense of regeneration and renewal, as new rulers will rise up to replace the older men and bring harmony to the politics of Italy.

The contrast and correspondences between individuals, the pattern of threes, and the harmony of reconciliation between alienated parties help to establish the significance of action and interaction in *The Tempest*. Relationships among and between characters are important for the play's structure and meaning, while the only two characters that seem to present any element of complexity in their connections with others are Prospero and Caliban. Curiously, as the most ennobled and the most degraded individuals, they raise the most questions about their attitudes toward others and the world around them. They help to create in Shakespeare's last play a maturity of vision that, although it may not match the intensity of the tragedies, imparts a richness of effect lacking in some of the earlier romantic comedies.

Theme

This richness of effect leads naturally into a discussion of theme. Theme is an expression or interpretation of the play's meaning. Because *The Tempest* has more than one meaning, it has many potential themes. Some of these thematic concerns have already been hinted at—the confusion between illusion and reality, and the significance of transformation and change. Others arise out of attention to character. Much of the focus on Prospero, for example, leads to an awareness of his power and to observations and questions about how he uses that power. His motives seem primarily good: a desire to return to his dukedom and to bring harmony to characters who are alienated. But he is also ruthless in his punishment of Caliban and even unkind in his threats to Ariel or his comments to Miranda and Ferdinand. Thematically, then, one can ask what role power plays in Prospero's hands and what kind of relationship is established between him and other characters. Power, it seems, depends on inequality and tempts one to overlook the shared humanity that would or should otherwise exist. Certainly, Prospero is not alone in his interest in power, for all the successful or unsuccessful attempts at treason are also based on a quest to wield power over others. *The Tempest* illuminates the corrupting influence of power, its proper authority, but also its limitations, as when the royal characters are powerless to still the storm or command respect from the sailors who endeavor to save the ship. Power is linked to ambition and points to both the civilizing and dehumanizing tendencies in human nature, made more apparent in the play by the fact that some characters behave in ways that seem barely human. If Antonio's corrupt ambition is the same as Caliban's, what does that say about Antonio's humanity or about Caliban's savagery? Shakespeare appears to integrate such questions into the structure of his plot.

A second related theme centers on the contrast between freedom and bondage. Prospero's servant and slave desire freedom but seek different means to achieve their ends. Prospero himself is guided by a dream to be freed from the island and reinstated in his dukedom. Ultimately, he chooses to free himself from his magic, an unsettling act because of what it suggests about his uses of magic throughout the play and what sort of liberty he will achieve when he has neither magic nor the sole government of Milan, which Ferdinand and Miranda will undertake. The young couple offers yet another perspective on the issue of liberty, for Ferdinand seems to take his bondage under Prospero in utterly good humor because of the love he has for Miranda. She, too, slants the question about freedom in the last scene when she accuses Ferdinand of cheating at chess but accepts it good-naturedly because of her love for him. The play suggests different avenues toward freedom and different definitions of bondage, love being a natural liberator in the face of oppression.

Another dichotomy that appears throughout the play exists between nature and two of its apparent opposites, nurture and art. There are numerous references to what is "natural." Miranda suggests that Caliban is unnatural or contrary to "good nature" as a "savage" from a "vile race" (1.2.355–360); she also indicates, however, that Ferdinand is so noble that he seems "A thing divine" and "nothing natural" (1.2.419). The meanings appear contradictory, for in one sense, nature is what has been made good by nurture or training, while in another sense, beauty or nobility can rise above that which is inherent or "natural." As different as Caliban and Ferdinand appear to Miranda, then, they are both to some degree "unnatural." She also assures Ferdinand, "My father's of a better nature, sir, / Than he appears by speech" (1.2.497–498), apologizing for his uncivil behavior. Through his characters' dialogue, Shakespeare engages questions about what is inbred or natural and what can be changed through nurture and achieved through art. By bringing the elements under his control, Prospero uses art to control nature and change both the weather and the behavior of human beings. His art is more powerful than nature and can create a thing of beauty, such as the wedding masque of the spirit goddesses. Shakespeare may even be alluding to his own craft as a playwright and commenting indirectly on the delightful and pleasant entertainment for the imagination that he is capable of creating. Nevertheless, Prospero is also limited, in spite of his art, in his efforts to nurture or train Caliban to civility and thus tame to his own purposes what exists in raw or natural form. One of the questions Shakespeare seems to pose is whether nature is a quality that human beings can and do spoil, or whether nature needs civilizing to improve it.

The ultimate direction of *The Tempest* is toward reconciliation; this is the prime focus of Prospero's art and one of the key thematic patterns in the play. Wrongs can be made right not by force, power, or ambition, but finally by grace and forgiveness. Prospero seems to want to bring his guilty characters, the "three men of sin" (3.3.53) to a place of awareness or contrition, as he sends Ariel to make a tempting banquet disappear before them and remind them of their past. But although the goal is not punishment, Prospero is certainly capable of it. The goal is not even simply guilt or regret but rather the right frame of mind for the wrongdoers to receive his pardon, which, when he has brought all the company together, he generously offers. His forgiveness is what makes possible the union of Miranda and Ferdinand and the promise of a new generation to bring hope for the future. Interestingly, even Antonio and Sebastian, who show no signs whatsoever of regret or acceptance of Prospero's mercy nevertheless receive it. As Shakespeare appears to suggest, grace is not dependent on repentance, although an unsettling cloud hovers over the unrepentant, leaving the ending of *The Tempest*, like some of Shakespeare's problem comedies, somewhat open-ended. If Antonio remains unrepentant, Caliban remains unreformed, and Prospero, the merciful, feels compelled to turn to the audience for mercy and applause, reminding Shakespeare's viewers that a play is a work of the imagination that requires the grace of the audience in order to take on life and succeed.

The Tempest has many themes, and this section only begins to touch on the possibilities. Theme should raise questions such as "What does the play mean?" "What is it about?" or "How does it make me feel?" This play challenges us as readers and viewers to consider these questions and to engage our imaginations as we explore some of the answers that seem most relevant to us.

TOPICS FOR WRITTEN AND ORAL DISCUSSION

1. Make two lists, one that describes what constitutes comedy and the other that defines tragedy. Then draw conclusions about ways in which *The Tempest* is tragic or comic, recognizing that comedy is not simply synonymous with humor.

2. Summarize what constitutes a Greek romance and discuss whether the phrase "escapist literature" could also apply to Shakespeare's *The Tempest* and if not, why not.

3. Find specific examples of events or circumstances in *The Tempest* that engender a sense of "wonder," "surprise," or the "miraculous." Discuss how these aspects cause you to respond to the play. If you have read or seen any other Shakespeare plays, how does your response to this one differ? Which one do you like better? Explain why.

4. Read the lines in this chapter quoted by the witch Medea in Ovid's *Metamorphoses*. Paraphrase the speech and then compare it to Prospero's in 5.1.33–57. How are they similar? Why do you suppose Shakespeare has Prospero echo the lines of a known literary enchantress or witch before he gives up his magic? What does the word "abjure" mean in 5.1.51 where Prospero announces that he will "abjure" his "rough magic"? How does this passage cause you to reflect on Prospero's role as a magician?

5. What kind of atmosphere does the setting of the island establish for the play? Is it positive, negative, or ambiguous? Provide specific examples of how the setting influences the play.

6. What is the effect of beginning the play with such a dramatic scene? Imagine how the play would be different if Prospero appeared first to explain what was happening and then the shipwreck occurred. Discuss the effect this change would have on the audience.

7. Language helps to distinguish characters in *The Tempest*. Find examples of various kinds of speech—both poetry and prose—and suggest how these patterns define or identify the characters.

8. Look specifically at Caliban's language and discuss how Shakespeare uses it to characterize this "mooncalf." How many different words can you find to describe Caliban? What do they suggest about his appearance and character?

9. Find as many references as you can to one of the natural elements in the play: earth, air, water, or fire. How do these images contribute to atmosphere, setting, and characterization?

10. Write a paragraph or two describing the significance of references to "dreams" in *The Tempest*. Consider, for example, what role sleep plays in *The Tempest*. What is the relationship between dream and art, dream and magic, or dream and illusion as opposed to reality?

11. Find as many references as you can to garments or clothing in the play. Why are they so important? What do they reveal about interactions between characters, and about contrasts between appearance and reality?

12.   Look for examples of dramatic irony in *The Tempest,* moments when the audience knows more than one or more characters. What effect does this irony have on your involvement in the play? Notice how often Prospero reveals his intentions and how often he keeps them a surprise from the audience. How does his concealment or revelation of his purposes affect your response to him and to the action as it unfolds?

13.   Select a scene that includes asides and/or soliloquies as well as dialogue. Draw diagrams indicating where the characters might be positioned in relation to one another and how they might move as they address each other and the audience. Who is meant to hear whom? As another option, act out a scene or portion thereof, determining how the characters stand, move, and speak to one another.

14.   Prospero speaks more than a quarter of the lines in the play. Notice how often he is also onstage without speaking or how often characters refer to him when he is offstage. What effect does this dominant presence have on your response to the play? On your response to Prospero? Are there any parts of the play that actually happen without Prospero's knowledge or interference? Write a character sketch for Prospero? Do you admire him, like him? Are you in any way critical of him?

15.   Consider the effect of contrasts and comparisons between characters and choose one of the following:

   a) Compare Ariel and Caliban as island creatures and as subordinates of Prospero.
   b) Compare the triangular relationship between Prospero, Ariel, and Miranda with Sycorax, Ariel, and Caliban. Consider uses of magic and parental influences on their children.
   c) Compare the treasonous pair, Antonio and Sebastian, with Stephano, Trinculo, and Caliban. How are they characterized differently and what do they have in common?
   d) Compare Alonso and Prospero as rulers and father figures. What kind of relationship do they have with their children and with their present and former subjects?
   e) Compare Caliban and Ferdinand in their relationships to Prospero and Miranda.

16.   Discuss in what ways Prospero and Caliban are the most complex and mysterious characters in the play. Is Prospero simply noble and Caliban degraded or are different perspectives available? Do these two characters seem black and white or is there room to discuss ambiguity?

17.   Debate whether Shakespeare celebrates the potential good of power in the play or criticizes its dehumanizing potential and danger? Argue your position using examples from the play.

18.   Discuss what the terms "nature," "natural," and "unnatural" signify in the play. What is the natural world like? Which characters are natural or unnatural and how? Look for possible ambiguities.

19.   What is the significance of art in *The Tempest*? How does it relate to nature? What is the role of Prospero's art? How might it relate to Shakespeare's art?

20.   Write one or two thematic statements about one of the following words: freedom, transformation, forgiveness. Suggest what *The Tempest* says about any of these topics. Then share your ideas with a classmate. What did you learn from each other's observations?

21.   Discuss whether you think Prospero is convincing in his forgiveness of the other characters. Does his mercy seem consistent with his earlier words and actions? Do you question or respect his choice? Antonio and Sebastian say nothing in response. How do you imagine they might appear in the final scene? If they are unresponsive, what does this suggest about Prospero's pardon? What might Shakespeare be implying about the happy ending of the play?

22.   Miranda is the only female character in *The Tempest*. Does this fact affect your response to the play in any way? How do you perceive her role and her qualities?

SUGGESTED READING

Boyce, Charles. *Shakespeare A to Z: The Essential Reference to His Plays, His Poems, His Life and Times, and More.* New York: Facts on File, 1990.

Hartwig, Joan. *Shakespeare's Tragicomic Vision.* Baton Rouge: Louisiana State UP, 1972.

Mowat, Barbara. *The Dramaturgy of Shakespeare's Romances.* Athens: U of Georgia P, 1976.

Olsen, Kirstin. *All Things Shakespeare: An Encyclopedia of Shakespeare's World.* Westport, CT: Greenwood Press, 2002.

Peterson, Douglas L. *Time, Tide, and Tempest: A Study of Shakespeare's Romances.* San Marino, CA: The Huntington Library, 1973.

Richards, Jennifer, and James Knowles. *Shakespeare's Late Plays: New Readings.* Edinburgh: Edinburgh UP, 1999.

Wells, Stanley. "Shakespeare and Romance." *Later Shakespeare.* Ed. John Russell Brown and Bernard Harris. London: Edward Arnold, 1966. 49–79.

2

Colonialism:
The Discoverer and
the Discovered

While *The Tempest* is explicitly set in the Mediterranean on an unidentified island somewhere between Tunis in Africa and Naples in Italy, Shakespeare introduces another possibility for the setting with his reference to the "still-vexed Bermoothes" (1.2.229), the islands of Bermuda where Ariel once fetched dew for Prospero. Setebos, the god of Caliban's mother, is specifically tied to the Indians of Patagonia in South America, and Caliban himself, identified in the cast of characters as "a savage and deformed slave" raises interest in the so-called savages whom explorers encountered on their expeditions to the New World of North and South America. Miranda's remark, "O brave new world / That has such people in't" (5.1.183–184) alerts audiences to the New World overseas, and Trinculo also draws connections between Caliban, that "strange fish" that he finds, and the English fascination with the strange inhabitants of North and South America and the West Indies, saying that in England, "When they will not give a doit to relieve a lame beggar, they will lay out ten to see a dead Indian" (2.2.32–34). Furthermore, in *The Tempest* Shakespeare alludes to the wreck of an English ship in the Bermudas, an event contemporary with the writing of his last romance. In a play that at first appears much more grounded in fantasy than history, Shakespeare seems intent on muddying the location of the enchanted island to augment not only its imaginary, but also, ironically, its historical significance. It has become popular in recent decades to accept the implications of an Atlantic as well as a Mediterranean setting, and to see *The Tempest* as a play about colonization, about the relationship between the discoverer and the discovered that was becoming a topic of such current relevance in the early seventeenth century as England joined other European nations in their quest to conquer, inhabit, and reap the wealth of new lands across the sea.

BUILDING AN EMPIRE

England was by no means the first European country to embark on building an empire beyond its own borders. Portugal and Spain share that claim to foreign resources, with Portugal for a time controlling commerce to the Far East and Spain dominating travel and acquisition of lands in the Pacific. Christopher Columbus is said to have discovered America for Spain in 1492. From then on, Spain began an aggressive campaign throughout the sixteenth century to claim and settle significant portions of North and South America and the West Indies. By 1574, five-eighths of Spain's population lived in North America (Bolton and Marshall 75). The earliest period of England's expansionism is marked by John Cabot's journey to North America in 1497, but England did not pursue its exploration as rapidly as Spain, for while Spain was building a vast empire, England's primary focus was on religious controversy and efforts to establish the Protestant Church of England.

In the second half of the sixteenth century, England began creating companies to engage in foreign trade in Russia and the Mediterranean, but not until the late 1570s and the 1580s did England begin to challenge Spain's dominance in the New World. Francis Drake became the first Englishman to circumnavigate the globe in 1577–1580; Martin Frobisher traveled to the northern part of North America in search of a northwest passage in 1576; and in 1584–1586 Walter Raleigh tried to establish an English claim on a broad area along the North American east coast known as Virginia. Because Spain had already declared its dominance in the New World, England's sailors had to be confrontational in their exploration, plundering Spanish ships and denying Spain's claim not only to new lands but to sea passages, as well. Still, by the end of Queen Elizabeth I's reign in 1603, England had not colonized or settled any part of the Americas. Raleigh's efforts in 1584–1586 failed as settlers deserted or simply failed to survive in their new environment.

The real beginnings of colonizing the New World for England began in King James's reign after 1603. Efforts were very much controlled by the crown as James granted charters or written contracts that allowed newly formed companies to settle in America in the king's name and with his permission. A new peace treaty with Spain in 1604 meant that officially England gave up some of its rights to trade and settle in certain areas of the

Americas and West Indies, although unofficially plunder, piracy, and trade still continued. The first British colony, however, was settled in 1606 in Virginia—a larger area than the state now known by that name—where Raleigh had earlier tried to put down English roots. One of the mandates of the Virginia Charter was to spread the Christian religion to Native Americans already inhabiting the area. In the harsh conditions of a new land, English settlers often depended on natives for food, but they also saw themselves as rightful inhabitants of the area, an attitude that created hostility among the indigenous people. Consequently, in the early years, while the British were trying to establish a government and new laws for their settlement, they were plagued by disease, starvation, Indian attacks, as well as Spanish resistance and fears of Spanish attacks. About the time that Shakespeare was writing *The Tempest,* the attitude among many of those directly involved in the colonizing efforts was, "Is this really worth it?"

THE SHIPWRECK

In May 1609, nine ships carrying 500 new colonists for John Smith's colony in Virginia set sail from England. Traveling with the colonists were Sir Thomas Gates, meant to be the new governor of Virginia, and Admiral Sir George Somers. While most of the ships arrived safely in America, the ship carrying Gates and Somers, called the *Sea-Venture,* became caught in a fierce sea storm on July 25 and landed on a Bermuda island. The ship was destroyed and everyone who reached Virginia assumed that the travelers on the *Sea-Venture* had been drowned at sea. But not only had they survived, they found themselves on an island that was very safe and comfortable, providing them with ample fresh fish, fowl, and water. Ironically, Bermuda had been considered an island of devils, and so the shipwrecked English travelers were more surprised than ever to find their surroundings so beautiful and welcoming. They began to make preparations to continue their journey to Virginia, building two new cedar boats in which they set sail, arriving in Virginia in May 1610, a year after they had left England. Everyone in Virginia was astonished to see them. News about the survivors traveled to London in September of 1610. Three documents, known as the Bermuda pamphlets, recorded the adventures of those on the shipwrecked boat. Although it was years before some of those documents were made public, Shakespeare probably had ready access to the material because he associated with members of the Virginia Company, including the earls of Southampton and Pembroke. Some details in *The Tempest* reveal Shakespeare's direct awareness of the *Sea-Venture's* journey to the New World in 1609–1610.

UTOPIA

The "New World" angle on *The Tempest* also draws attention to a sociopolitical concept—"utopia"—that had its beginnings in the sixteenth century. Utopia literally translated means "nowhere" but refers to an ideal human society. Englishman Sir Thomas More (1478–1535) first used the term as the title for a work in which he describes an ideal island society whose chief principle is that all property ought to be held in common. More's descriptions in *Utopia* (1516) indicate an awareness of the writings of explorers such as Christopher Columbus, not only with the idea of sharing possessions communally but in details such as the kind of "wine" New World inhabitants made, their great halls, their lack of interest in gold or jewels, and their frequent movement from place to place. Since More's time, an entire genre of utopian literature has developed, as well as "distopian" or anti-utopian works such as the modern novels *Brave New World* (Aldous Huxley, 1932) and *1984* (George Orwell, 1949). The utopian worlds of fiction usually represent freedom, justice, and equity as attainable and are both optimistic and visionary about the possibility of a reformed society. A geographically remote region creates the perfect setting for presenting an imaginary utopia.

The exploration of the New World in Shakespeare's *The Tempest* draws on the idea of a perfect society that More had established. Gonzalo is the chief spokesman for a new world order. While Sebastian and Antonio bait him and mock him, he surveys the island that becomes his inspiration for a commonwealth in which there is equality among all people, innocence, purity, and an abundance of food and goods supplied by nature with no toil or labor (2.1.152–173). As Sebastian and Antonio point out, Gonzalo contradicts himself in declaring equality among all people while he himself intends to be king over all. But Gonzalo does present one view of colonization in the play that is an alternative to the mastery and control that the discovery of the New World often assumed. He connects his vision to the Golden Age, which according to the classical myth of Ovid (43 B.C.–17 A.D.), occurred immediately after creation in the transition from chaos to order in the cosmos, when human beings lived freely without the need for laws, punishment, or hard labor. Ferdinand appeals to Christian typology rather than classical myth as he makes a similar observation about the island as an ideal society, saying, "Let me live here ever! / So rare a wond'red father and a wise / Makes this place Paradise" (4.1.122–124). Even Prospero offers a view of utopia in his betrothal masque with the mythic figures Iris, Ceres, and Juno. The world they represent contains all the richness and abundance of spring, summer, and harvest, without any winter. Shakespeare appears willing to give broad scope to the possibilities of a New World order by presenting a range of utopian views inspired by the island setting of the play, separated from the establishment of Old World politics.

"SAVAGES" OR CANNIBALS

Interestingly, the concept of utopia would have been viewed by most in Shakespeare's time as the antithesis of the New World with its Amerindian or Native American inhabitants, while others saw parallels between the two. To most explorers who discovered human beings in North and South America and the West Indies, the term "cannibal" or most often "savage" seemed fitting or appropriate. The information they brought back to Europe often developed into stories with as much grounding in fiction as in fact. Amerindians were identified as cannibals because of evidence that they killed and ate one another. They were labeled savages because they appeared to live like beasts, as nature produced them, with no refinements. For example, they ran virtually naked and ate roots and berries. According to European measures of religion, political organization, and technology, Amerindians were both morally and socially inferior for Christianity was deemed superior to non-Christianity or pagan practices, state superior to non-state, and the age of iron existing in Europe superior to the age of stone apparently still in place in the New World (Dickason 38). Europeans had a habit of describing the New World in negative terms according to what it did not have (Dickason 56). What they observed was no appreciation for art or beauty, no manners, and no natural affection or sensitivity to cruelty. From the time of Christopher Columbus's discovery of Amerindians in 1492, the European attitude was one of utter domination in which the "savages" were identified as creatures who would make good slaves.

A few outspoken individuals saw purity, perhaps even innocence, in Amerindian simplicity. Michel de Montaigne, a French essayist (1533–1592), for example, viewed "cannibals" as more natural in their social behavior and less cruel than Europeans who willingly tortured criminals and enemies, while Amerindians appeared to kill only their enemies and to eat them only after they were dead. Montaigne also spoke in support of the natives' reasoning powers and against colonization. He idealized natives but he was among a minority, and in his viewpoints he was more interested in critiquing European habits than advocating for native rights.

Shakespeare's *The Tempest* enters into this debate about the relationship between discoverer and discovered, between Old World and New World ways of living. The name Caliban is widely recognized as an anagram for "cannibal," and a question persists throughout the play about the association between nature and nurture. Many would argue that Caliban is nothing like the American "cannibal" or "savage." He has no cannibalistic traits; he has no trappings typically associated with Amerindians, such as feathers, arrows, body paint, or pipes. On the other hand, he also appears similar to a natural man who has not been civilized by Old World society. Although Prospero and Miranda attempt to teach him language and expose him to European culture, Prospero condemns him as "A devil, a born devil, on whose nature / Nurture can never stick; on whom my pains / Humanely taken, all, all lost, quite lost!" (4.1.188–190). Furthermore, he claims either ownership or responsibility when he says of Caliban, "this thing of darkness I / Acknowledge mine" (5.1.275–276). Caliban seems coarse and monstrous—beastlike, fishlike, doglike—in European terms, savage. He had tried to rape Miranda. Yet Shakespeare does not make Caliban completely unsympathetic, allowing Caliban to speak some of the most poetic lines about the island's beauty in the entire play. Moreover, the harsh relationship between him and Prospero, who deems himself lord of the island even though Caliban was there first, draws attention to the whole enterprise of New World colonization in which England had become more and more involved by the time Shakespeare crafted this romance with its story directed toward the potentially New World and toward the established Old World. The play raises questions about whether slavery is natural or cruel, whether civilization humanizes or corrupts individual ambitions, whether natural conditions are pure and simple or in need of reform, and whether exploitation is a right or an abuse.

Following a brief chronology, the remainder of this chapter includes excerpts from documents about the discovery of the New World and European reactions to it.

Brief Chronology of "New World" Events

1492	Christopher Columbus "discovers" the New World for Spain
1497	John Cabot journeys to North America for England
1516	Englishman Sir Thomas More writes *Utopia*
1576	Martin Frobisher searches for a northwest passage in North America
1577–1580	Englishman Francis Drake circumnavigates the globe
1584–1586	Walter Raleigh tries unsuccessfully to establish an English colony in Virginia
1603	John Florio translates Michel de Montaigne's French essays into English, including one on cannibals
1604	England makes peace with Spain
1606	England tries again—successfully—to establish a colony in Virginia
May, 1609	Nine ships leave England to take new colonists to Virginia
July, 1609	One of the nine ships is lost at sea and lands in Bermuda
May, 1610	Survivors of the shipwreck arrive in Virginia in new boats they made in Bermuda
1611	*The Tempest* performed in England

SHIPWRECK IN BERMUDA

William Strachey (1572?–1621), secretary to Thomas Gates, the governor of Virginia, provides one of the most vivid accounts of the *Sea Venture,* the ship that got caught in a storm in 1609 on its way to Virginia and landed on an island in Bermuda. His report of the experience, written in 1610 to an unknown lady in England, exists as one of three documents known as the Bermuda pamphlets that record the details of the "lost" colonists and their eventual arrival in Virginia in May, 1610. The following excerpt has been divided into four sections. The first section [1] describes the storm and the means by which the travelers managed to survive. Section [2] recounts the discovery of the miraculous fire that also appears in *The Tempest* as one of Ariel's tricks played upon the individuals in the storm-wracked ship from Naples. Section [3] records the surprising pleasantness and abundance of the island, and the last section [4] provides information about mutiny among traitors in the ship's party and how they were controlled. A final quotation is a marginal note included by Samuel Purchas (1577?–1626), editor of the report, who raises a question about the possibility or impossibility of civilizing "savages." Shakespeare likely had ready access to this letter because of his connections with members of the Virginia Company. Consider, as you read, parallels to the storm and the enchanted island in the fictionalized plot of *The Tempest.*

FROM WILLIAM STRACHEY, A TRUE REPERTORY OF THE
WRACK, AND REDEMPTION OF SIR THOMAS GATES,
KNIGHT; UPON, AND FROM THE ILANDS OF THE
BERMUDAS: HIS COMING TO VIRGINIA, AND THE ESTATE
OF THAT COLONY THEN, AND AFTER, UNDER THE
GOVERNMENT OF THE LORD LA WARRE, 1610, IN SAMUEL
PURCHAS, PURCHAS HIS PILGRIMES, VOL. XIX (1625)

(Glasgow: MacLehose; New York: Macmillan, 1906)

[1] Excellent Lady, know that upon Friday late in the evening, we brake ground out of the Sound of Plymouth, our whole Fleet then consisting of seven good Ships, and two Pinnaces, all which from the said second of June, unto the twenty three of July, kept in friendly consort together, not a whole watch at any time losing the sight each of other…we were within seven or eight days at the most, by Cap. Newport's reckoning of making Cape Henry upon the coast of Virginia: When on S. James his day, July 24 being Monday (preparing for no less all the black night before) the clouds gathering thick upon us, and the winds singing, and whistling most unusually, which

made us to cast off our Pinnace towing the same until then astern, a dreadful storm and hideous began to blow from out the North-east, which swelling, and roaring as it were by fits, some hours with more violence than others, at length did beat all light from heaven; which like an hell of darkness turned black upon us; so much the more fuller of horror, as in such cases horror and fear use to overrun the troubled, and over-mastered senses of all which (taken up with amazement) the ears lay so sensible to the terrible cries, and murmurs of the winds, and distraction of our Company, as who was most armed, and best prepared, was not a little shaken. For surely (Noble Lady) as death comes not so sudden nor apparent, so he comes not so elvish and painful (to men especially even then in health and perfect habitudes of body) as at Sea; who comes at no time so welcome, but our frailty (so weak is the hold of hope in miserable demon-strations of danger) it makes guilty of many contrary changes, and conflicts: For in-deed death is accompanied at no time, nor place with circumstances every way so uncapable of particularities of goodness and inward comforts, as at Sea....

For four and twenty hours the storm in a restless tumult, had blown so exceedingly, as we could not apprehend in our imaginations any possibility of greater violence, yet did we still find it, not only more terrible, but more constant, fury added to fury, and one storm urging a second more outrageous than the former; whether it so wrought upon our fears, or indeed met with new forces: Sometimes strikes in our Ship amongst women, and passengers, not used to such hurly and discomforts, made us look one upon the other with troubled hearts, and panting bosoms: our clamours drowned in the winds, and the winds in thunder. Prayers might well be in the heart and lips, but drowned in the outcries of the Officers: nothing heard that could give comfort, noth-ing seen that might encourage hope. It is impossible for me, had I the voice of Sten-tor, and expression of as many tongues, as his throat of voices, to express the outcries and miseries, not languishing, but wasting his spirits, and art constant to his own prin-ciples, but not prevailing. Our sails wound up lay without their use, and if at any time we bore but a Hollock, or half forecourse, to guide her before the Sea, six and some-times eight men were not enough to hold the whipstaff in the steerage, and the tiller below in the Gunner room, by which may be imagined the strength of the storm: In which, the Sea swelled above the Clouds, and gave battle unto Heaven. It could not be said to rain, the waters like whole Rivers did flood in the air. And this I did still observe, that whereas upon the Land, when a storm hath powered itself forth once in drifts of rain, the wind as beaten down, and vanquished therewith, not long after en-dureth: here the glut of water (as if throttling the wind ere while) was no sooner a lit-tle emptied and qualified, but instantly the winds (as having gotten their mouths now free, and at liberty) spake more loud, and grew more tumultuous, and malignant. What shall I say? Winds and Seas were as mad, as fury and rage could make them; for mine own part, I had been in some storms before,... Yet all that I had ever suffered gathered together, might not hold comparison with this: there was not a moment in which the sudden splitting, or instant over-settling of the Ship was not expected.

Howbeit this was not all; It pleased God to bring a greater affliction yet upon us; for in the beginning of the storm we had received likewise a mighty leak. And the Ship in every joint almost, having spewed out her Okam, before we were aware (a casualty more desperate than any other that a Voyage by Sea draweth with it) was grown five foot suddenly deep with water above her ballast, and we almost drowned within, whilest we sat looking when to perish from above. This imparting no less terror than danger, ran through the whole Ship with much fright and amazement, startled and turned the blood, and took down the braves of the most hardy Marriner of them all, insomuch as he that before happily felt not the sorrow of others, now began to sorrow for himself, when he saw such a pond of water so suddenly broken in, and which he knew could not (without present avoiding) but instantly sink him....

The Lord knoweth, I had as little hope, as desire of life in the storm, & in this, it went beyond my will; because beyond my reason, why we should labour to preserve life; yet we did, either because so dear are a few lingering hours of life in all mankind, or that our Christian knowledge taught us, how much we owed to the rites of Nature, as bound, not to be false to ourselves, or to neglect the means of our own preservation; the most despairful things amongst men, being matters of no wonder nor moment with him, who is the rich Fountain and admirable Essence of all mercy.

Our Governour, upon the Tuesday morning (at what time, by such who had been below in the hold, the Leak was first discovered) had caused the whole Company, about one hundred and forty, besides women, to be equally divided into three parts, and opening the Ship in three places (under the forecastle, in the waste, and hard by the Bitack) appointed each man where to attend; and thereunto every man came dully upon his watch, took the Bucket, or Pump for one hour, and rested another.... (5–9)

[2] During all this time, the heavens look'd so black upon us, that is was not possible the elevation of the Pole might be observed: nor a Star by night, nor Sun beam by day was to be seen. Only upon the Thursday night Sir George Summers being upon the watch, had an apparition of a little round light, like a faint Star, trembling, and streaming along with a sparkling blaze, half the height upon the Main Mast, and shooting sometimes from Shroud to Shroud, tempting to settle as it were upon any of the four Shrouds: and for three or four hours together, or rather more, half the night it kept with us; running sometimes along the Main-yard to the very end, and then returning. At which, Sir George Summers called diverse about him, and showed them the same, who observed it with much wonder, and carefulness: but upon a sudden, towards the morning watch, they lost the sight of it, and knew not what way it made. The superstitious Sea-men make many constructions of this Sea-fire, which nevertheless is usual in storms: the same (it may be) which the Graecians were wont in the Mediterranean to call Castor and Pollux, of which, if one only appeared without the other, they took it for an evil sign of great tempest. The Italians, and such, who lie open to the Adriatic and Tyrrene Sea, call it (a sacred Body) Corpo sancto: the Spaniards call it Saint Elmo, and have an authentic and miraculous Legend for it. Be it what it will, we laid other foundations of safety or ruin, then in the rising or falling of it, could it have served us now miraculously to have taken our height by, it might have strucken amazement, and a reverence in our devotions, according to the due of a miracle. But it did not light us any whit the more to our known way, who ran now (as do hoodwinked men) at all adventures, sometimes North, and North-east, then North and by West, and in an instant again varying two or three points, and sometimes half the Compass.

... Sir George Summers, when no man dreamed of such happiness, had discovered, and cried Land.... [W]e were enforced to run her ashore, as near the land as we could, which brought us within three quarters of a mile of shore....

[3] We found it to be the dangerous and dreaded Island, or rather Islands of the Bermuda: whereof let me give your Ladyship a brief description, before I proceed to my narration. And that the rather, because they be so terrible to all that ever touched on them, and such tempests, thunders, and other fearful objects are seen and heard about them, that they be called commonly, The Devil's Islands, and are feared and avoided of all sea travellers alive, above any other place in the world. Yet it pleased our merciful God, to make even this hideous and hated place, both the place of our safety, and means of our deliverance.

And hereby also, I hope to deliver the world from a foul and general error: it being counted of most, that they can be no habitation for Men, but rather given over to Devils and wicked Spirits; whereas indeed we find them now by experience, to be as habitable and commodious as most Countries of the same climate and situation: insomuch as if the entrance into them were as easy as the place itself is contending, it had longer ere this been inhabited, as well as other Islands. Thus shall we make it appear, That Truth is the daughter of Time, and that men ought not to deny everything which is not subject to their own sense.... (11–14)

Sure it is, that there are not Rivers nor running Springs of fresh water to be found upon any of them: when we came first we digged and found certain gushings and soft bubblings, which being either in bottoms, or on the side of hanging ground, were only fed with rain water, which nevertheless soon sinketh into the earth and vanished away....

A kind of web-footed Fowl there is, of the bigness of an English green Plover, or Sea-Mew, which all the Summer we saw not, and in the darkest nights of November and December (for in the night they only feed) they would come forth, but not fly far from home, and hovering in the air, and over the sea, made a strange hollow and harsh howling. Their colour is inclining to Russet, with white bellies (as are likewise the long Feathers of their wings Russet and White) these gather themselves together and breed in those Islands which are high, and so far alone into the Sea, that the Wild Hogs cannot swim over them, and there in the ground they have their Burrows, like Coneys in a Warren, and so brought in the loose Mould, though not so deep: which Birds with a light bough in the dark night (as in our Lowbelling) we caught. I have been at the taking of three hundred in an hour, and we might have laden our Boats. Our men found a pretty way to take them, which was by standing on the Rocks or Sands by the Sea side, and hollowing, and laughing, and making the strangest outcry that possibly they could: with the noise whereof the Birds would come flocking to that place, and settle upon the very arms and head of him that so cried, and still creep nearer and nearer, answering the noise themselves: by which our men would weigh them with their hand, and which weighed heaviest they took for the best and let the others alone, and so our men would take twenty dozen in two hours of the chiefest of them; and they were a good and well relished Fowl, fat and full as a Partridge... which

Birds for their blindness (for they see weakly in the day) and for their cry and hooting, we called the Sea Owl. . . .

The Tortoise is reasonable toothsome (some say) wholesome meat. I am sure our Company like the meat of them very well, and one Tortoise would go further amongst them, than three hogs. One Turtle (for so we called them) feasted well a dozen Messes, appointing six to every Mess. It is such a kind of meat, as a man can neither absolutely call Fish nor Flesh, keeping most what in the water. . . . (20–24)

[4] In these dangers and devilish disquiets (whilst the almighty God wrought for us, and sent us miraculously delivered from the calamites of the Sea, all blessings upon the shore, to content and bind us to gratefulness) thus enraged amongst ourselves, to the destruction each of other, into what a mischief and misery had we been given up, had we not had a Governour with his authority, to have suppressed the same? Yet was there a worse practice, faction, and conjuration afoot, deadly and bloody, in which the life of our Governour, with many others were threatened and could not but miscarry in his fall. But such is ever the will of God (who in the execution of his judgments, breaketh the firebrands upon the head of him, who first kindled them) there were, who conceived that our Governour indeed neither durst, nor had authority to put in execution, or pass the act of Justice upon anyone, how treacherous or impious so ever. . . . They persevered therefore not only to draw unto them such a number, and associates as they could work into the abandoning of our Governour and to the inhabiting of this Island. They had now purposed to have made a surprise of the Store house, and to have forced from thence, what was therein either of Meal, Cloth, Cables, Arms, Sails, Oars or what else it pleased God that we had recovered from the wreck, and was to serve our general necessity and use, either for the relief of us, while we stayed here, or for the carrying of us from this place again, when our Pinnace should have been furnished.

But as all giddy and lawless attempts, have always something of imperfection, and that as well by the property of the action which holdeth of disobedience and rebellion (both full of fear) as through the ignorance of the devisers themselves; so in this (besides those defects) there were some of the association, who not strong enough fortified in their own conceits, break from the plot itself, and (before the time was ripe for the execution thereof) discovered the whole order, and every Agent, and Actor thereof, who nevertheless were not suddenly apprehended, by reason the confederates were divided and separated in place, some with us, and the chief with Sir George Summers in his Island (and indeed all his whole company) but good watch passed upon them, every man from thenceforth commanded to wear his weapon, without which before, we freely walked from quarter to quarter, and conversed among ourselves, and every man advised to stand upon his guard, his own life not being in safety, whilst his next neighbour was not to be trusted. (32–33)

. . . . [marginal comment by Purchas] *"Can a Leopard change his spots? Can a Savage remaining Savage be civil? Were not we ourselves made and not born civil in our Progenitors' days? And were not Caesar's Britons as brutish as Virginians? The Roman swords were best teachers of civility to this & other Countries near us."* (62)

DISCOVERING THE ISLAND

Sylvester Jourdain, a survivor of the shipwreck, supplies one of the three Bermuda pamphlets available in 1610 before Shakespeare completed *The Tempest*. The following excerpt focuses on the surprising healthfulness of the island. Pay particular attention to references Jourdain makes to God and the devil as you consider his interpretation of the good fortune that the shipwrecked party encountered, landing as they did on an island reputed to be a place of devils. Consider how this language might be echoed by Shakespeare's characters' reaction to the island where they land.

FROM SYLVESTER JOURDAIN, *A DISCOVERY OF THE BARMUDAS, OTHERWISE CALLED THE ISLE OF DEVILS*

(1610. STC 14816) 4–10

...all our men, being utterly spent, tired, and disabled for longer labour, were even resolved, without any hope of their lives, to shut up the hatches, and to have committed themselves to the mercy of the sea (which is said to be merciless) or rather to the mercy of their mighty God and redeemer, (whose mercies exceed all his works) seeing no help, nor hope in the apprehension of man's reason, that any mother's child could escape that inevitable danger, which every man had...digested to himself, of present sinking. So that some of them having some good and comfortable waters in the ship, fetched them, and drunk one to the other, taking their last leave one of the other, until their more joyful and happy meeting, in a more blessed world; when it pleased God out of his most gracious and merciful providence, so to direct and guide our ship, (being left to the mercy of the sea) for her most advantage; that Sir George Sommers (sitting upon the poop of the ship)...most wishedly happily descried land; whereupon he most comfortably encouraged the company to follow their pumping, and by no means to cease bailing out of the water, with their buckets, baricos, and kettles, whereby they were so over wearied, and their spirits so spent with long fasting, and continuance of their labour, that for the most part they were fallen asleep in corners, and wheresoever they chanced first to sit or lie; but hearing news of land, wherewith they grew to be somewhat revived, being carried with wit and desire beyond their strength, every man hustled up, and gathered his strength and feeble spirits together, to perform as much as their weak force would permit him: though which weak means, it pleased God to work so strongly as the water was stayed for that little time, (which as we all much feared, was the last period of our breathing) and the ship kept from present sinking, when it pleased God to send her within half an English mile, of that land that Sir George Sommers had not long before descried: which were the Islands of the Barmudas. And there neither did our ship sink, but more fortunately in so great a misfortune, fell in between two rocks, where she was fast lodged and locked, for further budging.

But our delivery was not more strange in falling so opportunely and happily upon the land, as our feeding and preservation, was beyond our hopes and all men's expectations most admirable. For the islands of the Barmudas, as every man knoweth that hath heard or read of them, were never inhabited by any Christian or heathen people, but ever esteemed and reputed a most prodigious and enchanted place affording nothing but gusts, storms, and foul weather; which made every Navigator and Mariner to avoid [them], as Scylla and Charybdis, or as they would shun the Devil himself; and no man was ever heard to make for the place, but as against their wills, they have by storms and dangerousness of the rocks, lying seven leagues into the sea, suffered shipwrack; yet did we find there the air so temperate and the Country so abundantly fruitful of all fit necessaries, for the sustentation and preservation of man's life, that most in a manner of all our provisions of bread, beer, and victual being quite spoiled, in lying long drowned in salt water, notwithstanding we were there for the space of nine months (few days over or under) not only well refreshed, comforted, and with good satiety contented, but out of the abundance thereof, provided us some reasonable quantity and proportion of provision, to carry us for Virginia and to maintain ourselves, and that company we found there, to the great relief of them, as it fell out in their so great extremities... until it pleased God... that their store was better supplied. And greater, and better provisions we might have made, if we had better means for the storing and transportation thereof. Wherefore my opinion sincerely of this island is, that whereas it hath been, and is full accounted, the most dangerous, unfortunate, and most forlorn place of the world, it is in truth the richest, healthfulest, and pleasing land, (the quantity and bigness thereof considered) and merely natural, as ever man set foot upon.

TROUBLE IN THE VIRGINIA COLONY

The following is an excerpt from an authorized report of the Virginia colony recording some of the many problems that troubled the early settlers. The report, appearing in 1610, tries to explain the causes of unrest by blaming unruly settlers for their ambitious and unlawful behavior. Idleness, treason, and greed or covetousness are some of the concerns that leaders had to contend with in the early days of the settlement. Consider whether similar problems also surface among the island inhabitants in *The Tempest*.

FROM *A TRUE DECLARATION OF THE ESTATE OF THE COLONY IN VIRGINIA, WITH A CONFUTATION OF SUCH SCANDALOUS REPORTS AS HAVE TENDED TO THE DISGRACE OF SO WORTHY AN ENTERPRISE* (1610), PUBLISHED BY THE ADVICE OF THE COUNCIL OF VIRGINIA, IN GEOFFREY BULLOUGH, ED., *NARRATIVE AND DRAMATIC SOURCES OF SHAKESPEARE*, VOL. VIII

(London: Routledge & Kegan Paul, 1975) 297–298

The ground of all those miseries, was the permissive providence of God, who, in the fore-mentioned violent storm, separated the head from the body, all the vital powers of regiment being exiled with *Sir Thomas Gates* in those unfortunate (yet fortunate) Islands.... every man overvaluing his own worth, would be a Commander: every man underprising another's value, denied to be commanded...when therefore license, sedition, and fury, are the fruits of a heady, daring, and unruly multitude, it is no wonder that so many in our colony perished; it is a wonder, that all were not devoured....

The next fountain of woes was secure negligence, and improvidence, when every man sharked for his present booty, but was altogether careless of succeeding penury....

Unto idleness, you may join treasons, wrought by those unhallowed creatures that forsook the Colony, and exposed their desolate brethren to extreme misery. You shall know that 28 or 30 of the company...stole away the Ship..., they made a league amongst themselves to be professed pirates, with dreams of mountains of gold, and happy robberies: thus at one instant, they wronged the hopes, and subverted the cares of the Colony...: they created the Indians our implacable enemies by some violence they had offered:...they weakened our forces, by subtraction of their arms, and succours....

Unto Treasons, you may join covetousness in the Mariners, who for their private lucre partly embezzled the provisions, partly prevented our trade with the Indians, making the matches in the night, and forestalling our market in the day, whereby the Virginians were glutted with our trifles, and enhanced the prices of their Corn and Victual.

The state of the Colony, by these accidents began to find a sensible declining.

THE NATURAL WORLD OF CANNIBALS

French essayist Michel de Montaigne (1533–1592) wrote—among many other topics—about cannibals discovered in the New World. Much of his information came from a servant who had spent some years in America. Montaigne disputes the common conception of Native Americans as savage, describing them instead as pure and natural, uncorrupted by artifice and unsophisticated by civility. In his idealized view, the laws of nature are superior to the laws fashioned by humans living in a well-established society. Furthermore, he finds cannibalism itself less objectionable than some of the cruelties that the so-called civilized Europeans habitually practiced. Shakespeare obviously read John Florio's translation of Montaigne's essay. Some of Gonzalo's lines espousing an ideal commonwealth (2.1.152–173) come directly from Montaigne. See if you recognize those lines in this excerpt.

FROM MICHEL DE MONTAIGNE, "OF THE CANNIBALS," IN *THE ESSAYS OF MONTAIGNE*, TRANS. JOHN FLORIO (1603)

(1603; London: David Nutt, 1892)

Now (to return to my purpose) I find (as far as I have been informed) there is nothing in that nation [the Native American Indians], that is either barbarous or savage, unless men call that barbarism which is not common to them. As indeed, we have no other aim of truth and reason, than the example and Idea of the opinions and customs of the country we live in. There is ever perfect religion, perfect policy, perfect and complete use of all things. They are even savage, as we call those fruits wild, which nature of herself, and of her ordinary progress hath produced: whereas indeed, they are those which ourselves have altered by our artificial devices, and diverted from their common order, we should rather term savage. In those are the true and most profitable virtues, and natural properties most lively and vigorous, which in these we have bastardized, applying them to the pleasure of our corrupted taste. And if notwithstanding, in diverse fruits of those countries that were never tilled, we shall find, that in respect of ours they are most excellent, and as delicate unto our taste; there is no reason, art should gain the point of honour of our great and puissant mother Nature. We have so much by our inventions surcharged the beauties and riches of her works, that we have altogether over choked her: yet wherever her purity shineth she makes our vain and frivolous enterprises wonderfully ashamed. . . .

Ivies spring better of their own accord,
Unhaunted plots much fairer trees afford.
Birds by no art much sweeter notes record.

All our endeavour or wit, cannot so much as reach to represent the nest of the least
birdlet, its contexture, beauty, profit and use, no nor the web of a seely spider. 'All
things' (saith Plato) 'are produced, either by nature, by fortune, or by art. The greatest and fairest by one or other of the two first, the least and imperfect by the last.'
Those nations seem therefore so barbarous unto me, because they have received very
little fashion from human wit, and are yet near their original naturality. The laws of
nature do yet command them, which are but little bastardized by ours, and that with
such purity, as I am sometimes grieved the knowledge of it came no sooner to light,
at what time there were men, that better than we could have judged of it. I am sorry,
Lucurgus and Plato had it not: for me seemeth that what in those nations we see by
experience, doth not only exceed all the pictures wherewith licentious Poesie hath
proudly embellished the golden age, and all her quaint inventions to feign a happy
condition of man, but also the conception and desire of Philosophy. They could not
imagine a genuity so pure and simple, as we see it by experience; nor ever believe our
society might be maintained with so little art and human combination. It is a nation,
would I answer Plato, that hath no kind of traffic, no knowledge of Letters, no intelligence of numbers, no name of magistrate, nor of politic superiority; no use of service, of riches or of poverty; no contracts, no successions, no partitions, no occupation
but idle; no respect of kindred, but common, no apparel but natural, no manuring of
lands, no use of wine, corn, or metal. The very words that import lying, falsehood,
treason, dissimulations, covetousness, envy, detraction, and pardon, were never heard
of amongst them. How dissonant would he find his imaginary common-wealth from
this perfection? . . .

Furthermore, they live in a country of so exceeding pleasant and temperate situation, that as my testimonies have told me, it is very rare to see a sick body amongst
them; and they have further assured me they never saw any man there, either shaking
with palsy, toothless, with eyes dropping, or crooked and stooping through age.
(221–223)

[On cannibalism] . . . I am not sorry we note the barbarous horror of such an action, but grieved, that prying so narrowly into their faults we are so blinded in ours.
I think there is more barbarism in eating men alive, than to feed upon them being
dead; to mangle by tortures and torments a body full of lively sense, to roast him in
pieces, to make dogs and swine to gnaw and tear him in mammocks (as we have not
only read, but seen very lately, yea and in our own memory, not amongst ancient enemies, but our neighbours and fellow-citizens; and which is worse, under pretence of
piety and religion) than to roast and eat him after he is dead. (226)

TOPICS FOR WRITTEN AND ORAL DISCUSSION

1. What words does William Strachey use to describe the storm at sea in 1609, and what words does he use to describe the reactions of the people aboard the ship? Why, according to Strachey, are the ship's passengers surprised by what they find when they land on the Bermudan island? What do they find to their benefit?

2. What is St. Elmo's fire and how do the ship's passengers react to it?

3. What dangers developed on the island and how were these threats handled?

4. What does Samuel Purchas's marginal comment about leopards and savages suggest about his attitude toward the native inhabitants of the Americas?

5. Compare one of the following:

a) Strachey's account of the storm and the ship passengers' responses with Shakespeare's account of the shipwreck in act 1 in *The Tempest*. What similarities and differences do you see?

b) Strachey's record of the island compared to accounts of the island in *The Tempest*. How many different interpretations of Shakespeare's island can you find? Why do you suppose Shakespeare included a variety of descriptions?

c) Strachey's account of the mutineers and Shakespeare's description of unlawful traitors on the enchanted island. What do these stories—fact and fiction—suggest about human nature? How is order maintained?

6. What similarities do you find between Strachey's report of the storm and the island and Sylvester Jourdain's? What do these similarities suggest to you about the accuracy or truth of their accounts?

7. Part of what Strachey and Jourdain provide is fact and part is interpretation or how they perceive the facts. What role does God play in their interpretation of the facts? Find specific examples. What about the devil? Can you find similar views held by any of the characters in Shakespeare's play as they refer to God, providence, or the devil? Do you think Shakespeare offers a particularly Christian perspective in *The Tempest* or do characters simply use their beliefs about providence to justify their actions or attitudes? Explain.

8. *The True Declaration...of the Colony of Virginia* (1610) describes some of the social and political problems that troubled the new settlement in Virginia. What specifically were these problems? Compare these issues with a similar description in section [4] of Strachey's report. Although one account is of Virginia and the other of the "lost" settlers in Bermuda, what do the stories have in common? Are you surprised or not by the similarities? Why or why not?

9. In his essay "Of the Cannibals," how does Michel de Montaigne perceive Native Americans? What is his view of nature? What does he see as the opposite of nature? Which does he favor? Provide examples.

10.   Utopia is an ideal society. Describe Montaigne's view of an ideal society. Refer to Gonzalo's ideal commonwealth in *The Tempest* (2.1.152–173). What evidence do you find that Shakespeare borrowed Montaigne's ideas? Do you think we are meant to take Gonzalo's ideas seriously or mock him as Antonio and Sebastian do or react in another way? Explain why.

11.   If you are familiar with any distopian or anti-utopian literature such as Aldous Huxley's *Brave New World* or George Orwell's *1984,* discuss how these approaches to the world differ from Montaigne's in "Of the Cannibals" or even Shakespeare's in *The Tempest.*

12.   What is Montaigne's view of cannibalism? Why is he more offended by some European practices?

13.   Imagine Montaigne and Samuel Purchas discussing the habits of cannibals or "savages." (Refer to Montaigne's essay and Purchas's marginal comment at the very end of Strachey's excerpted report). Divide into two groups taking opposite views about cannibals and "savages" and hold a debate about whether they are to be admired or looked down upon and why. Remember that you are acting as seventeenth-century European people. Discuss, then, what effect your twenty-first-century perspective has on your involvement in such a debate. What made it easy or difficult?

14.   Notice references to "nature" or "natural" in *The Tempest.* Who would you describe as a natural man in the play and what does that mean? Point out if you notice any inconsistencies.

15.   Imagine you are a judge sent to decide who ought to be king or ruler of the island: Caliban or Prospero. Make a list of relevant evidence supporting each party, referring especially to 1.2.310–374. Give your ruling, providing reasons for your decision.

16.   Can you see Prospero as a colonizer? Explain what that means to you and how that affects your opinion of him and also of Caliban.

17.   Can you see Caliban as a native whose land has been taken away? How does that affect your opinion of him and also of Prospero? Debate the two views.

18.   As Montaigne says, "men call that barbarism which is not common to them." Explain how shockingly "uncommon" Caliban might appear to European settlers.

19.   Imagine Prospero and Montaigne having dinner together after Prospero returns to Milan. The conversation turns to the New World and its inhabitants. Even if Prospero had never left the Mediterranean, he no doubt has opinions based on his many years of island experience. How might the conversation develop between the two? Write a dialogue.

20.   Imagine you are either Caliban or Ariel on the island after all the Italians have left. Write a monologue for one or the other. How does it feel to be left alone on the island? How does it feel to be free or in control?

21.   Write a research essay about European efforts to colonize the New World. Did different countries have different approaches? What were their motivations and their methods? What is your response today to that period of history?

SUGGESTED READING

Bolton, Herbert Eugene, and Thomas Maitland Marshall. *The Colonization of North America, 1492–1783*. New York: Macmillan Company, 1920.

Dickason, Olive Patricia. *The Myth of the Savage: And the Beginnings of French Colonialism in the Americas*. Edmonton: University of Alberta, 1984.

Gallagher, Ligeia. *More's "Utopia" and Its Critics*. Chicago: Scott, Foresman and Co., 1964.

McFarlane, Anthony. *The British in the Americas, 1480–1815*. London: Longman, 1994.

Porter, H. C. *The Inconstant Savage: England and the North American Indian, 1500–1660*. London: Duckworth, 1979.

3

Magic: Religion, Art, and Science

Shakespeare's *The Tempest* is centrally about magic. Prospero is a mage or magus, a figure who seems larger than life because of the magical influence he has on the natural world, the spiritual world, and the actions and responses of all the other characters. With his extraordinary powers, he orchestrates the plot of the entire play: nothing seems to happen without his command, his knowledge, or his ability to manipulate the outcomes. Even the audience is not allowed to see beyond Prospero's plans, watching the events unfold without the foreknowledge that Shakespeare commonly gives to spectators of other plays where disguises are revealed before they are assumed or where tragic circumstances are disclosed before they happen. The audience knows, for example, that soldiers disguised as the forest of Birnan Wood are moving to Macbeth's castle before he does, that Iago has planted a false seed of distrust in Othello's mind, or that Juliet only seems dead when Romeo finds her in the tomb and decides to commit suicide. In *The Tempest,* Prospero's intent to shipwreck his enemies, separate them into groups on the island, and bring them to harmony and regeneration becomes apparent only as his magical spells and enchantments occur scene after scene. The island and its people are transformed by his apparent ability to tap into supernatural powers.

The centrality of magic raises questions about the believability of the plot and potential responses to it in its own time. What would Shakespeare's audience have understood, accepted, or experienced of the supernatural world and its relationship to human beings? At a time when religion was a strong social and political force as well as spiritual guide, and science was only experiencing its early birth pangs, magic was taken seriously as both a threat to traditional authorities and a possibility for expanded human knowledge, power, and discovery. The Renaissance or "rebirth" of classical learning and art that began in Italy and spread throughout Europe provided the foundation for renewed interest in magical thinking and learning. Following the thread of history from ancient Platonic Greece to continental Renaissance Europe and on to Elizabethan England indicates what spectrum of beliefs may have influenced Shakespeare as well as colored the thoughts of audience members watching Prospero don his magical robes and take up his powerful staff to shape the events that begin with the tempest at sea.

HERMES TRISMEGISTUS

In 1463, a Greek manuscript brought to Florence, Italy, was translated into Latin by a scholar of the court, Marsilio Ficino. This series of philosophical and religious texts was attributed to Hermes Trismegistus, a man thought to be a contemporary of Old Testament prophet Moses, a predecessor of Plato, and an Egyptian priest. The Renaissance had great respect for learning from ancient times, believing that older and more distant sources brought one closer to divine truth; the translations consequently had a profound effect on fifteenth- and sixteenth-century thought. The "Hermetic writings"—as they were called—emphasized the godlike potential of human beings. Although the manuscript told a creation story similar to the one in Genesis at the beginning of the Bible, it proclaimed more positively that humanity could be regenerated after the fall from paradise and regain divine knowledge and power.

Hermes became the most important figure in the Renaissance revival of magic. In earlier medieval times, the church had banned magic as evil and pagan, causing it to become a secretive practice. The Hermetic writings, however, raised the status of magic as a divine and learned art, lending it an aura of acceptability and even praise to replace its darkened reputation. Ironically, some of the major assumptions about Hermes Trismegistus turned out to be false. A later scholar discovered that the Hermetic writings were likely written between 100 and 300 A.D., not during the early Old Testament time of Moses. Also, probably various Greek authors were involved, not simply one. Nevertheless, these discoveries were made long after the legendary Hermes Trismegistus had influenced the Renaissance world. The adjective "Hermetic" is still used as a description of the tradition of magical beliefs that began in Renaissance Italy and spread rapidly throughout Europe.

ASTROLOGY

Marsilio Ficino (1433–1499), the translator of the Greek Hermetic writings, became a proponent of occult philosophy that emphasized the spirit world and its connection to human beings. Although the word "occult" today stirs up connotations of black magic or dark arts, the word as applied to Renaissance philosophy had less negative connotations, referring more neutrally to that which was secret, mysterious, supernatural, or inexplicable. Ficino and others became committed to reviving and making acceptable in their Christian era the works not only of Hermes Trismegistus but also of the prominent Greek philosopher, Plato (427–347 B.C.), who believed that human beings could ascend by degrees from contemplation to the discovery of truth. Ficino helped establish a Neoplatonic (i.e., Plato made new) school of thinking that was highly optimistic about humanity's divine and creative potential. The practice of magic was seen as a sign of the divinity within human beings, and this magic was based on the influence of the stars, which were thought to have sympathies or connections with plants, animals, stones, and all things. The stars, considered to be like living divine animals, were thought to rule the material world, and astrology, the study of the stars, became central to magical thinking.

Neoplatonism and astrology, however, ran counter to dominant Christian doctrine that declared humanity's limited nature as fallen creatures and asserted the need for God's redemptive power to liberate people from their sinfulness. Ficino best managed the tension between religion and the art of magic by trying to be cautious about the assertions of his philosophy, focusing on the positive celestial influences of stars and planets and resisting the harmful or maleficent forces. He distinguished between lawful, useful magic and unlawful, demonic magic, and identified his practice as the former. Still, his ideas were controversial. He claimed that human beings were at the center of the cosmos, mediating between the eternal and temporal worlds. He saw Christ not only as the Son of God, but also as a power that could exist in other human beings. Declaring magic as the noblest art, he thought that humans could use the spiritual power in the stars to enhance physical and mental well-being as well as transform the outside world, for example, by gathering clouds for rain or curing diseases.

Ficino suggested that talismans, objects believed to hold supernatural power, could be worn to attract the positive influences of the spirit world. He also believed in Orphic singing, a kind of music that was originally practiced by non-Christian cults to address pagan gods, but which he claimed could connect humans to the good influences of planets and stars, thus bringing about the perfect harmony of body and soul. The prominence of music in *The Tempest* suggests a strong astrological element to magic, which is made more explicit in the play by Prospero's comment about "a most auspicious star" (1.2.182) whose influence allows him to bring the shipwrecked party to his island for reformation and transformation. The problem with astrology and Neoplatonism, from a Christian standpoint, is that it seemingly allowed for human beings to achieve their own salvation through contemplation of the cosmos without needing God. Although such contradictions existed in Ficino's time, they became much more of a concern as other scholars and magicians adopted his philosophy and began to reshape it and share it farther abroad.

CABALA

Another Florentine, Giovanni Pico della Mirandola (1463–1494), introduced a mystical, religious aspect of magic, cabala, to Renaissance occult philosophy. Cabala means "tradition" and refers to a Jewish tradition of ancient secret wisdom presumably handed down orally from prophets contemporary with Moses. Cabalist magic relied on the Hebrew alphabet and names of God, and a symbolic set of numbers attached to these letters and words to communicate with angels or divine spirits as a way of trying to know God more deeply. Cabalists adhered to the idea that the universe was an organized whole governed by secret laws and hidden connections through which all things reflected God. Pico associated this magic with Christianity. Like Ficino, Pico differentiated between the good magic he practiced and the bad magic that involved devil worship. For him, Christian cabala helped to dissolve some of the fears around demonic or diabolical magic by emphasizing holy forces, angels, and the sacred names of God (Yates, *Occult Philosophy* 24). Pico saw cabalism as a way of showing God's love to all living creatures by freeing them from impurities. He did not believe magic could work without a cabalistic component. In *The Tempest*, Prospero's dependence on the spirit world of Ariel, the secrecy of his art, and the emphasis in his magic on good motives rather than harmful outcomes suggest something of the cabalist mystical or divine aspect of Renaissance magic.

ALCHEMY

Another magical belief system, alchemy, also had ancient origins. It was a practice that came to Europe from the Arabs and appears to have begun in Egypt, where it derived from Eastern mystical cults. It was also based on the skills of early metalworkers and craftsmen. There were, in fact, two branches to alchemy. One focused on speculative philosophy and the other was grounded in chemical science, but the two traditions were considered compatible and analogous rather than distinct.

The primary goal of the chemical or scientific tradition was to turn base metals into gold, and in so doing, to find a universal cure for all diseases and a way to prolong life. A substance known as the philosopher's stone or elixir was considered necessary in the transmutation or multiplication process that changed metals into gold; thus ardent alchemists searched continually for the elusive philosopher's stone. They were convinced that with divine assistance they could make the substance from raw materials by a lengthy chemical process. Alchemy upheld the ancient belief that the universe consisted of four basic elements: earth, air, water, and fire; it also insisted that all matter had three substances in common: mercury, salt, and sulfur. As a precursor to modern chemistry, it required a laboratory with furnaces, glasses, and vessels where experiments were conducted on metals and other substances. Alchemy was contrary to modern science, however, in that its primary assumption, that baser metals could be turned into gold, was entirely unscientific and eventually proven false. Prospero's attention to his books and his constant need for wood to light the fire in his cell indicate an alchemical aspect to his magic for he is likely dependent on his private "laboratory" for his charms and spells, and therefore dependent also on Caliban to continue to bring him fuel for his art. Furthermore, the many references to the four basic elements, especially the association of Caliban with earth and water and of Ariel with air and fire, add to the alchemical atmosphere of the play.

In Renaissance alchemy, seven metals were identified and related to seven stars: Sun, Moon, Venus, Jupiter, Mars, Mercury, and Saturn. This relationship between metals and celestial bodies helped to connect the chemical or experimental branch of alchemy with the second branch, the philosophical. Alchemists believed that everything in the universe had parallels in the earthly world. "As above, so below," they insisted, indicating a harmony that worked through everything. The philosophical tradition focused more on things above than below and was considered more important than the physical process of turning metals into gold; the philosophical goal was the purification or perfection of the soul. Gold, known as the perfect metal, began to symbolize excellence, wisdom, light, love, and perfection. In *The Tempest,* we sense that the philosophical aspect of alchemy is of paramount importance, for Prospero is interested not in changing the properties of metals but in using his magical knowledge and skills to change the souls or minds of the "three men of sin" (3.3.53), Antonio, Sebastian, and Alonso, who had conspired years before to rob him of his dukedom.

One of the most influential Renaissance alchemists, Zurich-born Paracelsus (1493–1541), held an ambiguous position between chemists and mystics because he practiced medical chemistry but held many mystical notions. As a physician he created a huge controversy when he burned books written by the accepted authorities on medicine at the time, namely, Galen, Avicenna, and Hippocrates. Paracelsus believed that nothing should be taken as an authority until it had been subjected to experiment and proof. His insistence on this "scientific" approach was revolutionary, and he introduced to his time a whole series of medicines based on chemicals, not simply on herbs that had been standard treatments before him. More interested in finding a cure for diseases than transmuting metals into gold, Paracelsus began a new school of medical chemistry. But he believed in a philosophy that involved the whole person, body, mind, and spirit, not simply the body. He claimed that spirits surrounded human beings with good and bad effects and that human nature was gradually being purged of bad influences in preparation for a return to the Golden Age or the beginning of a new millennium.

HENRICUS CORNELIUS AGRIPPA

Henricus Cornelius Agrippa (1486–1535) compiled the most substantial work on magic in the sixteenth century, combining natural magic with cabalism. Agrippa's *De Occulta Philosophia* or *The Occult Philosophy* divided magic into three parts: elemental magic, which dealt with ways to influence the planets using talismans and incantations; celestial magic, which taught how to attract and influence the stars using mathematics, geometrical figures, and music; and intellectual or ceremonial magic, which focused on ways to reach angels and spirits through cabalism. Agrippa's place in the history of Renaissance magic is easily confused because his two prominent works are entirely contradictory. While *The Occult Philosophy* (written in 1510 but not published until 1533) supports and explains magical practices, his other treatise, *On the Uncertainty and Vanity of the Arts and Sciences* (published in 1530), speaks strongly against the occult arts as dangerous and dismisses the learning of all arts and sciences in general as vain, proud endeavors resulting from too much intellectual curiosity.

It is not clear whether Agrippa changed his views or whether he was merely trying to protect his interest in magic by writing a document that disclaimed its power and significance. What is clear is that, while Agrippa was highly influential with Renaissance magicians and philosophers, he was constantly troubled by a reputation as a prominent black magician and sorcerer. In part, this reputation may have emerged from his own writing, for unlike his predecessors, he showed an interest in ways that magic could not only serve good ends but also bring magicians personal wealth, political power, or revenge. In part, his bad reputation may have also resulted from his willingness to be an outspoken critic of ruling classes and respected intellectual and religious authorities. Reproving those in power made him an unpopular figure among those who could damage his status and character.

JOHN DEE

John Dee, an Englishman (1527–1608) sometimes considered a model for Shakespeare's Prospero, was greatly influenced by Cornelius Agrippa's tripartite view of the universe and quoted from him extensively. Dee became the most important student of the supernatural in his country, owning England's largest library and having a well-equipped laboratory for alchemical experiments. He was both a scientist and a mystic, becoming the leading mathematician and navigational expert in Elizabeth's reign but also attempting to communicate with the spiritual world. There were three significant periods to his life (Yates, *Occult Philosophy* 79). In the first period, he was widely respected by nobles, explorers, and the queen herself as he used his brilliant mathematical and geographical skills to provide advice to navigators, artisans, and technicians. He believed that his expertise should serve his country and was the first to coin the phrase "the British Empire" as he supported an enlarged navy and a national goal to expand England's territory in order to improve the world. During this period, he also served as Elizabeth's court astrologer, although he never received the royal favors from the queen for which he hoped.

In his second period, from 1583 to 1589, John Dee traveled the continent of Europe where he became known more for his mysticism than his mathematics. His partner in magic, Edward Kelley, served as his medium in his efforts to communicate with angels by crystal gazing, known as scrying. Dee relied on Kelley's scrying abilities as the two conjured up visions of angels and spirits. Kelley claimed to have the philosopher's stone, and the two men became very intent on the alchemical goal of turning base metals into gold. They went from one European court to another, spending some time with Rudolf II, emperor of the Holy Roman Empire, who had a great passion for alchemy. But each time they failed to produce gold, their hosts sent them on their way. Kelley was, in fact, a fraud and a charlatan who took advantage of Dee's optimistic, trusting nature. In 1589 they parted ways, and Dee began the third and last period of his life in England from 1590 until his death in 1608. His former merit as a scientist had been discredited by his crystal gazing, and a growing mania against sorcerers and witches led to his disgrace. A mob destroyed his alchemical lab and witch-hunters burned his books; he had to defend himself against accusations that he was a conjurer. After being shunned and isolated, he died in poverty in 1608. As a possible model for Shakespeare's Prospero and other stage magicians, he presents a profile of a magus or mage with both a noble and a suspicious or even scandalous reputation.

KING JAMES

The change in English monarchs from Queen Elizabeth to King James in 1603 contributed to John Dee's downfall and disrepute. James was hostile to Dee because of his own views about magic and witchcraft. In 1591, while king of Scotland before also ascending England's throne, James became the subject of a treasonous plot in which a group was accused of using sorcery and witchcraft to take his life. First, they claimed to raise a storm at sea as the king returned from Denmark with his new bride, Queen Anne, and then they cast a spell on a wax effigy to try to kill him. King James became intimately involved in the trial of the offenders and later composed a treatise on demonology in which he theorized about how sorcerers and witches practiced their magic and how they ought to be punished. His treatise, *Demonology*, was republished in England in the early seventeenth century as he became the new English monarch.

In 1604, James also revised an old Elizabethan statute against witchcraft, imposing renewed harsh penalties on witches and sorcerers. He wanted to get rid of all enchanters in the nation. John Dee appealed to King James to put him on trial personally to see if the title of "conjuror" or "invocator of devils" could be proved, but the king ignored the request. In spite of a letter written in his own defense, Dee never saw his name cleared from suspicion before his ignoble death.

WITCHCRAFT

Concern about witchcraft came to England not only from Scotland as James became king of both countries, but also from the European continent where witch-hunts became an obsessive pastime in the late sixteenth century. On the continent, witch trials were extremely harsh and violent, using torture as a means of extorting confessions from accused women. Similar practices occurred in Scotland. In England, however, torture was illegal except in charges of treason; but on the continent, witchcraft was seen as treason against God as well as the state.

A general distinction was made throughout the Western world between witchcraft and magic or between black magic and white magic. Witches were said to have denied God and made a pact with the devil, exchanging their souls for extraordinary powers that they used to influence nature and harm other human beings. Among their abilities, they were believed to be capable of raising storms, moving from place to place through the air, and causing sterility or death. They allegedly took part in the rituals of witch Sabbaths. White magic, in contrast, did not require the denial of God; in fact, rites and rituals of magic often invoked the power of the Holy Spirit. In popular understanding, magic was a male art that required sophisticated learning while witchcraft was a disreputable practice primarily of lower-class women. Magicians emphasized exact knowledge of the secrets of nature and the influence of the stars rather than a pact with the devil. The magician's state of mind was important; he was supposed to prepare himself for his art—in a sense purify himself—by fasting, meditation, or repentance.

However, it was not always easy to distinguish between witchcraft and other magic. Theologians and other critics claimed no difference between them. Both witchcraft and magic involved powers of daemons who were supernatural beings or spirits thought to dwell between God and human beings, some of which were considered friendly and others of which were thought to be unfriendly or hostile. Sometimes it was difficult to tell the difference between good and evil spirits. Recall in Shakespeare's tragedy, Hamlet's struggle to determine whether the ghost who appeared to him had good or evil intentions. At any rate, it was difficult to control the outcome once one willingly began to conjure spirits as a way of transcending normal human powers. Unfriendly daemons may have been vigorously condemned as part of black magic, but the attempt to invoke spirits left one vulnerable to malevolent forces and open to accusations of sorcery or black magic even if motives were primarily good or holy. Furthermore, some practitioners of white magic raised their voices as sympathetic supporters of witches on trial. One thing is certain: in the sixteenth and seventeenth centuries magic and witchcraft—whether distinguished from each other or equated with each other—were taken seriously by people from all walks of life in European society.

In *The Tempest,* the distinction between Caliban's mother Sycorax and Miranda's father Prospero at first seems quite clear. Sycorax was a witch who had used her powers to trap Ariel in a pine tree for 12 years and who gave birth to Caliban, who displays devilishly uncivil behavior. Prospero, a skilled white magician, releases Ariel from the tree, if only to make him a longtime servant with a promise of future freedom. Prospero treats his daughter with affection and practices his art to bring men to repentance and to set the context for harmony and reconciliation. An apparent contrast exists between white magic used for good and black magic used for evil purposes. Nevertheless, Shakespeare does not allow the distinctions to be entirely straightforward. Both Prospero and Sycorax are banished from their respective homes, Naples and Algiers, as known practitioners of magic. Both have relied on the spirit world to act out their charms. And even if their motives are different, Prospero enacts some of the same deeds for which witches were known, raising storms and raising the dead. His soliloquy in which he describes his magical powers and practices echoes the words of the mythic witch, Medea (5.1.33–50; see chapter 1). Thus, while there appears to be no relationship between Prospero and the devil, and

Prospero's deeds, although sometimes appearing harsh, have a benevolent outcome or intent, the line between white and black magic in the play is potentially ambiguous, made all the more so when Prospero declares, "But this rough magic / I here abjure" (5.1.50–51), a strong statement that suggests he is giving up something that has become unacceptable or offensive.

THEATRICAL TRADITION

Prospero was not the only magician or magus on the Renaissance stage in England. Interest in mystical arts and controversy surrounding white and black magic inspired other dramatists to present their own renditions of theatrical magi. Two plays, Christopher Marlowe's *Doctor Faustus* (1592) and Ben Jonson's *The Alchemist* (1610), offer interesting alternative perspectives on stage magicians. *Doctor Faustus,* based on the German Faust legend, is an Elizabethan tragedy about the battle between good and evil in which the main character sells his soul to the devil to acquire magical skills and ends up condemned to hell because he cannot accept God's forgiveness for his choices. Jonson's *The Alchemist* offers quite a different tone as a satiric comedy that mocks alchemy and criticizes the underlying motivation of human greed through the main character, Doctor Subtle, a fraud who uses the pretense of magic for his own gain. In contrast to *The Tempest,* both of these plays censure magical arts as either dangerous or false and expose the human impulses that lead one to desire power beyond one's human limitations. All three plays, however, raise questions about what is illusion and what is real and demonstrate the "magicians'" power through language to conjure and to influence the actions of other characters. If Marlowe and Jonson were fairly conservative in their condemnation of magical arts, Shakespeare allowed himself to play with ambiguous possibilities while ultimately having Prospero reject the good effects of his magic for a more conventional life. The stage proved to be a place to engage with social and political issues that were contemporary, contentious, and relevant, including broad-sweeping curiosity and vigorous debate surrounding the study and practice of magic.

DECLINE OF MAGIC

Magic, as an art to be practiced, began its decline for reasons largely religious and scientific. Controversy over magic became especially intense from the 1570s to the early seventeenth century. From a religious perspective, occult efforts to Christianize ancient classical, pagan writings and fuse human powers of transcendence with God-centered traditions grew more and more suspicious. Reaction against magicians became stronger on the European continent in a backlash against both Neoplatonism and the theological challenges of the Protestant Reformation. In 1600, Giordano Bruno (b. 1548), a traveling occult missionary, was burned at the stake in Rome as a sorcerer. But his was an unusually celebrated case. The witch craze was more closely tied to condemnation of women practitioners of magical arts. Alleged female witches were routinely accused and tried successfully because they were easier targets to convict than educated men practicing occult philosophy and enjoying frequent ties to the courts of rulers in various European states. At any rate, most magicians defended themselves as practicing effective white magic, while most accusers saw them as evil sorcerers and an occasional few dismissed them as frauds.

Part of this trend developed because of ideas presented by magicians themselves. They advocated the view that humans had the potential to influence the natural world and explore the cosmos, whereas people in the earlier medieval period saw themselves as fixed figures in a cosmic hierarchy. This more active perspective of humanity, along with the pseudoscientific nature of much magic, seemingly bringing together fields such as early forms of chemistry, botany, zoology, mathematics, and astronomy, gradually fed a growing taste for true science. A leading English figure in this development, Francis Bacon (1561–1626), began to downplay the mysteriousness of the alchemist and emphasize the need for properly conducted experiments among groups of scientists from different fields. As this organized, institutional aspect of science began to take hold, the image of the all-powerful magus began to lose its luster, and occult practices were taken over primarily by cheats and impostors.

Shakespeare wrote *The Tempest* in 1610–1611 when religion and science were beginning to be seen as separate entities, when the witch craze was beginning to fade, when James—with his reputation for condemning sorcery—was on the throne, and when some of the most powerful advocates of occult philosophy were becoming figures of history. What this chapter's survey of Renaissance magic suggests is that Shakespeare and his audience had a variety of views to choose from in their response to human engagement with the supernatural world. The ambiguities in the play about attitudes toward magic and the practice of it draw from the controversies of the time while celebrating—in comic style—the good that can come from a mage using his skills to transform the world around him.

The remainder of this chapter includes a brief chronology of significant dates and excerpted documents including history books, treatises, letters, and plays that were current and relevant in Shakespeare's time.

Brief Chronology of the History of Magic in the Renaissance

1463	Florentine Marsilio Ficino translates Greek manuscript of "Hermes Trismegistus"
1463	Cabalist Pico della Mirandola born in Florence (died in 1494)
1486	Occult philosopher Henricus Cornelius Agrippa born (died in1535)
1493	Renaissance alchemist Paracelsus born (died in 1541)
1527	English magus John Dee born
1530	Agrippa's *On the Uncertainty and Vanity of the Arts and Sciences* published
1533	Agrippa's *The Occult Philosophy* published (written in 1510)
1561	Francis Bacon born (died in 1626)—a proponent of scientific experiment and critic of the secrecy and mysticism surrounding alchemy
1584	Reginald Scot's *The Discovery of Witchcraft* published, arguing that most fears of witchcraft and sorcery are unfounded
1591	Trial for treasonous witchcraft against James VI of Scotland
1592	Christopher Marlowe's *Doctor Faustus* composed
1597	King James VI's *Demonology* published, expressing his beliefs in sorcery and witchcraft
1600	Giordano Bruno, a magician, burned at the stake in Rome
1603	James VI of Scotland becomes James I of England
1604	James I imposes a new statute against witchcraft and sorcery; John Dee's letter of self-defense published (written in 1595)
1608	John Dee dies in poverty and disrepute
1610	Ben Jonson's *The Alchemist* performed by the King's Men
1610–11	Probable date of Shakespeare's *The Tempest*
1614	Sir Walter Raleigh's *History of the World* published, including a defense of magic

SIR WALTER RALEIGH'S DEFENSE OF MAGIC

Sir Walter Raleigh (1552–1618) was an English courtier, explorer, historian, and poet. He was a favorite of Queen Elizabeth and prospered under her reign, being granted lands, titles, and permission to colonize Ireland and North America. When James I became England's monarch, however, Raleigh's fortunes changed as King James despised him and soon charged him with a conspiracy to overthrow the king. Raleigh spent thirteen years imprisoned in the Tower where he wrote most of his works. *The History of the World* (1614) was an ambitious uncompleted project meant to trace the world's history from the story of Creation, through Greek mythology and Roman history to Raleigh's own times. The following excerpt is part of Raleigh's defense of magic. Although he had a reputation among his enemies as being an atheist, he is careful in this account to legitimize magic by connecting it with worship of God and dissociating it from the work of the devil. In S. 2 below, Raleigh describes three kinds of magic, noting their virtues and paying tribute to Zoroaster, a key figure in the history of magic. In S. 3, Raleigh defends the practice of magic against claims of the devil's meddling in it. Notice how he presents his case, arguing that the misuse of an art does not take away from its inherent goodness. Pay attention to the examples he offers to make this point about the inherent goodness of magic in spite of devilish abuses of it. Consider how good use and misuse of magic appear in *The Tempest* in the practices of Prospero and Caliban's mother, the witch Sycorax.

FROM SIR WALTER RALEIGH, *THE HISTORY OF THE WORLD*

(London: Printed for Walter Burre, 1614) Book 1, 199–205

Ch. XI, S. 1 Of Zoroaster, *supposed to have been the chief Author of Magic Arts: and of the diverse kinds of Magic*
S. 2 *Of the name of Magia: and that it was anciently far diverse from conjuring, and Witchcraft.*

Now for *Magic* itself; which Art (saith *Mirandola*) ... *Few understand, and many reprehend* ... *As dogs bark at those they know not:* so they condemn and hate the things they understand not: I think it not amiss ... to speak somewhat thereof. ...

Magus is a *Persian* word primitively; whereby is expressed such a one as is altogether conversant in things divine. And (as *Plato* affirmeth) the art of *Magic* is the art of worshipping God. To which effect *Apollonius*... addeth that *Magus*... is a name sometime of him that is a God by nature; sometimes of him that is in the service of God: in which latter sense it is taken *Matt. c.2.v.1.* And this is the first and highest kind: which *Piccolominie* calleth divine *Magic:* and these did the *Latins* newly entitle *Sapientes* or *wisemen: For the fear & worship of God is the beginning of knowledge.* These *Wisemen* the *Greeks* call *Philosophers:* the *Indians Brachmans:* which name they somewhat nearly retain to this day, calling their Priests *Bramines;* among the *AEgyptians* they were termed Priests; with the *Hebrews* they were called *Cabalists, Prophets, Scribes,* and *Pharisees:* amongst the *Babylonians* they were differenced by the name of *Chaldeans:* and among the *Persians Magicians*... .

A second kind of *Magic* was that part of *Astrology,* which had respect to sowing and planting, and all kinds of agriculture and husbandry: which was a knowledge of the motions and influences of the Stars into those lower elements....

The third kind of *Magic* containeth the whole Philosophy of nature; not the brabblings of the *Aristotelians,* but that which bringeth to light the inmost virtues, and draweth them out of nature's hidden bosom to human use,... *Virtues hidden in the center of the center,* according to the *Chymists*....

In all these three kinds which other men divide into four, it seemeth that *Zoroaster* was exceedingly learned: especially in the first and highest. For in his *Oracles* he confesseth God to be the Creator of the Universal: he believeth of the *Trinity,* which he could not investigate by any natural knowledge: he speaketh of Angels, and of *Paradise:* approveth the immortality of the soul: teacheth Truth, Faith, Hope, and Love, discoursing of the Abstinence and Charity of the *Magi,* which *Oracles* of his, *Psellus, Ficinus, Patritius,* and others have gathered and translated.... *Thus writeth Zoroaster, word for word. God the first incorruptible, everlasting, unbegotten, without parts, most like himself, the guide of all good, expecting no reward, the best, the wisest, the father of right, having learn'd justice without teaching, perfect wise by nature, the only inventor thereof*....

S.3 *That the good knowledge in the ancient Magic is not to be condemned: though the Devil here as in other kinds hath sought to obtrude evil things under the name and colour of good things.*

Seeing therefore it is confessed by all of understanding, that a *Magician* (according to the *Persian* word) is no other than... *A studious observer and expounder of divine things:* and the art itself (I mean the Art of natural *Magic*) no other... *Than the absolute perfection of natural Philosophy:* Certainly then it proceedeth from common ignorance, and no way sorteth with wise and learned men... and without difference and distinction, to confound lawful and praise-worthy knowledge with that impious, and (to use S. *Paul's* words) *with those beggarly rudiments,* which the Devil hath shuffled in, and by them bewitcheth and befooleth graceless men. For if we condemn natural *Magic,* or the wisdom of nature, because the Devil (who knoweth more than any man) doth also teach Witches and Poisoners the harmful parts of herbs, drugs, minerals, and excrements: then may we by the same rule condemn the Physician, and the Art of healing. For the Devil also in the Oracles of *Amphiaraus, Amphilochus, Trophonius,* and the like, taught men in dreams what herbs and drugs were proper for such and such diseases. Now no man of judgment is ignorant, that the Devil from the beginning hath sought to thrust himself into the same employment among the ministers and servants of God, changing himself for that purpose into an Angel of light. He hath led me to Idolatry as a doctrine of religion; he hath thrust in his Prophets among those of the true God; he hath corrupted the Art of *Astrology,* by giving a divine power to the Stars teaching men to esteem them as Gods, and not as instruments. And (as *Bunting* observeth) it is true, that judicial *Astrology* is corrupted with many superstitions: but the abuse of the thing takes not away the Art; considering that heavenly bodies (as even general experience showeth) have and exercise their operation upon the inferior. For the Sun, and the Star of *Mars* do dry; the Moon doth moisten, and govern the Tides of the Sea. Again, the Planets, as they have several and proper names, so have they several and proper virtues: the Stars do also differ in beauty and in magnitude; and to all the Stars hath God given also their proper names, which (had they not influences and virtues different) needed not: *He counteth the number of the Stars, and calleth them by their names.* But into the good and profitable knowledge of the celestial influences, the Devil ceaseth not to shuffle in his superstitions: and so to the knowledge of the secret virtues of nature hath he fastened his doctrine of *Characters,* numbers, and incantations; and taught men to believe in the strength of words and letters: (which without faith in God are but ink or common breath) thereby either to equal his own with the all-powerful word of God, or to diminish the glory of God's creating word, by whom are all things....

REGINALD SCOT'S SKEPTICAL VIEW OF WITCHCRAFT AND MAGIC

Reginald Scot's (1538?–1599) *The Discovery of Witchcraft* (1584) was the first strong argument against superstitions surrounding witchcraft and sorcery and existed as the sole rational argument in a time of public paranoia. Scot's unpopular position forced him to publish his work independently, and when King James ascended the throne in 1603, he insisted that all copies of *The Discovery of Witchcraft* be destroyed. Only a few copies survived to later record Scot's views. The first excerpt below is from Scot's introductory chapter in which he presents his main position that belief in witches is baseless because God is the only being with the superhuman power that people were readily attributing to witches. Scot focuses especially on storms and weather as he discounts the enchantments of witches. This is the very sort of spell that Prospero successfully casts over the ship near the island at the beginning of *The Tempest,* associating Prospero's art with popular beliefs about powers of witches.

The second excerpt from Book XI, Chapter XI describes the secrecy and complexity of cabalistic or spiritual magic and then discounts it by appealing to biblical authorities, and the third excerpt from Book IV, Chapter II recounts a tale from the medieval poet, Geoffrey Chaucer, in which a priest is deceived by a canon's yeoman who pretends to practice alchemy in order to swindle some money from the priest. In each of these accounts, Scot adopts a skeptical tone about the existence of magic, discrediting human abilities to influence the supernatural. His perspective would allow little room to engage in the tone of wonder surrounding Shakespeare's fictional tale of a magician conjuring spirits and practicing alchemical art.

FROM REGINALD SCOT, *THE DISCOVERY OF WITCHCRAFT* (1584), INTRO. BY HUGH ROSS WILLIAMSON

(1584; Arundel: Centaur Press, 1964)

Book I

Chapter I

An impeachment of Witches' power in meteors and elementary bodies tending to the rebuke of such as attribute too much unto them.

The fables of Witchcraft have taken so fast hold and deep root in the heart of man, that few or none can (nowadays) with patience endure the hand and correction of

God. For if any adversity, grief, sickness, loss of children, corn, cattle, or liberty happen unto them; by & by they exclaim upon witches. As though there were no God in Israel that ordereth all things according to his will; punishing both just and unjust with griefs, plagues, and afflictions in manner and form as he thinketh good: but that certain old women here on earth, called witches, must needs be the contrivers of all men's calamities, and as though they themselves were innocents, and had deserved no such punishments. . . .

Such faithless people (I say) are also persuaded, that neither hail nor snow, thunder nor lightning, rain nor tempestuous winds come from the heavens at the commandment of God: but are raised by the cunning and power of witches and conjurers; insomuch as a clap of thunder, or a gale of wind is no sooner heard, but either they run to ring bells, or cry out to burn witches; or else burn consecrated things, hoping by the smoke thereof, to drive the devil out of the air, as though spirits could be fraied away with such external toys. . . .

But certainly, it is neither a witch, nor devil, but a glorious God that maketh the thunder. I have read in the scriptures, that God maketh the blustering tempests and whirlwinds: and I find that it is the Lord that altogether dealeth with them, and that they blow according to his will. . . .

But little think our witchmongers, that the Lord commandeth the clouds above, or openeth the doors of heaven, as *David* affirmeth; or that the Lord goeth forth in the tempests and storms, as the Prophet *Nahum* reporteth: but rather that witches and conjurers are then about their business.

. . . But if all the devils in hell were dead, and all the witches in *England* burned or hanged; I warrant you we should not fail to have rain, hail and tempests, as now we have: according to the appointment and will of God, and according to the constitution of the elements, and the course of the planets, wherein God hath set a perfect and perpetual order.

I am also well assured, that if all the old women in the world were witches; and all the priests, conjurers: we should not have a drop of rain, nor a blast of wind the more or less for them. For the Lord hath bound the waters in the clouds, and hath set bounds about the waters, until the day and night come to an end: yea it is God that raiseth the winds and stilleth them: and he saith to the rain and snow; Be upon the earth, and it falleth. The wind of the Lord, and not the wind of witches, shall destroy the treasures of their pleasant vessels, and dry up the fountains; saith [*Hosea*]. Let us also learn and confess with the Prophet *David,* that we ourselves are the causes of our afflictions; and not exclaim upon witches, when we should call upon God for mercy. (25–26)

Book XI

Chapter XI

Of the Cabalistical art, consisting of traditions and unwritten verities learned without book, and of the division thereof.

Here is the place also for the Cabalistical art, consisting of unwritten verities, which the Jews do believe and brag that God himself gave to *Moses* in the mount *Sinai;* and afterwards taught only with lively voice by degrees of succession, without writing, until the time of *Esdras:* even as the scholars of *Archippus* did use wit and memory instead of books. They divide this in twain; the one expoundeth with philosophical reason the secrets of the law and the bible, where (they say) that *Solomon* was very cunning; because it is written in the Hebrew stories, that he disputed from the Cedar of *Libanus,* even to the Hisop, and also of birds, beasts &c. The other is as it were a symbolical divinity of the highest contemplation, of the divine and angel-like virtues, of holy names and signs; wherein the letters, numbers, figures, things and arms, the pricks, over the letters, the lines, the points, and the accents do all signify very profound things and great secrets. By these arts the Atheists suppose *Moses* wrote all his miracles, and that hereby they have power over angels and devils, as also to do miracles: yea and that hereby all the miracles that either any of the prophets, or Christ himself wrought, were accomplished.

But *C. Agrippa* having searched to the bottom of this art, saith it is nothing but superstition and folly. Otherwise you may be sure Christ would not have hidden it from his church. For this cause the Jews were so skilful in the names of God. But there is none other name in heaven or earth, in which we might be saved, but Jesus: neither is that meant by his bare name, but by his virtue and goodness towards us. These Cabalists do further brag, that they are able hereby, not only to find out and know the unspeakable mysteries of God; but also the secrets which are above scripture; whereby also they take upon them to prophesy, and to work miracles: yea hereby they can make what they list to be scripture. . . . And therefore these their revolutions are nothing but allegorical games, which idle men busied in letters, points, and numbers (which the Hebrew tongue easily suffereth) devise, to delude and cozen the simple and ignorant. And this they call Alphabetary or Arithmantical divinity, which Christ showed to his apostles only, and which *Paul* saith he speaketh but among perfect men; and being high mysteries are not to be committed unto writing, and so made popular. (175–176)

Book XIV

Chapter II

The Alchemister's drift, the Canon's yeoman's tale, of alchemystical stones and waters

Now you must understand that the end and drift of all their [the Alchemisters'] work, is to attain unto the composition of the philosopher's stone, called Elixir, and to the stone called Titanus; and to Magnatia, which is a water made of the four elements, which (they say) the philosophers are sworn neither to discover, nor to write of. And by these they mortify quicksilver, and make it malleable, and to hold touch: hereby also they convert any other metal (but especially copper) into gold. This science (forsooth) is the secret of secrets; even as *Solomon's* conjuration is said among the conjurors to be so likewise. And thus, when they chance to meet with young men, or simple people, they boast and brag, and say with *Simon Magus,* that they can work miracles, and bring mighty things to pass....

The tale of the canon's yeoman published by *Chaucer,* doth make (by way of example) a perfect demonstration of the art of Alchemistry or multiplication: the effect whereof is this. A canon being an Alchemister or cozenor, espied a covetous priest, whose purse he knew to be well lined, whom is assaulted with flattery and subtle speech, two principal points belonging to this art. At the length he borrowed money of the priest, which is the third part of the art, without which the professors can do no good, nor endure in good estate. Then he at his day repaid the money, which is the most difficult point in this art, and a rare experiment. Finally, to requite the priest's courtesy, he promised unto him such instructions, as whereby with expedition he should become infinitely rich, and all through this art of multiplication. And this is the most common point in this science; for herein they must be skilful before they can be famous, or attain to any credit. The priest disliked not his proffer; especially because it tended to his profit, and embraced his courtesy. Then the canon willed him forthwith to send for three ounces of quicksilver, which he said he would transubstantiate (by his art) into perfect silver. The priest thought that a man of his profession could not dissemble, and therefore with great joy and hope accomplished his request.

And now (forsooth) goeth this jolly Alchemist about his business and work of multiplication, and causeth the priest to make a fire of coals, in the bottom whereof he placeth a crosslet; and pretending only to help the priest to lay the coals handsomely, he foisteth into the middle ward or lane of coals, a beechen coal, within the which was conveyed an ingot of perfect silver, which (when the coal was consumed) slipped down into the crosslet, that was (I say) directly under it. The priest perceived not the fraud, but received the ingot of silver, and was not a little joyful to see such certain success proceed from his own handiwork wherein could be no fraud (as he surely conceived) and therefore very willingly gave the canon forty pounds for the receipt of this experiment, who for that sum of money taught him a lesson in Alchemistry, but he never returned to hear repetitions, or to see how he profited. (298–300)

KING JAMES'S VIEWS ON DEMONOLOGY

King James's *Demonology* (1597), composed after the trial against treasonous witchcraft in Scotland, addresses in learned style the seriousness of
witchcraft and the dangers of practicing magic or sorcery. In the first excerpt
from the introduction, James establishes the evil foundation of magic and
dismisses the skeptical views of men such as Reginald Scot. The main part
of the treatise is organized as a dialogue between two characters, Philomathes
and Epistemon. In the excerpts from the First Book below, in Chapter II,
Epistemon distinguishes between magic and sorcery or witchcraft according
to three passions that lead to these devilish arts; in Chapter III and Chapter
IV, he discourses on the distinction between lawful astrology and the unlawful black magic that arises under astronomy. The danger, he suggests, is
in too much curiosity that leads from studying simple natural causes to conjuring spirits and predicting the future. In the last excerpt from Book II,
Chapter V, Epistemon suggests why more women than men become witches,
describes some of the powers of witches, including raising storms, and spec-
ulates about three kinds of people who might suffer bewitchment. Consider,
as you read, where Prospero might fit into the scheme of lawful and unlawful practices and whether Epistemon might condemn or approve of Prospero's art.

FROM KING JAMES THE FIRST, *DEMONOLOGY* (1597), SEE ED. G. B. HARRISON, ELIZABETHAN AND JACOBEAN QUARTOS

(New York: Barnes & Noble, 1966)

The fearful abounding at this time in this country, of these detestable slaves of the
Devil, the Witches or enchanters, hath moved me (beloved reader) to dispatch in post,
this following treatise of mine, not in any wise (as I protest) to serve for a show of my
learning & engine, but only (moved of conscience) to press / thereby, so far as I can,
to resolve the doubting hearts of many; both that such assaults of Satan are most certainly practiced, & that the instruments thereof, merits most severely to be punished:
against the damnable opinions of two principally in our age, whereof the one called
SCOT an Englishman, is not ashamed in public print to deny, that there can be such
a thing as Witch-craft. (xi)

First Book

Chap. II

....

PHI[LOMATHES] Then this sin is a sin against the holy Ghost.

EPI[STEMON] It is in some, but not in all.

PHI[LOMATHES] How that? Are not all these that runs directly to the Devil in one Category.

EPI[STEMON] God forbid, for the sin against the holy Ghost hath two branches: The one a falling back from the whole service of GOD, and a refusal of all his precepts.... Now in the first of these two, all sorts of Necromancers, Enchanters or Witches, are comprehended....

PHI[LOMATHES] Then it appears there are more sorts nor one, that are directly professors of his service: and if so be, I pray you tell me how may, and what are they?

EPI[STEMON] There are principally two sorts, whereunto all the parts of that unhappy art are redacted; whereof the one is called *Magie* or *Necromancy,* the other *Sorcery* or *Witch-craft.*

PHI. What I pray you? and how many are the means, whereby the Devil allures persons in any of these snares?

EPI. Even by these three passions that are within ourselves: Curiosity in great engines: thirst of revenge, for some tortes deeply apprehended: or greedy appetite of gear, caused through great poverty. As to the first of these, Curiosity, it is only the enticement of *Magicians,* or *Necromancers:* and the other two are the allurers of the *Sorcerers,* or *Witches,* for that old and crafty Serpent, being a spirit, he easily spies our affections, and so conforms himself thereto, to deceive us to our wrack. (7–8)

Chap. III

....

PHI. What difference is there betwixt [*Magie* or *Necromancy*] and Witch-craft.

EPI. Surely, the difference vulgar put betwixt them, is very merry, and in a manner true; for they say, that the Witches are servants only, and slaves to the Devil; but the Necromanciers are his masters and commanders.

PHI. How can that be true, [that] any men being specially addicted to his service, can be his commanders?

EPI. Yea, they may be: but it is only [secondary]: For it is not by any power that they can have over him, but *ex pacto* allanerly; whereby he obliges himself in some trifles to them, that he may on the other part obtain the fruition of their body & soul, which is the only thing he hunts for.

PHI. An very inequitable contract forsooth: But I pray you discourse unto me, what is the effect and secrets of that art?

EPI. That is overlarge an field ye give me: yet I shall do good-will, the most summarily that I can, to run through the principal points thereof. As there are two sorts of folks, that may be enticed to this art, to wit, learned or unlearned: so is there two means, which are the first stirrers up & feeders of their curiosity, thereby to make them to give themselves over to the same: Which two means, I call the Devil's school, and his rudiments. The learned have their curiosity wakened up; and fed by that which I call his school: this is the *Astrology* judiciar. For diverse men having attained to a great perfection in learning, & yet remaining overbare (alas) of the spirit of regeneration and fruits thereof: finding all natural things common, as well to the stupid pedants as unto them, they essay to vindicate unto them a greater name, by not only knowing the course of things heavenly, but likewise to climb to the knowledge of things to come thereby. Which, at the first face appearing lawful unto them, in respect the ground thereof seemeth to proceed of natural causes only: they are so allured thereby, that finding their practice to prove true in sundry things, they study to know the cause thereof: and so mounting from degree to degree, upon the slippery and uncertain scale of curiosity; they are at last enticed, that where lawful arts or sciences fails, to satisfy their restless minds, even to seek to that black and unlawful science of *Magie.* Where, finding at the first, that such diverse forms of circles & conjurations rightly joined thereunto, will raise such diverse forms of spirits, to resolve them of their doubts: and attributing the doing thereof, to the power inseparably tied, or inherent in the circles: and many words of God, confusedly wrapped in; they blindly glory of themselves, as if they had by their quickness of engine, made a conquest of *Pluto's* dominion, and were become Emperors over the *Stygian* habitacles. Where, in the meantime (miserable wretches) they are become in very deed, bond-slaves to their mortal enemy: and their knowledge for all that they presume thereof, is nothing increased, except in knowing evil, and the horrors of Hell for punishment thereof, as *Adam's* was by the eating of the forbidden tree. (9–11)

Chap. IV

. . . .

PHI. But methinks these means which ye call the School and rudiments of the Devil, are things lawful, and have been approved for such in all times and ages: As in special, this science of *Astrology,* which is one of the special members of the *Mathematics.*

EPI. There are two things which the learned have observed from the beginning, in the science of the Heavenly Creatures, the Planets, Stars, and such like: The one is their course and ordinary motions, which for that cause is called *Astronomia:* . . . that is to say, the law of the Stars: And this art indeed is one of the members of the *Mathematics,* & not only lawful, but most necessary and commendable. The other is called *Astrologia,* . . . which is to say, the word, and preaching of the stars: Which is divided in two parts: The first by knowing thereby the powers of simples and sicknesses, the course of the seasons and the weather, being ruled by their influence; which part depending upon the former, although it be not of itself a part of *Mathematics:* yet it is not unlawful, being moderately used, suppose not so necessary and commendable as the former. The second part is to trust so much to their influences, as thereby to fore-tell what common-weals shall flourish or decay: what persons shall be fortunate or un-fortunate: what side shall win in any battle: What man shall obtain victory at singular combat: What way, and of what age shall men die: What horse shall win at match-running; and diverse such like incredible things, wherein *Cardanus, Cornelius Agrippa,* and diverse others have more curiously then profitably written at large. Of this root last spoken of, springs innumerable branches; such as the knowledge by the nativi-ties.... And this part of *Astrology* whereof I have spoken, which is the root of their branches, was called by them *pars fortunae.* This part now is utterly unlawful to be trusted in, or practiced among Christians, as leaning to no ground of natural reason: & it is this part which I called before the devil's school.

PHI But yet many of the learned are of the contrary opinion.

EPI. I grant, yet I could give my reasons to fortify & maintain my opinion, if to enter into this disputation it would not draw me quite off the ground of our discourse; be-sides the mis-spending of the whole day thereupon: One word only I will answer to them, & that in the Scriptures (which must be an infallible ground to all true Chris-tians) That in the Prophet *Jeremiah* it is plainly forbidden, to believe or hearken unto them that Prophesies & forespeaks by the course of the Planets and Stars. (12–14)

Second Book

Chap. V

. . . .

PHI. What can be the cause that there are twenty women given to [witchcraft], where there is one man?

EPI. The reason is easy, for as that sex is frailer than man is, so is it easier to be en-trapped in these gross snares of the Devil, as was over well proved to be true, by the Serpent's deceiving of *Eve* at the beginning, which makes him the homlier with that sex sensine.... They can raise storms and tempests in the air, either upon Sea or land, though not universally, but in such a particular place and prescribed bounds, as God will permit them so to trouble: Which likewise is very easy to be discerned from any other natural tempests that are meteors, in respect of the sudden and violent raising thereof, together with the short enduring of the same.... They can make folks to be-come frenetic or Maniac, which likewise is very possible to their master to do, since they are but natural sicknesses: and so may he lay on these kinds, as well as any oth-ers. They can make spirits either to follow and trouble persons, or haunt certain houses, and affray often times the inhabitants: as hath been known to be done by our Witches at this time. And likewise they can make some to be possessed with spirits, & so to become very Demoniacs: and this last sort is very possible likewise to the Devil their Master to do, since he may easily send his own angels to trouble in what form he pleases, any whom God will permit him so to use.

PHI. But will God permit these wicked instruments by the power of the Devil their master, to trouble by any of these means, any that believes in him?

EPI. No doubt, for there are three kind of folks whom God will permit so to be tempted or troubled: the wicked for their horrible sins, to punish them in the like measure; The godly that are sleeping in any great sins or infirmities and weakness in faith, to waken them up the faster by such an uncouth form: and even some of the best, that their patience may be tried before the world as JOB'S was. For why may not God use any kind of extraordinary punishment, when it pleases him; as well as the ordinary rods of sickness or other adversities. (43–47)

JOHN DEE'S DEFENSE OF HIS MAGICAL ARTS

Englishman John Dee, philosopher, alchemist, and mathematician (1527–1608), suffered much criticism and condemnation—especially later in life—for his practice of magic. The following document is a letter he wrote and addressed to the Archbishop of Canterbury, defending his "studious exercises" in philosophy against all the attacks he received. The letter was written in 1595 in the reign of Queen Elizabeth—and thus he mentions "her Majesty"—but was published in 1604, early in James's reign when Dee likely felt the mood of intolerance was on the rise. He deliberately associates his study and practice with the beliefs of Christianity and portrays himself as a loyal servant of the English monarch. Try to gauge the tone of his letter and decide whether you find him credible and sympathetic or otherwise.

FROM JOHN DEE, *A LETTER, CONTAINING A MOST BRIEF DISCOURSE APOLOGETICALL, WITH A PLAIN DEMONSTRATION, AND FERVENT PROTESTATION, FOR THE LAWFULL, SINCERE, VERY FAITHFULL AND CHRISTIAN COURSE, OF THE PHILOSOPHICAL STUDIES AND EXERCISES, OF A CERTAIN STUDIOUS GENTLEMAN: AN ANCIENT SERVANT TO HER MOST EXCELLENT MAJESTY ROYAL*

(written in 1595; London: 1604)

To the most Reverend father in God, the Lord Archbishop of Canterbury, Primate and Metropolitan of all England, one of her Majesty's most honorable privy Counsel: my singular good Lord.

Most humbly and heartily I crave your Grace's pardon, if I offend anything, to send, or present unto your Grace's hand, so simple a discourse as this is: Although by some sage and discreet my friends their opinion, it is thought not to be impertinent, to my most needful suits, presently in hand, (before her most excellent Majesty Royal, your Lordship's good Grace, and other the Right honorable Lords of her Majesty's Privy Counsel) to make some part of my former studies, and studious exercises... to be first known and discovered unto your Grace, and other the Right honorable my good Lords, of her Majesty's Privy Counsel: And, Secondly, afterwards, the same to be permitted to come to public view: Not so much, to stop the mouths; and, at length to stay the impudent attempts, of the rash, and malicious devisors and contrivers of most untrue, foolish, and wicked reports, and fables, of, and concerning my foresaid studious exercises, passed over, with my great, (yea incredible) pains, travels, cares, and costs, in the search, and learning of true Philosophy; As, therein, So, to certify, and satisfy the godly and unpartial Christian hearer, or reader hereof: That, by his own judgment, (upon his due consideration, and examination of this, no little parcel, of the particulars of my foresaid studies, and exercises philosophical annexed) He will, or may, be sufficiently informed, and persuaded; That I have wonderfully labored, to find, follow, use, & haunt the true, straight, and most narrow path, leading all true, devout, zealous, faithful, and constant Christian students.... All thanks, are most due, therefore, unto the Almighty: Seeing, it so pleased him, (even from my youth, by his divine favor, grace, and help) to insinuate into my heart, an insatiable zeal, & desire, to know his truth: And in him, and by him, incessantly to seek, and listen after the same; by the true philosophical method and harmony; proceeding and ascending, (as it were) *gradatim,* from things visible, to consider of things invisible: from things bodily, to conceive of things spiritual: from things transitory, & momentary, to meditate of things permanent: by things mortal...to have some perceiverance of immortality. And too conclude, most briefly; by the most marvelous frame of the *whole World,* philosophically viewed, and circumspectly weighted, numbered, and measured (according to the talent, & gift of God, from above allotted, for his divine purposes effecting) most faithfully to love, honor, and glorify always, the *Framer,* and *Creator* thereof. In whose workmanship, his infinite goodness, unsearchable wisdom, and Almighty power, yea, his everlasting power, and divinity, may (by innumerable means) be manifested and demonstrated.

· · ·

But the great losses and damages which in sundry sorts I have sustained, do not so much grieve my heart, as the rash, lewd, fond, and most untrue fables and reports of me and my studies philosophical, have done, & yet do: which commonly, after their first hatching, and devilish devising, immediately with great speed, are generally all the Realm overspread; and to some, seem true; to other, they are doubtful: and to only the wise, modest, discreet, godly, and charitable (and chiefly to such as have some acquaintance with me) they appear, and are known to be fables, untruths, and utterly false reports, and slanders. Well, this shall be my last charitable giving of warning, and fervent protestation to my Countrymen and all other in this case:

Before the Almighty our God, and your Lordship's good grace, this day, on the peril of my soul's damnation (if I lie, or take his name in vain herein) I take the same God, to be my witness; that, with all my heart, with all my soul, with all my strength, power, and understanding (according to the measure thereof, which the Almighty hath given me) for the most part of the time, from my youth hitherto, I have used, and still use, good, lawful, honest, Christian, and divinely prescribed means, to attain to the knowledge of those truths, which are meet, and necessary for me to know; and wherewith to do his divine Majesty such service, as he hath, doth, and will call me unto, during this my life: for his honor and glory advancing, and for the benefit, and commodity public of this kingdom; so much, as by the will, and purpose of God, shall lie in my skill, and ability to perform: as a true, faithful, and most sincerely dutiful servant, to our most gracious and incomparable Queen Elizabeth, and as a very comfortable fellow-member of the body politic, governed under the Scepter Royal of our Supreme head (Queen Elizabeth) and as a lively sympathicall, and true symmetrical fellow-member, of that holy mystical body, Catholic extended and placed (wheresoever) on the earth: in the view, knowledge, direction, protection, illumination; and consolation of the Almighty, most blessed, most holy, most glorious, comajestical, coeternal, and coessential Trinity: The head of that body, being only our Redeemer, Christ Jesus, perfect God and perfect man: whose return in glory, we faithfully await, and daily do very earnestly cry unto him, to hasten his second coming, for his elects' sake: iniquity doth soon this earth, abound, and prevail, and true faith with charity, and Evangelical simplicity, have but cold, slender, and uncertain entertainment, among the worldly-wise men of this world.

Therefore (herein concluding) I beseech the Almighty God, most abundantly to increase and confirm your grace's heavenly wisdom, and endue you with all the rest of his heavenly gifts, for the relieving, refreshing, and comforting, both bodily and spiritually, his little flock of the faithful, yet militant here on earth. Amen.

MAGIC ON THE RENAISSANCE STAGE

In Christopher Marlowe's tragedy, *Doctor Faustus* (1592), the title character is a gifted German scholar who decides that all forms of learning are no longer satisfying and that magic is the only practice left for him to pursue. He conjures up a devil, Mephistophilis, and offers to sell his soul to the devil for 24 years of rich living and obedience from Mephistophilis. Two angels, one good and the other evil, attempt to influence Faustus, but Faustus listens to the evil angel and spends his allotted time enjoying tricks of his magic until the devil sends fiends to carry him to hell. The following excerpt from the first scene shows Faustus making his choice and reveals his motives for desiring magical powers. Consider how his ambitions compare with Prospero's motives and practice of magic in *The Tempest*.

FROM CHRISTOPHER MARLOWE, *DOCTOR FAUSTUS* (1592), SEE IN *THE COMPLETE PLAYS*, ED. J. B. STEANE

(London: Penguin Books, 1986) 267–269

FAUSTUS: These necromantic books are heavenly,
　　　　Lines, circles, scenes, letters and characters:
　　　　Ay, these are those that Faustus most desires.
　　　　Oh, what a world of profit and delight,
　　　　Of power, of honour of, omnipotence,
　　　　Is promised to the studious artizan!

GOOD ANGEL: Oh Faustus, lay that damned book aside,
　　　　And gaze not on it lest it tempt thy soul
　　　　And heap God's heavy wrath upon thy head.
　　　　Read, read the scriptures: that is blasphemy.

EVIL ANGEL: Go forward, Faustus, in that famous art
　　　　Wherein all nature's treasure is contained.
　　　　Be thou on earth as Jove is in the sky,
　　　　Lord and commander of these elements.

Exeunt ANGELS.

FAUSTUS: How am I glutted with the conceit of this!
　　　　Shall I make spirits fetch me what I please,
　　　　Resolve me of all ambiguities,

Perform what desperate enterprise I will?
I'll have them fly to India for gold.
Ransack the ocean for orient pearl,
And search all corners of the new-found world
For pleasant fruits and princely delicates.
I'll have them read me strange philosophy,
And tell the secrets of all foreign kings.
I'll have them wall all Germany with brass,
And make swift Rhine circle fair Wittenberg.
I'll have them fill the public schools with silk,
Wherewith the students shall be bravely clad.
I'll levy soldiers with the coin they bring,
And chase the prince of Parma from our land,
And reign sole king of all the provinces. (1.1.49–93)

Ben Jonson's play *The Alchemist* is a satiric comedy on alchemy and the underlying motivation of human greed. The play was performed by Shakespeare's company, the King's Men, in 1610 shortly before the first recorded appearance of *The Tempest* (1611). Shakespeare would have, therefore, been intimately familiar with Jonson's play and his mocking portrayal of magic on stage. In *The Alchemist,* Doctor Subtle, a self-proclaimed alchemist who is actually a cheat and a fraud, convinces Face, Lovewit's butler, to allow him to set up his alchemical laboratory at Lovewit's house while Lovewit is away in the country. Subtle and Face dupe a variety of greedy and naive individuals seeking riches and counsel. The scheme comes to an end when Lovewit returns, disposes of the rogues, and collects their winnings.

   In the following excerpt, Doctor Subtle describes in detail the alchemical process for Mammon, a knight seeking gold and riches, and his skeptical companion, Surly. Subtle's account indicates the way alchemists believed that gold could be made or transubstantiated by a slow process involving the elements, air, water, fire, and earth, and the three substances, mercury, sulfur, and salt. He appears knowledgeable while intending to confuse and deceive. Mammon may seem convinced of the mystical practice, but Surly argues and questions Subtle's explanations. Note the reason Subtle offers for the obscurity and complexity of the alchemical practice and what would happen, as Mammon explains, if the art were much simpler.

FROM BEN JONSON, *THE ALCHEMIST* (1610),
SEE ED. F. H. MARES

(Cambridge, MA: Harvard University Press, 1967) 68–71

Sub[tle]   It is, of the one part,
                        A humid exhalation, which we call
                        Materia liquida, or the unctuous water;

On th' other part, a certain crass and viscous
Portion of earth; both which, concorporate,
Do make the elementary matter of gold:
Which is not, yet, *properia materia,*
But common to all metals, and all stones.
For, where it is forsaken of that moisture,
And hath more dryness, it becomes a stone;
Where it retains more of the humid fatness,
It turns to sulphur, or to quicksilver,
Who are the parents of all other metals.
Nor can this remote matter, suddenly,
Progress so from extreme unto extreme,
As to grow gold, and leap o'er all the means.
Nature doth, first, beget th' imperfect; then
Proceeds she to the perfect. Of that airy,
And oily water, mercury is engender'd;
Sulphur o' the fat and earthy part: the one,
(Which is the last) supplying the place of male,
The other of the female, in all metals.
Some do believe in hermaphrodeity,
That both do act, and suffer. But these two
Make the rest ductile, malleable, extensive.
And, even in gold, they are; for we do find
Seeds of them, by our fire, and gold in them:
And can produce the species of each metal
More perfect thence, than nature doth in earth.
Beside, who doth not see, in daily practice,
Art can beget bees, hornets, beetles, wasps,
Out of the carcasses, and dung of creatures;
Yea, scorpions, of an herb, being ritely plac'd:
And these are living creatures, far more perfect,
And excellent, than metals.

Mam[mon]   Well said, Father!
Nay, if he take you in hand, sir, with an argument,
He'll bray [pound] you in a mortar.

Sur[ly]   'Pray you, sir, stay.
Rather than I'll be bray'd, sir, I'll believe
That alchemy is a pretty kind of game
Somewhat like tricks o' the cards, to cheat a man
With charming.

Sub[tle]   Sir?
Sur[ly]   What else are all your terms
Whereon no one o' your writers 'grees with other?
Of your elixir, your *lac Virginis,*

Your stone, your med'cine, and your chrysosperm,
Your salt, your sulphur, and your mercury,
Your oil of height, your tree of life, your blood,

. . . .

Powder of bones, scalings of iron, glass,
And worlds of other strange ingredients,
Would burst a man to name?

Sub[tle]   And all these, nam'd,
Intending but one thing: which art our writers
Us'd to obscure their art.

Mam[mon]   Sir, so I told him,
Because the simple idiot should not learn it,
And make it vulgar.

Sub[tle]   Was not all the knowledge
Of the Egyptians writ in mystic symbols?
Speak not the Scriptures, oft, in parables?
Are not the choicest fables of the poets,
That were the fountains, and first springs of wisdom,
Wrapp'd in perplexed allegories? (2.3.142–207)

TOPICS FOR WRITTEN AND ORAL DISCUSSION

1.   What are some of the other names for "magician" that Walter Raleigh identifies in *The History of the World* S. 2? In your opinion, how does the fact that magic seemed so widely practiced throughout the world affect its acceptability or credibility?

2.   What three kinds of magic does Raleigh identify in S. 2, and how does he relate magic to the recognition and worship of God?

3.   In S. 3 of Chapter I in *The History of the World*, why does Raleigh suggest that magic should not be condemned though the devil may use it? In what ways does he say superstitions have corrupted potentially good arts or beliefs? Consider this argument in light of *The Tempest*. Seemingly, Prospero practices good magic while Sycorax had practiced black magic. How might Raleigh defend Prospero's art?

4.   In Book I, Chapter I of *The Discovery of Witchcraft*, why does Reginald Scot dismiss the power of witchcraft? With what contrasting examples does he conclude, as a way of reinforcing his argument?

5.   How does Scot describe cabalistic art in Book XI, Chapter XI? Why might he appeal to Cornelius Agrippa as an authority? (See earlier information in this chapter on magic.) What biblical basis does Scot use to refute cabalistic art? How is Prospero's magic spiritual or spirit-related?

6.   In Book XIV, Chapter II, how would you describe the tone of Scot's description of alchemy and the canon's yeoman's practice of the art in Chaucer's tale? What is the chief deception that occurs?

7.   What evidence is there that Prospero practices alchemy? What seems to be his primary aim or goal in using magic?

8.   Imagine a meeting between Reginald Scot and Prospero. What might they say to each other? How might each try to prove his point by actions or words?

9.   In Chapter II of the First Book of *Demonology*, what does James indicate magicians, sorcerers, and witches have in common and by what passions does he distinguish them? How does James elaborate on these distinctions in Chapter III and what ultimately happens to those who go to "the Devil's school"?

10.   In Chapters III and IV of *Demonology*, how does Epistemon explain to Philomathes the difference between lawful and unlawful practices, between astrology and astronomy?

11.   Why does James feel that more women than men become witches? How does he describe the kind of powers they have? Why might he, as king, feel the need to report on witchcraft?

12.   What "three kind of folks" does Epistemon suggest might be tempted by witchcraft? Consider the "three men of sin" (3.3.53) who are under Prospero's magical influence in *The Tempest*. Do they fit any of Epistemon's categories? How, then, might Shakespeare's view of magic differ from James's view of witchcraft? Are there any similarities?

13.   Discuss the role of gender in perceptions about magic in the sixteenth and seventeenth centuries.

14.   Reginald Scot and King James both appeal to God while offering very different arguments about sorcery and witchcraft. As a skeptic, how does Scot use his faith in God? In contrast, how does James apply his faith to confirm the dark powers of the supernatural?

15.   Describe the tone John Dee establishes for his letter of defense simply by its lengthy title. Although he is very formal and therefore wordy, in brief summary what are the key points he wishes to make?

16.   Dee asked for a trial before King James as an opportunity to defend himself against charges of conjuring and invoking devils but James refused. Imagine that instead he had agreed. Act out the trial, based on information in this chapter about both historical figures. What might be the arguments of the Crown prosecutor, and would Dee defend himself or hire a lawyer? Create some reputable witnesses for both sides and script a final response from King James.

17.   Write a diary entry for John Dee at the end of his life in which he looks back on his years of fame and fall from grace. What might some of his reflections be?

18.   Prospero has been compared sometimes to John Dee and sometimes to King James. Discuss why either comparison might be fitting or inappropriate. How would either comparison affect the characterization of Prospero? How might King James respond to either parallel? Given that *The Tempest* was performed by the King's Men before King James, what do you suppose Shakespeare might be considering as he shaped Prospero's character, knowing whom the audience would include?

19.   What motives does Doctor Faustus express for his desire to pursue magic? Are they noble or reprehensible? Why do you suppose his condemnation to hell at the end of the play is considered tragic rather than simply just?

20.   Imagine Doctor Subtle in Jonson's *The Alchemist* dressed up as a traveling salesperson bent on selling his skills as an alchemist. How might you deliver his speech, so full of alchemical jargon, considering that he is a fraud and a cheat? Add the other two characters, Mammon as a convinced "buyer" and Surly as a skeptic. Dramatize the short scene; then discuss in what ways the scenario might seem very modern though written 400 years ago.

21.   Choose one of Prospero's speeches and compare it with the excerpted lines from Doctor Faustus and Doctor Subtle. How are the three magicians alike or different? Consider how the differences among the genres—*The Tempest* as romance, *Doctor Faustus* as tragedy, and *The Alchemist* as satire—might be reflected in the characters' lines. What do you think each playwright's view of magic is?

Alternatively, script a dialogue between two of the magicians that reveal what they have in common or how they are different.

22.   Why might Prospero abandon his magic at the end of the play? Consider his speech in 5.1.33–57. Does Shakespeare portray Prospero's magic positively, negatively, or ambiguously? Explain your position.

23.   Imagine Prospero and Sycorax had an opportunity to meet. What might they say to each other or try to do to one another? How might they be similar or different? How might you use costumes to characterize them?

SUGGESTED READING

Holroyd, Stuart, and Neil Powell. *Mysteries of Magic.* London: Bloomsbury Books, 1991.

Levack, Brian P. *Renaissance Magic.* New York: Garland Publishing, Inc., 1992.

Mebane, John S. *Renaissance Magic and the Return of the Golden Age: The Occult Tradition and Marlowe, Jonson, and Shakespeare.* Lincoln: U of Nebraska P, 1989.

Shumaker, Wayne. *The Occult Sciences in the Renaissance: A Study in Intellectual Patterns.* Berkeley: U of California P, 1972.

Srigley, Michael. *Images of Regeneration: A Study of Shakespeare's* The Tempest *and Its Cultural Background.* Stockholm: Uppsala, 1985.

Thomas, Keith. *Religion and the Decline of Magic.* New York: Charles Scribner's Sons, 1971.

Yates, Frances A. *Giordano Bruno and the Hermetic Tradition.* London: Routledge, 1964.

———. *The Occult Philosophy in the Elizabethan Age.* London: Routledge and Kegan Paul, 1979.

4

Power: Legitimacy and Treachery

The Tempest dramatizes a world in which power defines many of the relationships. The context of the play is political. Not only does Prospero govern the small and mostly uninhabited island as his own kingdom but the politics of the Italian courts of Milan and Naples become relevant as the shipwrecked party from those states enters Prospero's world. One of the chief inquiries and sources of conflict in the play revolves around the legitimate and illegitimate uses of power. In the past that precedes the play, Prospero's legitimate position as duke of Milan was usurped by his brother Antonio with the assistance of Alonso, king of Naples. Once the play begins, acts of treason and accusations of treachery abound. Antonio and Sebastian attempt to take Alonso's life; Caliban invites Stephano and Trinculo into a plot against Prospero's life. Prospero charges Ferdinand with a false claim of treason, compelling him to take a menial, subservient role while Prospero himself exercises great control through magical influence over everyone on the island. He demands absolute obedience from Ariel and Caliban as servant and slave, both of whom chafe at their plight and seek after their own freedom. Resolution comes only when power seems to be returned to its rightful hands, with Prospero regaining his dukedom and the relationship between Milan and Naples being made legitimate through the unifying bonds of marriage between Miranda and Ferdinand.

But the resolution does not answer all the questions that the play dramatizes. Does Prospero gain much if the reinstatement of his dukedom simply puts new power in Ferdinand's hands as future king of Naples? Is the conclusion satisfactory if Antonio and Sebastian remain unrepentant and corrupt power mongers? Does a duke deserve his power if he shirks his political responsibilities? Is treason ever justifiable? Is a deliberately false accusation of treason any less wrong than a planned act of treachery? Is Prospero's use of power on the island appropriate and justifiable? These are potential questions that *The Tempest* constantly raises. They are political questions about right and wrong that evade simple responses. They elicit even more inquiries about the political world in which the play appeared. One might ask, for example, how the pattern of power relationships in the play reflects or responds to concerns of legitimate authority and illegitimate force. Such issues certainly interested Shakespeare and his audience. Furthermore, plays were subject to government regulation or censorship and political topics were particularly suspicious. How did *The Tempest,* with such a political edge to it, not only escape censorship but find acceptance before King James at court performances? An exploration into crises of power both in Britain and in continental Europe prove illuminating in revealing some of the various attitudes toward treason and legitimacy that were current when Shakespeare wrote his final romance. Moreover, an examination of parliamentary ferment in England on the eve of the play's public appearance sheds some light on how Shakespeare's contemporaries may have engaged with issues of power sharing that inevitably characterize the world of politics and unfold in the development of the play. The following discussion establishes the relevance of questions in *The Tempest* to the early seventeenth century both on England's soil and abroad.

JAMES I AND TREASONOUS PLOTS

King James was no stranger to treason, nor was England before his governance free of such concerns. While Elizabeth I's extended reign from 1558 to 1603 provided England with longed-for stability after years of uncertainty and unrest regarding succession, legitimate claims to the throne, and the role of religion in politics, her government continued to suffer from threats that never reached their full potential for damage. There were several plots to take the queen's life. The crux of the matter was religion in a post-Reformation society. Elizabeth was a Protestant, as was her brother, King Edward VI, who assumed the throne after their father, Henry VIII, established the Protestant Church of England and broke ties with the Catholic Church in Rome. Between the reigns of Edward and Elizabeth, however, their sister Mary I ruled as a Catholic queen and gained a reputation as "Bloody Mary" for her harsh persecution of Protestant subjects. Although Elizabeth compelled the nation to return to Protestantism with her reign, staunch Catholics remained in the country and tried to overthrow her and replace her with a monarch sympathetic to their religion. In 1578, the pope passed a decree known as a papal bull, in which he excommunicated Elizabeth from the Catholic Church. The result was that Catholics in England were then perceived to be traitors because they could not swear complete loyalty to their queen while they professed loyalty to the church in Rome. Government attacks against the Catholics were sometimes severe, including imprisonment and even death. As a result, many Catholics became secretive about their religion. The continued presence of Catholics in the country, however, became not simply a matter of religious heresy but of national security as a power struggle, sometimes overt, sometimes covert, characterized Elizabeth's reign.

James, who was King James VI of Scotland before he also became England's James I at Elizabeth's death in 1603, was also familiar with threats of treason and political extremists. His father, Lord Darnley, had been murdered in a conspiracy, and his mother, Mary, Queen of Scots, was a Catholic monarch who was executed by the Protestants in England. In 1591, a group of alleged witches were charged in a treasonous plot against King James's life. On April 15, 1600, someone attempted to kidnap him while he was visiting a subject, the earl of Gowrie, but James was rescued before he was harmed. That event became known as the Gowrie Conspiracy, and the earl of Gowrie was blamed and executed for the treachery. By the time James reached England and became its monarch, he was well-versed in the dangers of treason, as were his new subjects who had lived under Elizabeth's reign.

English Catholics were hopeful that James, a Protestant with a Catholic mother, would be more sympathetic to their cause than Elizabeth was, and initially he seemed to give them reasons for encouragement. He strongly desired peace rather than war or civil unrest and adopted as his kingly motto *Beati Pacifici*, "Blessed are the peacemakers." Catholic extremists were not patient, however, and before long hatched several conspiracies, including the Bye Plot and the Main Plot—failed attempts against James's life. They put an end to any tolerance on James's part. He tightened security, and on February 22, 1604, he ordered all Jesuits and other Catholic priests to leave the country, while increasing fines for Catholic subjects. All these steps were precursors to one of the greatest and most controversial scandals in James's reign, the Gunpowder Plot.

The plan of the conspirators in the Gunpowder Plot was to blow up Parliament House with a huge stock of gunpowder in its cellar on the opening day of the legislative session on November 5, 1605. Had they been successful, they would have killed not only the king, but also his sons who were his heirs, as well as all the lords attending the session. In short, they would have created anarchy, by not simply annihilating their king but destroying the system of constitutional monarchy in place. Their goal was to replace James with a Catholic ruler. Their plan failed, however, in a rather dramatic sequence of events.

The Crown received an anonymous bomb threat a month before Parliament opened. Then on the eve of the legislative session, Guy Fawkes, the man appointed to ignite the explosives, was caught in the cellar ready to do his deed. The other conspirators fled London but were soon also captured, charged with treason, convicted, and hanged. November 5 became known as Guy Fawkes Day—an occasion still recognized with fireworks in England today—in which the country celebrated the Crown's victory but which also in the early years following the event reminded the government and its people of the fear and controversy surrounding threats to public safety and national security.

In 1611, when *The Tempest* reached the stage, the victory over the Gunpowder Plot would no doubt have still excited thoughts and feelings about the real dangers of treason. A play about the Gowrie Conspiracy was attempted on stage in 1605 but was immediately suppressed because it touched too directly on current politics. If *The Tempest,* with its multiple treasonous plots, managed to escape censorship, the reasons no doubt lay partly in the fictionalized version of treachery and perhaps also in the strong impression that the plots are overshadowed by Prospero's sweeping control and the return of his dukedom at the play's conclusion. Antonio and Sebastian never show remorse, however, for their part in the past treason and the attempted regicide on stage. Their silence leaves somewhat open-ended the sense of peace and reconciliation, suggesting that this particular power struggle may be over but that the power hungry never completely disappear nor find appeasement on the political scene. Moreover, Prospero's suitability as an effective and astute political leader remains questionable from his comments at the beginning and the end of the play.

RUDOLF II AND THE HOLY ROMAN EMPIRE

These questions about Prospero's political authority point to an interesting parallel in the current affairs of Europe when *The Tempest* was written. One of the main centers of power in Europe was the Holy Roman Empire, a loose assembly of over a thousand European territories. These many states and provinces, comprising the general geographical area of Germany, Austria, and Bohemia, exercised a significant degree of autonomy and independence, although an emperor nominally ruled the whole. The emperor was elected by seven electors, who governed over some of the territories within the empire. Traditionally, the Catholic Hapsburg dynasty held the emperor's position, having family members chosen by the electoral princes from 1452 until 1806 except for a brief period in the eighteenth century. The empire functioned not by formal instruments of power but by negotiation, compromise, collaboration, and persuasion.

When Shakespeare's *The Tempest* was being dramatized on English stages, a European crisis was brewing over control of the empire. The emperor, Rudolf II, was a reclusive ruler interested more in his library and the practice of magic than the government of his realm. As early as 1606, the Hapsburg family agreed that Rudolf should be deposed for his inattention to his political responsibilities. In 1608, he was forced to give up the crowns of Austria, Hungary, and Moravia to his brother Matthias, leaving him only the imperial crown as emperor and the crown of Bohemia which Matthias coveted. In March 1611, the crisis erupted as Matthias entered Prague with a Catholic army to usurp his brother's position entirely; by April, Matthias was declared king of Bohemia. Rudolf went into hiding in his palace where he remained a virtual prisoner until he died—some say of madness—in January of 1612. England became a part of the ferment when a gathering of Protestant princes in the empire tried to foster support for Rudolf and sent a messenger to King James seeking influence to reinstate Rudolf. James had positive feelings toward Rudolf although he would not likely have approved of Rudolf's neglect of his political responsibilities. Both saw themselves as peacemakers and believed in seeking a middle way between Protestant or Catholic extremes. Part of the proposal to support Rudolf included the marriage of James's daughter Elizabeth to one of the Protestant princes, Frederick, the elector of Palatine, an arrangement that ultimately took place on February 14, 1613 (see chapter 5), a year after Rudolf's death. There were hopes among the Protestant rulers that Frederick might take Rudolf's place as emperor, a dream that never came to fruition.

This European political scene shares some obvious parallels with *The Tempest* in which Prospero, like Rudolf II, lost control of his government partly because of inattention to its administration. Antonio, like the usurping brother Matthias, connives to take over Prospero's political role. While Antonio is portrayed as the false and evil brother, Prospero admits to Miranda that he himself "neglecting worldly ends, all dedicated / To closeness and the bettering of [his] mind" (1.2.89–90). Antonio's ambitions are never portrayed positively, but Prospero's suitability to his position of leadership is certainly portrayed ambiguously. Perhaps he trusted his brother more than Antonio deserved; that was the very least of his faults. But even at the end of the play, having regained his dukedom and abjured his magic, Prospero seems unlikely to assume the powers of state when Ferdinand and Miranda are placed to take over his responsibilities. He indicates he plans to "retire me to my Milan where / Every third thought shall be my grave" (5.1.311–312). The question subtly presented is whether a duke unwilling to govern should bear the title of duke or at the very least, What precautions should a duke take to ensure his authority if he intends to pursue interests other than the political governance that falls within his jurisdiction? If Rudolf II seems partly to blame for his own demise, how should one consider the consequences of Prospero's choices? Whether Shake-speare deliberately intended this comparison or not, it is unlikely that James and his court audience would not have recognized the similarities, given the prevalence of European concerns and instability, and England's involvement in the political fray especially through marriage, the same plan that helps to bring about reconciliation in *The Tempest*.

JAMES I AND PARLIAMENT

While a history of treason in England and Scotland and rebellion in the Holy Roman Empire depict the extremes of political threat in times contemporary with *The Tempest*, the more normalized activity of political legislation and relationships of day-to-day power sharing in England are also illuminating. England was a constitutional monarchy. That meant that while a king or queen sat on the throne and wielded significant power, the monarch was still accountable to the people through representatives who sat in Parliament where laws were passed. This accountability focused especially on money because the monarch could not tax the public without the approval of Parliament and had limited means to acquire finances without parliamentary support. James was a profligate spender; he was also vocal about his own view that he held absolute power, a view contrary to the constitution under which he governed and increasingly unpopular the more adamantly he expressed it. On February 14, 1610, he called his fourth session of Parliament largely because he needed a significant sum of money for debts and for continued support of his expenditures. Most people at the time recognized that a new financial settlement was needed, but the debate centered on concerns about the amount and about fears that James was using the terms of a settlement to gain more independent political power. Because of James's extravagance, royal expenditures had increased by more than 70 percent in five or six years. Costs stemmed not only from necessary royal responsibilities but also from his many festivities, his support of Scottish favorites housed at court, and his generosity to his servants. Furthermore, whereas Queen Elizabeth, the previous unmarried monarch, had only one royal household to support, in James's time, there were three: the king's, his wife the queen's, and his eldest son Prince Henry's. James was looking for a lump sum to retire his debt plus an annual sum to keep him out of further debt.

The king was willing to make concessions in order to receive the money he was seeking. Two issues were at stake. One was a system of wardships in which if the land held by a knightly tenant succeeded to a minor, the land and rights to arrange a marriage were taken by the Crown. This fiscal agreement profited the monarch. The second issue was called purveyance, an arrangement in place since the Middle Ages by which the Crown could force subjects to sell produce and products to the royal household at a discount. After months of negotiations, the two sides came to an initial agreement called the Great Contract that would give the monarchy a sum of money in return for abolishing wardships and purveyance. James then suspended Parliament until the fall with the details of the agreement to be worked out. When Parliament resumed on October 16, however, the two sides seemed farther apart than ever. The parliamentary House of Commons grew more fearful that James might be using the Great Contract to gain financial independence from them, and James, for his part, added new demands to the agreement. Distrust grew and in February of 1611, the king dissolved Parliament without having reached any resolution about overhauling the financial system and providing the Crown with a steady income. He did not recall Parliament again until 1614.

While the Parliament of 1610, the year before *The Tempest* was first performed, was substantially about finances, the language of debate was largely about the legitimate or illegitimate uses of power and the rights of the people. James declared that kings were like gods, a comparison that emphasized the great scope of legitimate power he believed belonged to him, while he contended that subjects had no right even to dispute the extent of his power. The members of the House of Commons, for their part, found the king's efforts to silence them wholly objectionable and concluded that to be so silenced made them little more than slaves at his command. This debate sheds some light on the rhetoric of power and control in *The Tempest*. Prospero governs his island like a king—or a tyrant, depending on one's perspective. He treats Caliban as his slave and Ariel as an indentured servant. He allows no protests from either of them, threatening to encase Ariel in an oak tree for raising the promise of his impending freedom and constantly punishing Caliban with cramps and pains. At play is a power struggle not unlike the one between King James and his Parliament (Hamilton 70). When Prospero brings the relationship between Miranda and Ferdinand under his control, as well, he temporarily makes Ferdinand his slave and then admonishes the couple to exercise restraint and chastity. Interestingly, restraint and self-discipline are hardly words that subjects would readily apply to King James, and the fact that Shakespeare introduces these values to his play suggests both a nod to the English subjects trying to rein in James's profligacy and a potential compliment to the king because it is, after all, the ruler Prospero who demands and represents these values in the play (Hamilton 70). One of the questions that the play seems to invite regards Prospero's use of his extraordinary powers as he governs the island in a way that he never governed his own dukedom. One could say that he uses his powers to good ends and thus the actions are suitable and justifiable, but one could also debate the issue, questioning the reasonableness of his demands and the superior attitude with which he engages his various "subjects." Furthermore, Caliban declares the island is his from Sycorax his mother (1.2.331), and Prospero provides no answer whatsoever that would legitimate his claims to power over Caliban. Awareness of issues of legitimacy and power surrounding James and Parliament on the contemporary political scene enrich an understanding of the political dynamics in Shakespeare's romance by suggesting a greater complexity in the relationships portrayed.

METAPHORS OF GOVERNMENT

Every age has its ideology, its explanation for its particular system of social order. Most often a dominant ideology, belonging to those in power, subordinates ideologies of those who believe the system should be run differently. In Elizabethan and Jacobean England, various metaphors explained or confronted the constitutional monarchy as a political system. Related to public order, these metaphors underlie conflicts involving both legitimate conflict of parliamentary debate and illegitimate conflict of rebellion and treason. Three such metaphors offered here to amplify the discussion about power are the "chain of being," the king's two bodies, and the lion and the fox.

The "chain of being" is a metaphor that sees the universe as a hierarchical chain descending from God to angels, to human beings, to animals, plants, and inanimate objects. Degree and order are emphasized as the chain links everything in its proper place. Furthermore, this cosmology served as a scheme for smaller units of order as well. The commonwealth, for example, was seen to be a miniature cosmos in which the king—like God—was at the top and the subjects descended according to class beneath him. Should anyone within the system threaten the order through rebellion from below or tyranny from above, such action caused disorder or disease in the whole system. This metaphor worked in favor of those in power because as long as they avoided tyranny they had a God-ordained right to govern and command obedience from their subjects. Dubbed the Elizabethan World Picture (by scholar F.M.W. Tillyard), this view of politics provided monarchs such as James support for his argument in favor of the divine right of kings.

The second metaphor, the king's two bodies, offered similar support for monarchs' authority. According to this view of order, the king has two bodies, one his natural, physical body and the other his political body as ruler of the state. Early in the conception of this metaphor the body politic was seen to be comprised of the king as head and the subjects as part of the corporate body having some influence. As the monarchical system strengthened in the sixteenth and seventeenth centuries, however, the two bodies theory came to represent solely the king and encouraged the view that he was answerable only to God and not to the people. This view fostered a related idea of nonresistance or absolute obedience in which subjects had no right to rebel for any reason because even a tyrant was seen to be God's agent sent to punish or cleanse and rebuild the nation. James favored this view, although not all of his subjects agreed; some critics even wrote documents in support of tyrannicide, the subjects' right to overthrow the king. In fact, when James's son Charles succeeded to the throne, that is exactly what happened as he was eventually beheaded in 1649 during the English civil war.

The third metaphor comes from the pen of the influential Italian political advisor, Niccolo Machiavelli, in the early sixteenth century. While most English doctrines of monarchy presented an ideal view of how things ought to be, Machiavelli focused on the realistic view of how things were. At a time when Italian city-states were unstable and virtually ungovernable, Machiavelli suggested that leaders should rule by whatever means necessary even if that included force, fear, and false appearances. He relied on a metaphor of the lion and the fox, indicating that a ruler or prince ought to have the strength of a lion and the cunning of a fox. Machiavelli's views were negatively received in England; many regarded his practical measures as anti-Christian and immoral. The word "machiavellian" retains the idea of deception or double-dealing even today. Nevertheless, there was some growing support for some of his advice in the 1600s, and thus the responses varied considerably.

While none of these three metaphors appears overtly in *The Tempest,* they offer a philosophical background for the political perspectives being presented. The "chain of being" and the king's two bodies support absolute power of a ruler over his subjects, the kind of power Prospero seems to display on the island if not while duke of Milan. If one accepts these metaphors, one not only sees the treason of Antonio and Sebastian as reprehensible but also agrees that even Ariel is wrong to question Prospero's command over him. But if one questions the absolute power of the head of state, as many in England's constitutional monarchy did, then Prospero's insistence on his complete control of public and private affairs is subject to scrutiny. The play seems to allow the possibility of either interpretation. As for mixed reaction to Machiavelli's metaphors of power, the lion and fox, they open up issues in the play, as well. From the negative perspective of a "machiavellian" as a corrupt and deceptive politician, Antonio nicely fits the bill, but when one considers the "machiavellian" as an astute ruler, Prospero seems to emulate that pattern, although at times he, too, is dishonest and deceptive, allowing the ends to justify the means. One can ask whether *The Tempest* presents ideal or practical views of power and what distinguishes a tyrant from a just, legitimate ruler. Such questions necessarily spark debate because Shakespeare created a complex enough dynamic on stage to yield more than one response.

Following a chronology of relevant dates and events, excerpts from a Gunpowder Plot trial, King James's writing, speeches in Parliament, and Machiavelli's document on government contribute to this chapter's discussion of the politics at play in Shakespeare's drama about the legitimate and illegitimate uses of power.

Brief Chronology of Significant Historical and Political Events

1558	Elizabeth becomes queen of England
1578	The pope passes a decree that excommunicates Elizabeth from the Roman Catholic Church
1591	Trial in Scotland of witches in alleged treason against King James
1600	Gowrie Conspiracy against King James in Scotland
1603	James VI of Scotland becomes James I of England
1604	James tightens security and orders Catholic priests to leave England
Nov. 5, 1605	Guy Fawkes Day, when the Gunpowder Plot was obstructed
March 28, 1606	Father Garnet tried in the Gunpowder Plot; hanged on May 3
1608	Rudolf II of the Holy Roman Empire compelled to give up crowns of Austria, Hungary and Moravia to his brother Matthias
Feb. 14, 1610	King James calls his fourth session of Parliament; dissolves it in July
Oct. 16, 1610	King James reopens Parliament to vote on Great Contract
Feb. 1611	James dissolves Parliament with no new financial agreement being made
March 1611	Matthias marches to Prague with Catholic army and usurps his brother Rudolf's power
Nov. 1, 1611	*The Tempest* performed at court
Jan. 1612	Rudolf II of the Holy Roman Empire dies
Feb. 14, 1613	James's daughter Elizabeth marries Frederick, elector of Palatine

A TRIAL IN THE GUNPOWDER PLOT

Henry Garnet, a Jesuit priest, was believed by many to be the chief instigator behind the Gunpowder Plot although no evidence ever clearly indicted him. He was captured hiding in a house in England after an extensive manhunt by the authorities. From his capture on March 28, 1606, to his execution on May 3, he was examined more than 20 times by the king's council, who ultimately resorted to torture to obtain a questionable confession. The following account records the charges against Garnet as one of the traitors in the plot and his final response before his execution. Consider whether he seems a remorseful or deceptive captive. Try to relate his response to the traitors in *The Tempest* who are exposed by Ariel in the banquet table scene.

FROM *A TRUE AND PERFECT RELATION OF THE WHOLE PROCEEDING AGAINST THE LATE MOST BARBAROUS TRAITORS, GARNET A JESUIT AND HIS CONFEDERATES*

(London: Robert Barker, 1606. STC 11618) Fff2–Fff3

That this *Garnet*...together with *Catesby* lately slain in open Rebellion and with *Oswald Tesmond a Jesuit*, otherwise *Oswald Greenwell*, as a false Traitor against the most mighty, & most renowned king our sovereign Lord King James, the 9 of June last, traitorously did conspire and compass,

To depose the King and to deprive him of his government

To destroy and kill the King, and the noble Prince *Henry*, his eldest Son: such a King and such a Prince, such a Son of such a Father, whose virtues are rather with amazed silence to be wondered at, than able by any speech to be expressed

To stir sedition and slaughter throughout the kingdom

To subvert the true Religion of God, and whole government of the kingdom

To overthrow the whole State of the Commonwealth....

This *Garnet*, together with *Catesby* and *Tesmond*, had speech and conference together of these treasons, and concluded most traitorously, and devilishly. (O–O2)

Then *Garnet* said, Good countrymen, I am come hither this blessed day of *The invention of the holy Cross,* to end all my crosses in this life. The cause of my suffering is not unknown to you; I confess I have offended the King, and am sorry for it, so far as I was guilty, which was in concealing it, and for that I ask pardon of his Majesty; The treason intended against the King and State was bloody, myself should have detested it, had it taken effect. And I am heartily sorry, that any Catholics ever had so cruel a design. . . .

Then addressing himself to execution, he kneeled at the Ladder foot, and asked if he might have time to pray, and how long. It was answered, he should limit himself: none should interrupt him. It appeared he could not constantly or devoutly pray; fear of death, or hope of Pardon even then so distracted him: For oft in those prayers he would break off, turn and look about him, and answer to what he overheard, while he seemed to be praying. When he stood up, the Recorder finding his behaviour as it were an expectation of a Pardon, wished him not to deceive himself, nor beguile his own soul, he was come to die, and must die; requiring him not to Equivocate with his last breath, if he knew anything that might be danger to the King and State, he should now utter it. *Garnet* said, It is no time now to Equivocate: how it was lawful, and when, he had showed his mind elsewhere. But saith he, I do not now Equivocate, and more than I have confessed, I do not know. . . . Being upon the Gibbet, he used these words, I commend me to all good Catholics, and I pray God preserve his Majesty, and Queen, and all their posterity, and my Lords of the Privy Counsel, to whom I remember my humble duty, and I am sorry that I did dissemble with them: but I did not think they had such proof against me, till it was showed me; But when it was proved, I held it more honour at that time to confess, than before, to have accused.

KING JAMES'S POLITICAL ADVICE

King James was an intellectual who had both a practical and a theoretical interest in kingship and issues of power. He wrote extensively about his views. The following excerpt is from his book of advice to his son, Prince Henry, called *Basilicon Doron,* meaning "kingly gift." James believed that kings, not subjects nor Parliament, should make the laws and execute them. In the quotation below, he distinguishes between a good king and a tyrant, contrasting the two to teach his son how to govern well. James expresses an ideal view of government in which he places great faith in the godly benevolence of the ruler. Consider whether Prospero seems more like a just ruler or a tyrant according to James's distinctions.

FROM KING JAMES I, *BASILICON DORON* (1599), CHARLES HOWARD MCILWAIN, ED. *THE POLITICAL WORKS OF JAMES I*

(Cambridge, MA: Harvard UP, 1918) 18–19

For the part of making, and executing of Laws, consider first the true difference betwixt a lawful good King, and an usurping Tyrant....The one acknowledgeth himself ordained for his people, having received from God a burden of government, whereof he must be countable: The other thinketh his people ordained for him, a prey to his passions and inordinate appetites, as the fruits of his magnanimity: And therefore, as their ends are directly contrary, so are their whole actions, as means, whereby they press to attain to their ends. A good King, thinking his highest honour to consist in the due discharge of his calling, employeth all his study and pains, to procure and maintain, by the making and execution of good Laws, the welfare and peace of his people; and as their natural father and kindly Master, thinketh his greatest contentment standeth in their prosperity, and his greatest surety in having their hearts, subjecting his own private affections and appetites to the weal and standing of his Subjects, ever thinking common interest his chiefest particular: whereby the contrary, an usurping Tyrant, thinking his greatest honour and felicity to consist in attaining...to his ambitious pretences, thinketh never himself sure, but by the dissension and factions among his people, and counterfeiting the Saint while he once creep in credit, will then (by inverting all good Laws to serve only for his unruly private affections) frame the commonweal ever to advance his particular: building his surety upon his people's misery: and in the end (as a stepfather and an uncouth hireling) make up his own hand upon the ruins of the Republic. And according to their actions, so receive they their reward: For a good King (after a happy and famous reign) dieth in peace, lamented by his subjects, and admired by his neighbours; and leaving a reverent renown behind him in earth, obtaineth the Crown of eternal felicity in heaven. And although some of them (which falleth out very rarely) may be cut off by the treason of some unnatural subjects, yet liveth their fame after them, and some notable plague faileth never to overtake the committers in this life, besides their infamy to all posterities hereafter: Whereby the contrary, a Tyrant's miserable and infamous life, armeth in end his own Subjects to become his burreaux: and although that rebellion be ever unlawful on their part, yet is the world so wearied of him, that his fall is little meaned by the rest of his Subjects, and but smiled at by his neighbours. And besides the infamous memory he leaveth behind him here, and the endless pain he sustaineth hereafter, if oft falleth out, that the committers not only escape unpunished, but farther, the fact will remain as allowed by the Law in diverse ages thereafter. It is easy then for you (my Son) to make a choice of one of these two sorts of rulers, by following the way of virtue to establish your standing; yea, in case ye fell in high way, yet should it be with the honourable report, and just regrate of all honest men.

KING JAMES'S SPEECH TO PARLIAMENT

The following document is a portion of King James's speech to his fourth session of Parliament in 1610 that he assembled to increase the "supply" or financial support for the Crown from the people. [I] He begins with three comparisons to define his power and authority, likening himself as king to God, a father, and the head of the body. [II] While James believes it is the king's right to make laws, he declares that the king must then abide by those laws. Under such conditions, he insists that subjects have no right to question the monarch's ways of government. [III] Finally, he explains his financial reasons for calling Parliament. Try to gauge the tone of James's speech, bearing in mind that he comes to Parliament with a request that only they have power to grant. Consider what kind of power relationship he is establishing. (Note: The date 1609 in the title below is based on the old Julian Calendar; according to the Gregorian Calendar we now use, the year is 1610.)

FROM KING JAMES VI AND I, *A SPEECH TO THE LORDS AND COMMONS OF THE PARLIAMENT AT WHITE-HALL, ON WEDNESDAY THE XXI OF MARCH. ANNO 1609* [1610], CHARLES HOWARD MCILWAIN, ED., *THE POLITICAL WORKS OF JAMES I*

(Cambridge, MA: Harvard UP, 1918)

[I] The State of MONARCHY is the supremest thing upon earth: For Kings are not only GOD'S Lieutenants upon earth, and sit upon GOD'S throne, but even by GOD himself they are called Gods. There be three principal similitudes that illustrates the state of MONARCHY: One taken out of the word of GOD; and the two other out of the grounds of Policy and Philosophy. In the Scriptures Kings are called Gods, and so their power after a certain relation compared to the Divine power. Kings are also compared to Fathers of families; for a King is truly *Parens patriae*, the politic father of his people. And lastly, Kings are compared to the head of this Microcosm of the body of man.

Kings are justly called Gods, for that they exercise a manner or resemblance of Divine power upon earth: For if you will consider the Attributes to God, you shall see how they agree in the person of a King. God hath power to create, or destroy, make, or unmake at his pleasure, to give life, or send death, to judge all, and to be judged nor accomptable to none: To raise low things, and to make high things low at his pleasure, and to God are both soul and body due. And the like power have Kings: they make and unmake their subjects: they have power of raising, and casting down: of life, and of death: Judges over all their subjects, and in all causes, and yet accomptable to none but God only. They have power to exalt low things, and abase high things, and make of their subjects like men at the Chess; A pawn to take a Bishop or a Knight, and to cry up, or down any of their subjects, as they do their money. And to the King is due both the affection of the soul, and the service of the body of his subjects....

As for the Father of a family, they had of old under the Law of Nature *Patriam potestatem*...over their children or family (I mean such Fathers of families as were the lineal heirs of those families whereof Kings did originally come:) For Kings had their first original from them, who planted and spread themselves in *Colonies* through the world. Now a Father may dispose of his Inheritance to his children, at his pleasure; yea, even disinherit the eldest upon just occasions, and prefer the youngest, according to his liking; make them beggars, or rich at his pleasure; restrain, or banish out of his presence, as he finds them give cause of offence, or restore them in favour again with the penitent sinner: So may the King deal with his Subjects.

And lastly, as for the head of the natural body, the head hath the power of directing all the members of the body to that use which the judgment in the head thinks most convenient. It may apply sharp cures, or cut off corrupt members, let blood in what proportion it thinks fit, and as the body may spare, but yet is all this power ordained by God....For although God have power as well of destruction, as of creation or maintenance; yet will it not agree with the wisdom of God, to exercise his power in the destruction of nature, and overturning the whole frame of things, since his creatures were made, that his glory might thereby be the better expressed: So were he a foolish father that would disinherit or destroy his children without a cause, or leave off the careful education of them; And it were an idle head that would in place of physic so poison or phlebotomize the body as might breed a dangerous distemper or destruction thereof.

[II] But now in these our times we are to distinguish between the state of Kings in their first original, and between the state of settled Kings and Monarch, that do at this time govern in civil Kingdoms....how soon Kingdoms began to be settled in civility and policy, then did Kings set down their minds by Laws, which are properly made by the King only; but at the rogation of the people, the Kings grant being obtained thereunto. And so the King became to be *Lex loquens,* after a sort, binding himself by a double oath to the observation of the fundamental Laws of his kingdom: *Tacitly,* as by being a King, and so bound to protect as well the people, as the Laws of his Kingdom; And *Expressly,* by his oath at his Coronation: So as every just King in a settled Kingdom is bound to observe that paction made to his people by his Laws, in framing his government agreeable thereunto....And therefore a King governing in a settled Kingdom, leaves to be a King, and degenerates into a Tyrant, as soon as he leaves off to rule according to his Laws. In which case the King's conscience may speak unto him, as the poor widow said to Philip of Macedon; Either govern according to your Law, *Aut ne Rex sis.* And though no Christian man ought to allow any rebellion of people against their Prince, yet doeth God never leave Kings unpunished when they transgress these limits: For in that same Psalm where God saith to Kings, *Vos Dij estis,* he immediately thereafter concludes, *But ye shall die like men.* The higher we are placed, the greater shall our fall be....the taller the trees be, the more in danger of the wind; and the tempest beats sorest upon the highest mountains. Therefore all Kings that are not tyrants, or perjured, will be glad to bound themselves within the limits of their Laws; and they that persuade them the contrary, are vipers, and pests, both against them and the Commonwealth....As for my part, I thank God, I have ever given good proof, that I never had intention to the contrary: And I am sure to go to my grave with that reputation and comfort, that never King was in all his time more careful to have his Laws duly observed, and himself to govern thereafter, than I.

....So is it sedition in Subjects, to dispute what a King may do in the height of his power: But just Kings will ever be willing to declare what they will do, if they will not incur the curse of God. I will not be content that my power be disputed upon: but I shall ever be willing to make the reason appear of all my doings, and rule my actions according to my Laws. (307–310)

[III] And now the third point remains to be spoken of; which is the cause of my calling of this Parliament. And in this I have done but as I use to do in all my life, which is to leave mine own errand hindmost.

It may be you did wonder that I did not speak unto you publicly at the beginning of this Session of Parliament, to tell you the cause of your calling, as I did (if I be rightly remembered) in every Session before. But the truth is, that because I call you at this time for my particular Errand, I thought it fitter to be opened unto you by my Treasurer, who is my public and most principal Officer in matters of that nature, than that I should do it myself: for I confess I am less naturally eloquent, and have greater cause to distrust mine elocution in matters of this nature, then in any other thing. I have made my Treasurer already to give you a very clear and true accompt both of my having, and expenses: A favour I confess, that Kings do seldom bestow upon their Subjects, in making them so particularly acquainted with their state. If I had not more than cause, you may be sure I would be loath to trouble you: But what he hath affirmed in this, upon the honour of a Gentleman, (whom you never had cause to distrust for his honesty,) that do I now confirm and avow to be true in the word and honour of a King; And therein you are bound to believe me. Duty I may justly claim of you as my Subjects; and one of the branches of duty which Subjects owe to their Sovereign, is Supply; but in what quantity, and at what time, that must come of your loves. I am not now therefore to dispute of a King's power, but to tell you what I may justly crave, and expect with your good wills. I was ever against all extremes; and in this case I will likewise wish you to avoid them on both sides. For if you fail in the one, I might have great cause to blame you as Parliament men, being called by me for my Errands: And if you fall into the other extreme, by supply of my necessities without respective care to avoid oppression or partiality in the Levy, both I and the Country will have cause to blame you. (316–317)

PARLIAMENT SPEAKS

The following excerpts indicate the response of members of Parliament to King James's views about his power over his people. Mr. Wentworth primarily insists that the King's prerogative should be open to dispute from Parliament, and suggests that otherwise the people are no more than slaves. His fellow members of Parliament, Hoskin and Yelverton, raise similar issues, contending that the king must not have unlimited power because he is accountable to the people through Parliament. Only a brief statement of the import of their speeches is available but helps to indicate that Wentworth was not alone in his position. Compare these views with James's position in the previous passage as you try to understand why the differences between king and Parliament ultimately led to the two sides leaving the table without any agreement on the financial issue they came to address. Consider how the relationships of power and obedience or resistance play out in *The Tempest;* think about who might be considered subjects as opposed to rulers, and how they respond to one another.

FROM ELIZABETH READ FOSTER, ED., *PROCEEDINGS IN PARLIAMENT* (1610), VOL. 2

(New Haven, CT: Yale UP, 1966) Vol. 2, 82–83

[Friday, May 11, 1610]

On Friday the 11th day of May 1610, Mr. SPEAKER delivered a message from the King to this effect, that we should not entertain into our consideration any disputation touching the prerogative of the king in the case of impositions for that was determined by judgment in the proper court and could not be undone but by error. But if there were any cause for us to complain in regard of the time, the nature of the merchandise or the unproportionableness of the imposition, his Majesty would be as ready to afford grace as we should be to petition him for grace.

This done Mr. WENTWORTH rose and spake. That judgments given in any of the king's courts indeed are not reversible but by error or attaint. But he perceived his Majesty was misinformed in our proceedings in this business for no man went about to reverse the judgment given against Bate. But if he did not or was not able or durst not bring a writ of error, let that judgment on God's name bind him, for that seizure of his goods etc. But no other man in England is bound by that judgment; but he may try the law in a new action. And shall all other courts be at liberty notwithstanding this judgment to dispute the law and shall this court be barred and tied not to dispute it? Is not the king's prerogative disputable? Do not our books in 20 cases argue what the king may do and what not do by his prerogative as join a demurrer the same term, but not in another, etc. and put some other cases to that purpose. Nay if we shall once say that we may not dispute the prerogative, let us be sold for slaves.

SAMUEL RAWSON GARDINER, *PARLIAMENTARY DEBATES IN 1610, EDITED, FROM THE NOTES OF A MEMBER OF THE HOUSE OF COMMONS*

(Camden Society, 1862) no. 81

Hoskin's Speech (June 23–28): The regal power from God, but the actuating thereof is from the people.

   To have this power illimitated is contrary to reason. (76)

   Yelverton's Speech (June 29): Mr. Yelverton's position: an arbitrary, irregular, unlimited, and transcendent power of the King is imposing. (88)

MACHIAVELLI'S PERSPECTIVE

The following selections are from Niccolo Machiavelli's political treatise that he addresses to an Italian prince in the early sixteenth century. He bases his advice on the practical reality that corruption and ambition exist in the political sphere. Therefore, he suggests that cruelty or evil may be justified if it quickly brings about peace and stability. He also indicates that it is better to be feared than to be loved because fear inspires greater loyalty and security than admiration. Finally, he advises the deception of a fox for an effective governor, noting that it is only necessary to appear good rather than to be good. Machiavelli's ideas sparked strong negative reaction in England but also converted some to admiration as they realized that in the real and imperfect world godliness was not as important as a secular approach to political interaction. Think about which characters in *The Tempest* seem most "machiavellian" and whether they seem so in a positive, practical way or a negative, abusive way.

FROM NICCOLO MACHIAVELLI, *THE PRINCE* (1513), HARVARD CLASSICS COLLECTION

(New York: Collier, 1910)

It may be asked how Agathocles and some like him, after numberless acts of treachery and cruelty, have been able to live long in their own country in safety, and to defend themselves from foreign enemies, without being plotted against by their fellow-citizens, whereas, many others, by reason of their cruelty, have failed to maintain their position even in peaceful times, not to speak of the perilous times of war. I believe that this results from cruelty being well or ill employed. Those cruelties we may say are well employed, if it be permitted to speak well of things evil, which are done once for all under the necessity of self-preservation, and are not afterwards persisted in, but so far as possible modified to the advantage of the governed. Ill-employed cruelties, on the other hand, are those which from small beginnings increase rather than diminish with time. They who follow the first these methods, may, by the grace of God and man, find, as did Agathocles, that their condition is not desperate; but by no possibility can the others maintain themselves.

Hence we may learn the lesson that on seizing a state, the usurper should make haste to inflict what injuries he must, at a stroke, that he may not have to renew them daily, but be enabled by their discontinuance to reassure men's minds, and afterwards win them over by benefits. Whosoever, either through timidity or from following bad counsels, adopts a contrary course, must keep the sword always drawn, and can put no trust in his subjects, who suffering from continued and constantly renewed severities, will never yield him their confidence. Injuries, therefore, should be inflicted all at once, that their ill savour being less lasting may the less offend; whereas, benefits should be conferred little by little, that so they may be more fully relished. (33–34)

And here comes in the question whether it is better to be loved rather than feared, or feared rather than loved. It might perhaps be answered that we should wish to be both; but since love and fear can hardly exist together, if we must choose between them, it is far safer to be feared than loved. For of men it may generally be affirmed that they are thankless, fickle, false, studious to avoid danger, greedy of gain, devoted to you while you are able to confer benefits upon them, and ready, as I said before, while danger is distant, to shed their blood, and sacrifice their property, their lives, and their children for you; but in the hour of need they turn against you. The Prince, therefore, who without otherwise securing himself builds wholly on their profession is undone. For the friendships which we buy with a price, and do not gain by greatness and nobility of character, though they be fairly earned are not made good, but fail us when we have occasion to use them.

Moreover, men are less careful how they offend him who makes himself loved than him who makes himself feared. For love is held by that tie of obligation, which, because men are a sorry breed, is broken on every whisper of private interest; but fear is bound by the apprehension of punishment which never relaxes its grasp.

Nevertheless a Prince should inspire fear in such a fashion that if he do not win love he may escape hate. For a man may very well be feared and yet not hated, and this will be the case so long as he does not meddle with the property or with the women of his citizens and subjects. And if constrained to put any to death, he should do so only when there is manifest cause or reasonable justification.

But since a Prince should know how to use the beast's nature wisely, he ought of beasts to choose both the lion and the fox; for the lion cannot guard himself from the toils, nor the fox from wolves. He must therefore be a fox to discern toils, and a lion to drive off wolves.

To rely wholly on the lion is unwise; and for this reason a prudent Prince neither can nor ought to keep his word when to keep it is hurtful to him and the causes which led him to pledge it are removed. If all men were good, this would not be good advice, but since they are dishonest and do not keep faith with you, you, in return, need not keep faith with them; and no prince was ever at a loss for plausible reasons to cloak a breach of faith. Of this numberless recent instances could be given, and it might be shown how many solemn treaties and engagements have been rendered inoperative and idle through want of faith in the Princes, and that he who was best known to play the fox has had the best success.

It is necessary, indeed, to put a good colour on this nature, and to be skilful in simulating and dissembling. But men are so simple, and governed so absolutely by their present needs, that he who wishes to deceive will never fail in finding willing dupes....

It is not essential, then, that a Prince should have all the good qualities which I have enumerated above, but it is most essential that he should seem to have them; I will even venture to affirm that if he has and invariably practises them all, they are hurtful, whereas the appearance of having them is useful. Thus, it is well to seem merciful, faithful, humane, religious, and upright, and also to be so; but the mind should remain so balanced that were it needful not to be so, you should be able and know how to change to the contrary. (60–61)

TOPICS FOR WRITTEN AND ORAL DISCUSSION

1. Summarize the history of treason familiar to King James's England at the time *The Tempest* was originally performed.

2. What is Henry Garnet, the Jesuit priest, accused of in the Gunpowder Plot of 1605? Summarize his response on his execution date. Note that to "equivocate" is to evade the truth by answering ambiguously through mental reservations so that the truth remains unclear. Do you find that Garnet equivocates or does he seem openly repentant and remorseful? Does he seem sympathetic? Use evidence to support your answer.

3. Compare as traitors Henry Garnet and Shakespeare's "three men of sin" (3.3.53) in *The Tempest,* Alonso, Antonio, and Sebastian. What are their crimes? How are they punished or pardoned? How do they respond when accused of their treasonous acts? How does the word "remorse" suit them?

4. How does the treasonous plot of Stephano, Trinculo, and Caliban contribute to the theme of political treachery in *The Tempest*? How does their plot help to characterize Prospero and his role as the governor of the island?

5. Imagine Antonio and Sebastian have an opportunity for a private dialogue after Prospero pardons them for their wrongs, takes back his dukedom, and lets them know his awareness of their attempt to take Alonso's life. What might they say to each other? Script a dialogue or script two possible alternative responses and let the class judge which one is more convincing and believable.

6. Imagine a dialogue between Emperor Rudolf II and Prospero about their similar political plights. Both lovers of magic have had their political powers usurped by their brothers. How might they empathize with each other? Is either one of them in a position to offer advice or counsel to the other or are they both somewhat naive or misguided? Let your words reflect your opinion.

7. Supporters of Rudolf II sought help from England's king, and James I had good feelings toward the emperor. Write a letter from James to Rudolf. What might James say to Rudolf given Rudolf's circumstances, James's relationship to his own subjects, his views on power and rulers, and his ideals about good government. (Refer to the documents by King James in this chapter.)

8. Put yourself in the shoes of Matthias, brother to Rudolf II, emperor of the Holy Roman Empire. Rudolf is not fulfilling his responsibilities as political ruler. Write an open letter to convince all the princes in the empire that you are justified in taking Rudolf's place. What arguments and political rhetoric will you use? Second, write a diary entry that honestly expresses your personal views or expectations. Third, write a letter to Rudolf to explain to him your plans or to accuse him of his faults or both. Decide before you begin whether to make Matthias sympathetic as a political figure or overly ambitious as a traitor.

9. What difference does King James identify between a good king and a tyrant in *Basilicon Doron*? What reward or response does each receive for his actions?

10.   Discuss whether you think Prospero's actions as governor of the island are those of a good ruler or a tyrant. Then choose sides and hold a debate justifying your position according to details from the play. Does Prospero use his power appropriately or not? By what right does he rule?

11.   List the three comparisons King James uses to explain his role as monarch over his people in his speech to Parliament in 1610. How does each comparison legitimize his assertion of power?

12.   Declaring monarchs to be makers of laws, what role does James I grant to subjects and what limitations does he put on them?

13.   In explaining his reasons for calling Parliament, what kind of relation does James assume and establish with members of Parliament? Does he seem arrogant or humble? Find examples to support your position. How would you describe the tone of his entire speech? What would you expect the reaction of the House of Commons to be?

14.   What is your impression of Parliament's response to James in 1610 based on the short excerpts entitled "Parliament Speaks" in this chapter? What are the primary complaints from the House of Commons?

15.   Consider that Shakespeare was probably writing *The Tempest* at the time that the parliamentary debate of 1610 took place. In a relationship of power and service between Prospero and his subjects, Caliban and Ariel, what does Prospero want from them and what do they want from him? How might their relationship parallel the power struggle between James and Parliament?

16.   How do you suppose James I might react to the portrayal of Prospero as ruler in the play? Obviously, the play was not badly received for it was performed at least twice before the king. Imagine yourself as James and write a letter to William Shakespeare, expressing your response to *The Tempest* and its characters based on attitudes James relays in this chapter's documents.

17.   Responses to Machiavelli in England were mixed from admiration to hatred. Can you find reasons for the range of reactions in the excerpts from *The Prince* quoted in this chapter? Do you think his advice seems practical and necessary or immoral and evil? Explain why.

18.   Consider which characters appear "machiavellian" in *The Tempest* given that the term generally connotes cunning and deception although it could otherwise mean one who uses power effectively through shrewdness. Discuss how the ambiguous response to Machiavelli could reflect some ambiguities in the play. Consider, for example, whether Prospero is wise in choosing to forgive his enemies and whether his arrangement of the betrothal between Miranda and Ferdinand reflects political opportunism or idealism. What does he gain from the marriage and what will he lose?

19.   If Prospero and Machiavelli sat down to share their views on power and good government, what might they say to one another? Would they agree or disagree? Provide evidence for your position.

20.   Write an essay in which you either defend Prospero as a good ruler or accuse him as a bad ruler, explaining what criteria you will use to assess his performance and drawing from speeches in act 1 and act 5 about the past and the future as well as from actions on the island.

SUGGESTED READING

Gardiner, Samuel Rawson. *What the Gunpowder Plot Was* (1897). Rpt. New York: Greenwood Press, 1969.

Hamilton, Donna B. "Shakespeare's Romances and Jacobean Political Discourse," in *Approaches to Teaching Shakespeare's* The Tempest *and Other Late Romances.* New York: MLA, 1992. 65–71.

Parker, Geoffrey. *Europe in Crisis, 1598–1648.* Ithaca, NY: Cornell UP, 1979.

Parkinson, C. Northcote. *Gunpowder, Treason and Plot.* London: Weidenfeld and Nicholson, 1976.

Raab, Felix. *The English Face of Machiavelli, A Changing Interpretation.* London: Routledge, 1964.

Tillyard, E.M.W. *The Elizabethan World Picture.* New York: Random House, 1944.

5

Society: Marriage and the Court

Prospero's great social plan involves regaining his dukedom and offering pardon to his enemies. A crucial part of that plan is to ensure the marriage of his daughter Miranda to Ferdinand, the son of his enemy, King Alonso. Miranda and Ferdinand immediately fall in love with each other, and their betrothal represents the typical sign of closure and harmony that ends a comedy. But their promised marriage also represents a political act that legitimizes the reconciliation of the two states, Milan and Naples, and promises a future government under one ruler, Ferdinand. Shakespeare brings love and politics together in his final play, combining the playful, communal celebration of comedy with the serious public concerns more often found in his histories and tragedies. The happy encounter between Ferdinand and Miranda emerges in the foreground of the play while at the background the recent wedding of Alonso's daughter Claribel to the king of Tunis reinforces the importance of marriages as public alliances designed for the well-being of the state more than for the happiness of the couple. Alliances through marriage were the hallmark of European government in Shakespeare's time, for the sake of building kingdoms, ensuring peace, protecting against war, and promoting economic prosperity. During James's reign in England such concerns were significant, imposing much weight on the marriage possibilities for his children. The following discussion will explore romantic traditions and political practicalities that provide a context—both literary and historical—for the plot of *The Tempest*.

COURTLY LOVE

Chapter 1 already outlines some of the qualities of "romance" as a term de-riving from early Greek literature and eventually gaining currency in reference to Shakespeare's last four plays. Here it is useful to say more about "love" as a romantic concept combined with the kind of idealism that characterized it. A literary convention identified as the "courtly love tradition" began in early me-dieval literature among eleventh-century French poets writing about knights seeking the love of beautiful ladies. In courtly love poetry, the lovers are of royal lineage; they are not peasants or commoners. The woman is perceived as being like a goddess, placed on a pedestal and worshipped from afar. The knight who seeks her and idolizes her is typically not the woman's husband but often a man engaged in an impossibly adulterous longing that is guaran-teed to remain unfulfilled. The distance between him and the lady he loves is a sign of the purity of their love. Thus, while he displays gentlemanly behav-ior of courtesy, humility, and service, his desire has a quality of untried per-fection but may also include a sense of desperation or despair because the knight will never be able to consummate his desire.

This literary convention of courtly love found its way to the English Re-naissance period through the influence of Italian love poetry. English poets imported poems known as sonnets from the Italian writer Petrarch and then composed their own verses about women worshipped for their love and pu-rity, and desired for their perfection. Shakespeare became one of the chief writ-ers of sonnets in England. He modified the form, however, sometimes addressing the relationship of male friendship rather than the love between a man and a woman, and even when he chose the latter, he explored many sides of a complex relationship rather than simply idealizing love. In the Renais-sance, marriage began to be seen as the culmination of courtly love rather than the antithesis of it.

In *The Tempest*, Ferdinand and Miranda express in fairly simple, undevel-oped terms, romance deriving from the courtly tradition. They fall in love at first sight, and speak in exalted language when they describe one another. Mi-randa thinks at first that Ferdinand is a spirit and says, "I might call him / A thing divine; for nothing natural / I ever saw so noble" (1.2.418–420). Ferdi-nand calls Miranda a "goddess" and a "wonder" (1.2.422, 427). He is imme-diately ready to make her the queen of Naples until Prospero intervenes to slow down their interaction by making Ferdinand his temporary slave or ser-vant. Ferdinand delights in the labor as service to the maid he loves; she weeps to see him suffer under the burden. Their gestures are the epitome of courtesy and indulgence. Shakespeare's emphasis on Miranda's virginity only heightens the element of romance in the relationship between his two young lovers. They can easily be seen as figures of a courtly literary tradition that Shakespeare has translated from the page to the stage.

MARRIAGE LAWS AND CUSTOMS

The context of *The Tempest,* however, is not simply literary. Attitudes toward courtship and marriage during Shakespeare's time can also shed light on the relationship between the two lovers. Discrepancies and conflicts existed between customs and laws about courtship and marriage. Although there is no particular element of controversy surrounding Miranda and Ferdinand's short courtship, Miranda's forwardness when she believes she is alone with Ferdinand and his comparable initiative before awaiting Prospero's consent to their marriage commitment raise questions from the perspective of Renaissance marriage laws and traditions.

On the one hand, the earlier medieval secular view of marriage as an economic, social contract emphasized the parents' role in arranging a match for their children and establishing positive financial conditions. On the other hand, the church, with its increasing influence prior to the Reformation, stressed the binding sacred power of two individuals consenting to a holy union before God without the need for parental influence. After Henry VIII broke away from the Roman Catholic Church and established the Protestant Church of England, conflicting secular and sacred views of marriage continued to coexist. Church or "canon" law remained the final arbiter and all that it required legally to make a marriage was the verbal pledge of a man and a woman to each other before witnesses, including the traditional words, "I do." Families, however, maintained a social, if not a legal, influence in directing their children's choices, and even the church firmly advised children to honor and obey their fathers and mothers.

Parental guidance was strongest in upper classes because the economic and social outcome of marriage was much more significant for people with rank and status. This was especially true of royalty, for the matches made between princes and princesses were often designed with a political purpose in mind. The tradition of parental consent was also stronger for daughters than for sons because England was governed by a patriarchal system in which men were granted supreme authority in politics, community, and family. In this male-dominated society, inheritances passed from father to son, and the family was seen as a miniature commonwealth mirroring the larger commonwealth or state of England. Daughters were traditionally recognized as property, making their care and welfare dependent first on their fathers' and then on their husbands' position. Into this mixture of laws and customs, of individual choice and family consent, there was a growing perception that marriage not only could have—but should have—love rather than economic, social, or political gain as its most powerful binding force. Consequently, even when family guidance and approval were recognized and practiced, the feelings of the couple began to be a more important and respected premarital consideration.

Sacred and secular attitudes intermingled, and many handbooks or conduct books for courtship and marriage were written during the English Renaissance. In the male-dominated hierarchy of the patriarchal system, not only were fathers and husbands traditionally granted supreme authority over their daughters and wives, but women were also regarded as the weaker sex, physically and morally. The handbooks, whose authors were typically male, often gave more attention to women's roles than to men's. A woman's virginity was considered her greatest virtue before marriage. After marriage her greatest virtue was her fidelity. She was repeatedly reminded to be chaste, silent, and obedient. Conduct books warned against women being too outspoken and harshly condemned adulterous wives, loose women, and unwed mothers, while a man's adultery was not judged with the same severity nor his virginity prior to marriage given much concern. These opposing sexual expectations of men and women presented a double standard that some male writers even in Shakespeare's time began to acknowledge as discriminatory. And yet many others continued to uphold traditional sexual categories as part of the ideal and necessary model of gender relationships.

In fact, against traditional sixteenth-century views of spousal duties, virtues, and indiscretions, opposing perspectives began to emerge with the religious and political changes following the Reformation and during the Renaissance or humanist revival with which it coincided. Historically, the pre-Reformation church viewed marriage as less admirable than a single celibate life but necessary for procreation and advisable to avoid the temptation of unlawful sexual relations. After the Reformation, leaders within the newly established Protestant church began to stress the dignity of marriage. A view of marriage that acknowledged the companionship or partnership of the relationship became more popular. The Puritans, a group within the Protestant church, even encouraged private morality and spiritual equality between husbands and wives. Simultaneously, the secular humanism of the Renaissance promoted individualism, recognizing, to a limited degree, the values of freedom and education for women as well as for men. Consequently, although the male hierarchy remained largely intact, women had a greater possibility for self-expression and self-assertion. Nevertheless, traditional assumptions of domestic hierarchy were not simply replaced by growing expressions of individualism and spiritual equality.

How does the match between Miranda and Ferdinand reflect or challenge this social and political context? Since Prospero orchestrates the meeting between the couple and intends that they desire to marry each other, one could simply say that his plan succeeds because Miranda and Ferdinand do exactly what he wants them to do. However, he does impose temporary restrictions, and whether he expects them to be obeyed or not, the significant point is that as soon as the young couple believes they have a corner of the island to themselves, they take matters into their own hands. Miranda dismisses the traditional daughter's role as one who is silent and obedient when first she tells Ferdinand her name. Then, she expresses her feelings for the prince. She immediately asks him outright about his regard for her: "Do you love me?" (3.1.67). Finally, she asks him to marry her. She confesses in the midst of their conversation that she disobeys her father's orders and forgets his precepts, and yet she persists. Ferdinand, for his part, believes he has no fatherly authority to consult since Alonso has supposedly drowned at sea, but he gives no indication that he intends to seek Prospero's approval before agreeing to marry Miranda. In short, the young couple acts completely contrary to the familial expectations of the time. Instead, they act of their own accord, in line with a growing perception that love should be a key element of marriage. Prospero admits in an aside that he is surprised by their initiative but pleased with the outcome. As he sanctions and blesses their betrothal, he emphasizes the importance of chastity before marriage and celebrates the political benefit of the union.

THE MARRIAGE OF PRINCESS ELIZABETH AND FREDERICK V, ELECTOR OF PALATINE

The political aspect of the betrothal between Miranda and Ferdinand has striking parallels with the marriage arrangement of King James's daughter, Princess Elizabeth, and Frederick V, the elector of Palatine. When James replaced Elizabeth I on the English throne in 1603, the public was introduced to an entirely new dynamic at court. Elizabeth had been the ruling monarch for 45 years, and remained single to the end, although early in her reign her advisors tried to marry her to a foreign prince in order to form a favorable political alliance and create the possibility of an obvious heir to the throne. James arrived in London with a wife and three children. Consequently, the familial aspect of court life became newly significant. Almost immediately, James and influential court leaders began to consider possible marriage arrangements especially for the eldest son and heir to the throne, Prince Henry, and the second child, Princess Elizabeth. James's motivations were purely political. England had remained largely isolated from European continental politics during Elizabeth's reign, and James wanted to establish new political ties. Religion played a key role with nation-states identifying themselves as either Protestant or Catholic and often struggling with internal religious factions that created unrest. James wanted to promote peace on the continent as well as ensure the Protestant identity of England. Initially, he thought of arranging a marriage between Prince Henry and a Catholic princess, while matching Princess Elizabeth with a Protestant prince, thus promoting peaceful ties with both religions and giving England a prominent political presence in Europe. Prince Henry, however, was staunchly Protestant and not in favor of a Catholic alliance. But before any arrangement could be made, tragedy struck the Stuart family as Prince Henry died of a sudden illness in 1612 at the age of 18.

The youngest prince, Charles, then became heir to the throne, but all eyes turned to Elizabeth and the marriage plans being made for her. For several years, James had been negotiating a match between his daughter and potential suitors. In 1611, the newly appointed Frederick V, 15-year-old elector of Palatine showed interest in Princess Elizabeth. Primarily German, the Palatinate region that he governed was one of approximately a thousand separate territories loosely joined under a political body known as the Holy Roman Empire. Frederick had more influence than many of the affiliated territories because he was one of seven electors with the power to elect the Holy Roman emperor when the throne became vacant. More important, from a British standpoint, he was the staunchly Protestant head of the Union of German Protestant Princes, established in 1608. His religious association pleased the Protestant majority in England, while he, too, was looking for Protestant supporters to shore up strength for the German Union. In spring of 1612 marriage negotiations began in earnest. Not until then did Elizabeth have any personal involvement in the plans for her future. Previous suitors had approached James, leaving his daughter entirely out of any proposals affecting her. By the middle of October, Frederick arrived in England for marriage preparations, and Elizabeth met him for the first time. Prince Henry's sudden death on November 6 delayed wedding plans but only temporarily, and the betrothal ceremony between Elizabeth and Frederick V took place on December 27, 1612, with the wedding following on Valentine's Day, February 14, 1613.

Between the betrothal and the wedding, the couple enjoyed all kinds of activities together including boat trips, hunting, playing cards, and watching plays. In spite of the fact that the match between the two had been strictly a political alliance, Elizabeth and Frederick appeared to be quite fond of each other and compatible in interests as well as in age. Fourteen plays by Shakespeare's company, the King's Men, are listed as being performed at court for the betrothed couple, one of which was *The Tempest*. While it is unlikely that Shakespeare could have foreseen the royal match that took place more than a year after he wrote *The Tempest*, evidence indicates that interest in marriage negotiations between Frederick and Elizabeth began as early as 1608, and Shakespeare, like the rest of the public, would have been aware of the negotiations. Furthermore, the plot of *The Tempest* simply serves as an appropriate performance for an engaged royal couple. Many scholars have pointed out the parallels between the play's action, in which the usurped duke arranges a marriage between his daughter and a young prince who will provide a favorable political alliance. Some have even suggested that the entertainment Prospero conjures up for them of spirits acting as mythological characters coming to bless the couple was added to the original play for its 1613 performance. Others maintain that the performance within the play is congruent with the direction of *The Tempest*'s plot and need not have been an afterthought. Either way, the play became part of a significant event in English history: the first royal marriage for decades, filled with hopes and expectations of peaceful government and a new generation of young rulers. However, Frederick eventually accepted the throne of Bohemia in 1619, an act that intensified conflict leading to Europe's Thirty Years War and made him and Elizabeth political refugees. Thus, many of the hopes expressed at the marriage of the young couple were later dashed, although nobody could foresee such distress at the time of the wedding.

COURT MASQUES

The entertainment Prospero creates for Miranda and Ferdinand is known as a masque, a form of activity that became very popular at the English court during James's reign. A masque is a semi-dramatic performance involving music, dance, elaborate costumes, sets, and pageantry, and including allegorical figures such as Peace or Malice, folklore characters such as fairies and nymphs, and mythological characters such as Neptune or Venus. The acting is elaborate and formal, and the main purpose of the masque is to honor and praise the monarch who is the primary audience of the performance. Unlike conventional theater, the actors are not professional players, but rather members of the court who have donned masks and costumes for the special occasion of the masque. The performance is focused not on story line or plot but rather on music and spectacle. The king is included in the masque in the sense that he is recognized as the one with power to connect to the deities of the supernatural world in the performance and to bring harmony and peace to the world being presented. The masquers eventually draw court spectators into their performance, including nobles, ladies, diplomats, and foreign ambassadors, leading them onto the dance floor, thus making an obvious connection between the entertainment and the real life and relationships of elite political society rather than offering illusion separate from reality.

Queen Anne was the chief instigator of masque performances at court. She loved the spectacle and costumes and was a proficient dancer. She appointed two men to create masques for her pleasure, Ben Jonson who wrote the poetry and Inigo Jones who was the scene designer. Together these men produced lavish and elite entertainments that were characterized by mystery and wonder. The first of the queen's masques was *The Masque of Blackness,* performed in 1605. In it, Queen Anne and her ladies appear as 12 blackamoors or Ethiopians who are daughters of the Niger River. They receive a vision that they are to travel to a land ending in "tania" where their complexion will be refined and they will become beautiful. The place they seek is Britannia or Britain, and the power to transform them rests not only in England's temperate climate but also in King James's idealized power, which is like the "sun" whose light represents divine wisdom (Parry 46). A second significant Jonson and Jones masque is *The Masque of Queens* performed in 1609. In it, Jonson introduces an element known as an anti-masque that precedes the main masque and displays chaos and disorder in contrast to the peace and order ushered in by the masque proper. The anti-masque in *The Masque of Queens* centered on 12 witches from hell who represent the grotesque and dark arts in wild dances before 12 less threatening masquers take their place. The anti-masque was performed by professional actors, while the masque that followed continued to be portrayed by members of the nobility. Jonson's masques always moved toward the resolution of conflict through symbolic figures. The entertainments represented a ceremonial and celebratory idealization of political life at court.

Masques were often presented for the celebratory political occasion of a noble wedding. Three such masques were performed at the wedding of Princess Elizabeth and Frederick V. Shakespeare introduces this contemporary court tradition to *The Tempest* by having Prospero offer a masque for the pleasure of Miranda and Ferdinand at their betrothal. Like the masques in James's court, this one is defined as much by its spectacle as by its poetry. Thus, it is difficult to imagine its effect without actually seeing it performed. The masque involves three mythological figures: Ceres, goddess of vegetation and fertility, represents the regeneration of nature; Iris is the goddess of the rainbow representing hope and providing a pathway for the gods between heaven and earth; Juno is the goddess of marriage and protector of women. The three come together to bless the love between Miranda and Ferdinand. Juno who descends from above in an elaborate stage apparatus, says, "Spring come to you at the farthest / In the very end of harvest" (4.1.114–115), expressing a wish that the young couple experience no winter but only spring, summer, and autumn. The nymphs and reapers who join the celebration perform a dance befitting the grace and hope of earthly paradise. An abrupt end to the masque occurs when Prospero remembers "Caliban and his confederates" (4.1.140) and turns his attention toward them. What comes next is very much like an anti-masque that follows rather than precedes the masque. Caliban and his cohorts are earthy and grotesque, and rather than a dance, they get run through a wild and noisy chase in which spirits in the form of dogs hunt them down and capture them. Shakespeare's incorporation of a masque into *The Tempest* reveals his awareness of a contemporary entertainment and his willingness to play with various styles and forms of entertainment. The appeal of the masque form for his drama about an enchanted island is that it heightens the sense of wonder and mystery created by Prospero's supernatural power, while adding to the visual and musical effects that are prominent throughout the play.

The remainder of this chapter includes poetry and excerpted documents that help to draw connections between the betrothal in *The Tempest* and the social and literary contexts of marriage and court society in England in the early seventeenth century.

SHAKESPEAREAN LOVE POETRY

Shakespeare wrote many sonnets, the love poetry of the English Renaissance that grew out of the courtly love tradition. A sonnet is a fourteen-line poem with a set rhyme scheme and a fixed rhythm of iambic pentameter. Shakespeare organized his sonnets into three quatrains or four-line sections followed by a concluding rhyming couplet that often posed a question about the preceding lines or offered a summary or reversal for the poem as a whole. Sonnet 18 below expresses the love between a man and a woman in which the lover compares his beloved to a summer's day and finds the nature of the beloved to be greater and more lasting than the beautiful day. The speaker concludes by indicating that the poem itself helps to immortalize the beloved by making her loveliness lasting in memory. Pay attention to the various images the speaker uses to describe the beloved and consider whether the tone of the sonnet might suit the interaction between Miranda and Ferdinand.

FROM WILLIAM SHAKESPEARE, SONNET 18 (C. 1590S), SEE IN *THE RIVERSIDE SHAKESPEARE*, ED. G. BLAKEMORE EVANS ET AL.

(Boston: Houghton, 1974) 1752

SONNET 18

> Shall I compare thee to a summer's day?
> Thou art more lovely and more temperate:
> Rough winds do shake the darling buds of May,
> And summer's lease hath all too short a date;
> Sometime too hot the eye of heaven shines,
> And often is his gold complexion dimm'd,
> And every fair from fair sometime declines,
> By chance or nature's changing course untrimm'd:
> But thy eternal summer shall not fade,
> Nor lose possession of that fair thou ow'st,
> Nor shall Death brag thou wand'rest in his shade,
> When in eternal lines to time thou grow'st.
>> So long as men can breathe or eyes can see,
>> So long lives this, and this gives life to thee.

THE DUTIES OF CHILDREN BEFORE MARRIAGE

Thomas Becon (1512–1567), a Protestant minister, wrote the first significant guide book or conduct book after the Reformation. His advice remained
relevant into the seventeenth century. In the excerpt below, he emphasizes the
popular Renaissance view that women were to be chaste, silent, and obedient.
He also expresses his view on marriage, strongly recommending that young
men and women ensure that they have the approval of their parents or others
in authority before they commit themselves to each other. To do otherwise is
not only an act of disobedience, but also an "offence against God." Consider
how Miranda and Ferdinand measure up to Becon's standards of model behavior.

FROM THOMAS BECON, A NEW CATECHISM

(London, 1564. STC 1710)

"Of the Duty of Maids and Young Unmarried Women"

FROM *SILENCE IN A MAID IS GREATLY COMMENDABLE*

[T]his also must honest maids provide, that they be not full of tongue, and of much
babbling, nor use many words, but as few as they may, yea, and those wisely and dis-
creetly, soberly and modestly spoken, ever remembering this common proverb: A maid
should be seen and not heard. Except that the gravity of some matter do require, that
she should speak: or else an answer is to be made to such things as are demanded of
her: let her keep silence. For there is nothing that doth so much commend, advance,
set forth, adorn, deck, trim, and garnish a maid as silence. And this noble virtue may
the virgins learn of that most holy, pure, and glorious virgin Mary: which when she
either heard or saw any worthy and notable thing, blabbed it not out straightaways to
her gossips, as the manner of women is at this present day, but being silent, she kept
all those sayings secret and pondered them in her heart, saith blessed Luke. Fol.
ccccc.xxxvi

FROM *CHILDREN OUGHT NOT TO CONTRACT MATRIMONY WITHOUT CONSENT OF THEIR PARENTS*

Finally, when the time cometh, that they feel themselves apt unto marriage, and are desirous to contract matrimony to them, that they may avoid all uncleanness and bring forth fruit according to God's ordinance, as their parents have done before them: they must diligently take heed, that they presume not to take in hand so grave, weighty, and earnest matter, nor entangle themselves with the love of any person, before they have made their parents, tutors, friends, or such as have governance of them privy of their intent, yea and also require their both counsel and consent in the matter, and by no means to establish or appoint any thing in this behalf without the determination of their rulers. For this part of the honor that the children owe to their parents and tutors by the commandment of God, even to be bestowed in marriage, as it pleaseth the godly, prudent, and honest parents or tutors to appoint: with this persuasion, that they for their age, wisdom, and experience, yea and for the tender love, singular benevolence, and hearty good will that they bear toward [the children], both know and will better provide for them, than they be able to provide for themselves. The histories of the Holy Bible teach evidently, that the godly fathers in times past appointed the marriages of their children, and that the children attempted nothing in this behalf without counsel, consent, determination, and appointment of their parents. And that authority, which parents at that time had over their children, have fathers and mothers also at this present. And as the children then did not take upon them to marry without the consent of their parents: no more ought they to do so in this our age. The children which presume to marry without the counsel of their parents, do greatly offend God, and are fallen away from the obedience, which they owe their parents or tutors in this behalf, by the commandment of God. Let all godly maids take heed therefore, that they snarl not themselves with the love of any other, nor marry with any person before they have the good will of their parents. Fol. ccccc xxxiiiir

THE CONSENT AND CONTRACT OF MARRIAGE

One of many popular conduct books written in England after the Reformation, John Dod and Robert Cleaver's *A Godly Form of Household Government* (1598) is typical in its stance on marriage contracts. Unlike Becon's *A New Catechism*, Dod and Cleaver's advice takes into consideration the desires of the couple promised in marriage as well as the views of the parents. While they indicate what constitutes a legitimate marriage and the potential harm that can arise from a secret or untimely marital contract, they also point out the wisdom of a marriage in which the couple willingly chooses one another rather than being forced into consent by those in authority over them. Note the importance of voluntary consent as well as the role that parents are assigned in the marriage contract.

FROM JOHN DOD AND ROBERT CLEAVER, *A GODLY FORM OF HOUSEHOLD GOVERNMENT: FOR THE ORDERING OF PRIVATE FAMILIES, ACCORDING TO THE DIRECTION OF GOD'S WORD*

(London: 1598. STC 5383)

A Contract, is a voluntary promise of marriage, mutually made between one man and one woman, both being meet and free to marry one another, and therefore allowed so to do by their Parents.

....[W]e call this promise of marriage, voluntary, because it must not come from the lips alone, but from the well-liking and consent of the heart: for if it be only a verbal promise, without any will at all, (and so mere hypocritical and dissembled) though it bindeth the party that promiseth, to the performance of his promise, made before God and man: yet if the Parents afterwards shall certainly know this, and that there was no will, nor unfeigned meaning at all in the party, neither yet is, but rather a loathing and abhorring of his spouse betrothed, though he be not able to render just and sufficient cause thereof, they may upon this occasion, either defer the day of marriage the longer, to see if God will happily change the mind of the party, or utterly break and frustrate the promise....Wherefore this promise must be in this respect, at least, willing, and voluntary. For...if it be voluntary and unfeigned, it is enough, and fully sufficient, to make a true contract in the Lord....Secondly, we call it voluntary, in respect of constraint and compulsion, contrary to a free consent: for if either party be urged, constrained, or compelled, by great fear of their Parents, or others, by threatening of loss or preferment, of health, of limb, of life, or of any such other like, or by any other violent manner of dealing whatsoever, to yield their promise clean contrary to the motion of good liking of their hearts. This kind of promise, as it doth not bind the party to keep it: so it ought to be frustrated and broken by the Parents themselves, or by such masters as may and ought, to command and rule them in such cases. (116–121)

But if [a marriage contract] be mutual, then it doth mutually and inviolably bind both: so that in this regard, neither Parent, Magistrate, nor any other, can or ought to break it. For this being fully performed and accomplished, is one principal cause of making two one flesh....(123)

...it is a calamity infernal...to be in company with those that a man would not be withall, and yet cannot be separated nor depart from them. Hereof cometh, as we do see in some marriages, so great ruins, so wicked and vile deed, as maims, & murders committed by such desperate persons, as are loath to keep, and yet cannot lawfully refuse, nor leave them: Therefore young folks ought not to be too rash and hasty in their choice, but to have the good advice and direction of their parents and trusty friends in this behalf, who have better judgment, and are more free from the motions of all affections, than they are. And they must take heed, lest following the light and corrupt judgment of their own affections and minds, they change not a short delectation and pleasure, into a continual sorrow and repentance. For we do learn, by great and continual use and experience of things, that the secret contracts made between those that be young do seldom prosper, whereas contrariwise, those marriages that are made and established by the advice of wise and religious parents, do prosper well. (151–152)

PRINCESS ELIZABETH AND PRINCE FREDERICK

The occasion of the marriage between James I's daughter Princess Elizabeth to the elector of Palatine, Prince Frederick V, generated many lavish celebrations at court from December 1612 until after the wedding on February 14, 1613. This was the first royal wedding in England since Henry VIII's many marriages in the first half of the sixteenth century, and the youth and comparative innocence of the young couple in 1612 encouraged a spirit of hope and expectation. King James was an extravagant monarch from the outset and spared no cost in the entertainments for the courtship, including plays, masques, and pageantry. The following account, first printed in 1613 and then reprinted by John Anstis much later in 1733, provides a record of some of the court recreations and the wedding ceremony. The first celebration was an elaborate fireworks display along the Thames River on February 11; the second was a mock sea battle between the "infidel" Turks and conquering English navy on February 13. Finally, on February 14, the marriage ceremony itself took place, with court dignitaries and the royal family gathered for the solemn occasion in their finest garments. Notice the importance of ritual throughout and the prominence of the king who was always center stage even when the activities were designed for his daughter's wedding. Think of the prominence of Prospero in all the ceremonial or ritual events in *The Tempest*, especially related to Miranda and Ferdinand's meeting and betrothal.

FROM "THE MAGNIFICENT MARRIAGE OF THE TWO
GREAT PRINCES FREDERICK COUNT PALATINE, &C. AND
THE LADY ELIZABETH DAUGHTER TO THE IMPERIAL
MAJESTIES KING JAMES AND QUEEN ANNE TO THE
COMFORT OF ALL GREAT BRITAIN", IN JOHN NICHOLS,
*THE PROGRESSES, PROCESSIONS, AND MAGNIFICENT
FESTIVITIES OF KING JAMES THE FIRST, HIS ROYAL
CONSORT, FAMILY, AND COURT*, VOL. II

(New York: Burt Franklin, 1828) 536–549

Being desirous to give satisfaction to certain of my acquaintance in the country most willing to understand the manner of the Triumphs holden at the Royal Marriage of his Majesty's Daughter, Princess Elizabeth, I have made means for the true intelligences thereof; and, I hope according to the content of the reader, I have set forth here a true discourse of the same; first of the Shows and Fireworks upon the water before the Marriage performed upon Thursday night, being the eleventh of February; then the imitation of a Sea-fight upon Saturday following; also of the Royal and Princely passage of Prince Palsgrave with his renowned Bride to his Highness' Chapel at White-hall, where, in the presence of his Majesty and the Noble State, they were married, to make us rejoice with a wished happiness, with the Masques and Revels following, shows of more Royalty than ever in this age was seen in the Court of England. There-fore let the reader hereof prepare himself to entertain them with extraordinary joy, and receive the good will of the writer for a tribute to be paid as due to his country.

The manner of the Fire-works showed upon the Thames, upon the Thursday
before the Wedding.

To begin these Triumphant Sports, his Highness, the Queen's Majesty, Prince Charles, Prince Frederick, with the Princess Elizabeth his Royal Bride, and the rest of the Nobility of England, upon Thursday the eleventh of February in the evening, being placed in the galleries and windows about his Highness' Court of Whitehall, where, in the sight of many thousands of people many artificial conclusions in Fire-works were upon the Thames performed, and that the pleasurable sights on the water might equal the sumptuous Shows on the land, thus they proceeded. First, for the wel-come of the beholders, a peal of ordnance like unto a terrible thunder, rattled in the air, and seemed as it were to shake the earth; immediately upon this a rocket of fire burst from the water, and mounted so high into the element, that it dazzled the be-holders' eyes to look after it. Secondly, followed a number more of the same fashion, spreading so strangely with sparkling blazes, that the sky seemed to be filled with fire, or that there had been a combat of darting stars fighting in the air; and all the time these continued, certain cannons planted in the fields adjoining made thundering music to the great pleasure of the beholders. After this, in a most curious manner, an artificial Fire-work with great wonder was seen flying in the air, like unto a Dragon, against which another fiery vision appeared, flaming like to St. George on horseback, brought in by a burning Enchanter, between which was there fought a most strange battle continuing a quarter of an hour or more; the Dragon being vanquished, seemed to roar like thunder, and withall burst in pieces and so vanished; but the Champion, with his flaming horse, for a little time made a show of a triumphant conquest, and so ceased. After this was heard another rattling sound of cannons, almost covering the air with fire and smoke, and forthwith appeared out of a hill of earth made upon the water a very strange fire, flaming upright like unto a blazing star. After which flew forth a number of rockets so high in the air, that we could not choose but approve by all reasons that Art hath exceeded Nature, so artificially were they performed, and still as the chambers and culverines played upon the earth, the Fire-works danced in the air to the great delight of his Highness and the Princes....When Kings' commands be, art is stretched to the true depth, as the performance of these engineers have been approved....

*The manner of a Sea-fight, showed upon the Thames, upon the Saturday
before the Wedding*

Between the hours of two and three of the clock the same day in the afternoon,
being Shrove Saturday, the King's Majesty accompanied with the Queen, the rest of
the Princes and Peers of Estate, to add the more glory to these pre-intended shows,
placed themselves in great Royalty upon the Privy Stairs of Whitehall, where after a
while expecting the beginning of the desired Fire-works, the Lord Admiral sent forth
two or three Gentlemen in a whirrie with a flag or banner to signify the King and the
Nobilities' tarriance for the representations, which was answered with an intelligence
by the report, from a great cannon; whereupon a certain Venetian man of war, and a
ship called a carvell, came proudly with their flags and colours sailing up, in the sight
of seventeen Turkish galleys, which lay hovering upon Lambeth side, betwixt whom
was a most Royal and praise-worthy imitation of a Sea-fight in such a sort performed,
as if the danger of such an enterprise had been by true action attempted; all which explains the honours of martialists, and made his Majesty with many thousands of people of all sorts of many nations, eye-witnesses of the true manner of such like
encounters. But, not to be troublesome in my discourses, I will briefly explain the encounters as they passed.

There was a bar or kind of artificial fence made upon the river Thames, with barges
and lighters chained together, to keep out passengers, which otherwise with much un-
ruliness would have hindered the pastimes and much troubled the performers; but,
being thus hemmed in as it were upon the main seas, the two Venetian ships, as I said
before, falling within danger of the Turkish galleys, endured a fresh encounter, and
long time most worthily defended themselves; but, by reason of the number of the
galleys, they were at last boarded, taken, and carried as booty and prize under the command of a Turkish castle, which represented and bare the name of the Castle of Argeir,
furnished with twenty-two well-approved great pieces, which was contributed and
built upon Lambeth side, at a place named Stand-gates, environed with craggy rocks
as the Castle is now situate in Turkey. After the galleys had taken these Venetian ships
and delivered them into the Turkish Admiral's command, they had sight of another
argosay or galliaza which seemed to be of Spain, which likewise, after a fierce conflict,
they made prize of, and with much triumph tendered the same up also to the Turkish Admiral. After this, upon a sudden, was a thundering peal of ordinance or chambers placed on Lambeth Marsh, whereupon the scouts and watches of the Castle
discovered an English navy, to the number of fifteen sail of the King's pinnaces, making up towards the point, with their red-crossed streamers most gallantly waving in
the air, to the great delight of all the beholders, which as then seemed to cover over
the Thames in boats and barges....In the meantime, the King's pinnaces and the Turkish galleys joined, between whom were shown many strange attempts, even as if they
had ventured their very lives for their country's safety; they spared neither powder nor
policy to sack one another, but on both sides bestirred themselves so bravely, that his
Highness with all the rest of his attendants were therewith much delighted. At last the

galleys, being overcharged with long and forward encounters of the English Navy, for refuge and shelter made now into the Castle. . . . The fight for a time continued fiercely, the victory leaning to neither side, either of them attempting to assault and board each other, but at last the galleys, being sore bruised and beaten, began to yield, where upon the English Admiral fell down, and cast anchor before the Castle, and then spared not in the best manner to thunder off their ordnance, whereat the Turks yielded both Castle and galleys, and submitted to the conquest of the English Admiral, who fired many of the said galleys, sacked the Castle, and took prisoner the Turk's Admiral, with diverse Bashaws and other great Turks, and also recovered the Venetian and Spanish ships before taken by the galleys. . . . Thus ended Saturday's shows upon the waters, being the eve of this great Marriage-day.

The manner of the Marriage upon Shrove Sunday, with the Royal Passage of Prince Frederick and his Bride, to his Majesty's Chapel at Whitehall.

But now to relate and make known the Royal Passage of the renowned Bridegroom and his fair Bride (for the satisfying many thousands) as they entered into his Highness' Chapel at Whitehall, the next day, being Sunday, even overcomes me with a rejoicing description. The Court being placed full of people of many estates, sorts, and nations; and their eyes and hearts fixed to behold the pompous glory of this Marriage in great Royalty, . . . the Palsgrave from the new-built Banquetting-house, attired in a white suit, richly beset with pearl and gold, attended on by a number of young gallant Courtiers, both English, and Scottish, and Dutch, all in rich manner, every one striving to exceed in sumptuous habiliments fit for the attendance of a Princely Bridegroom. After came [preceded by Lord Harington of Exton, her Tutor], the Lady Elizabeth, in her virgin-robes, clothed in a gown of white satin, richly embroidered, led between her Royal Brother Prince Charles and the Earl of Northampton [both Bachelors]; upon her head a crown of refined gold, made Imperial by the pearls and diamonds thereupon placed, which were so thick beset that they stood like shining pinnacles upon her amber-coloured hair, dependently hanging plaited down over her shoulders to her waist; between every plait a roll or list of gold-spangles, pearls, rich stones, and diamonds; and withall, many diamonds of inestimable value, embroidered upon her sleeves, which even dazzled and amazed the eyes of the beholders; her train in most sumptuous manner carried up by fourteen or fifteen Ladies, attired in white satin gowns, adorned with many rich jewels. . . . After went a train of Noblemen's daughters in white vestments, gloriously set forth; which virgin Bridesmaids attended upon the Princess like a sky of celestial stars upon fair Phoebe. After them came another train of gallant young Courtiers, flourishing in several suits embroidered and pearled, who were Knights, and the sons of great Courtiers; after them came four Heralds at Arms, in their rich coats of Heraldry; and then followed many Earls, Lords, and Barons, as well of Scotland as England, in most noble manner; then the King of Heralds, bearing upon his shoulder a mace of gold; and then followed the honourable Lords of his Highness' Privy Council, which passed along after the Train towards the Chapel; and then came four reverend Bishops of the land in their Church-habiliments;

after them four Sergeants of the Mace in great state, bearing upon their shoulders four rich enamelled maces. Then followed the right honourable the Earl of Arundell, carrying the King's sword; and then in great Royalty the King's Majesty himself in a most sumptuous black suit, with a diamond in his hat of a wonderful great value; close unto him came the Queen, attired in white satin, beautified with much embroidery and many diamonds; upon her attended a number of married Ladies, the Countesses and wives of Earls and Barons, apparelled in most noble manner, which added glory unto this triumphant time and Marriage. These were the passages of our States of England, accompanying the Princely Bride and Bridegroom to his Highness' Chapel....

This Royal Assembly being in this sort settled in the Chapel, the organ ceased, and the Gentlemen of the Chapel sung a full anthem; and then the Bishop of Bath and Wells, Dean of his Majesty's Chapel, went into the pulpit, which stood at the foot of the step before the Communion-table, and preached upon the second of St. John, the Marriage of Cana in Galilee; and the Sermon being ended,... the Choir began another anthem, which was the psalm, "Blessed art thou that fearest God," &c. While the Choir was singing the anthem, the Archbishop of Canterbury and Dean of the Chapel went into the vestry, and put on their rich copes, and came to the Communion-table, where they stood till the anthem was ended.

They then ascended the hautpas, where these Two great Princes were married by the Archbishop of Canterbury, in all points according to the Book of Common Prayer; the Prince Palatine speaking the words of marriage in English after the Archbishop. The King's Majesty gave the Bride....

The Garter Principal King of Arms published the styles of the Prince and Princess to this effect: All health, happiness, and honour be to the high and mighty Prince, Frederick the Fifth, by the grace of God, Count Palatine of the Rhine, &c.; and to Elizabeth his wife, only Daughter of the high, mighty, and right-excellent James, by the grace of God, King of Great Britain, &c.

Then joy was given by the King and Queen, and seconded with the congratulations of the Lords there present....

And then fell to dancing, masking, and revelling, according to the custom of such assemblies, which continued all the day and part of the night in great pleasure.

THE COURT MASQUE

Ben Jonson was one of the chief poets of court masques in James's reign. *The Masque of Blackness* established Jonson and Inigo Jones, the scene designer, as royal masque composers for the Stuart family. Queen Anne asked for an opportunity to appear in a popular disguise with black faces, and Jonson penned *The Masque of Blackness* to meet her request. The following excerpt provides first a stage direction that gives some sense of the visual spectacle that played such an important part in the performance. Then the River Niger in Africa converses with AEthiopia, the moon, about the vision that Niger's daughters must go to Britannia to be made white and beautiful. Notice near the end of AEthiopia's speech reference to the "sun" that rules Britannia. This is King James, and as in all royal masques, Jonson pays tribute to the monarch, the main audience of the masque, the one whom the masque is meant to honor and praise. Consider the betrothal masque that Prospero conjures up in *The Tempest*. Note the similar mythic splendor and sense of wonder.

FROM BEN JONSON, THE MASQUE OF BLACKNESS (1605), SEE *IN COURT MASQUES: JACOBEAN AND CAROLINE ENTERTAINMENTS*, ED. DAVID LINDLEY (1995)

(Oxford: Clarendon, 1995) 5–7

At this the moon was discovered in the upper part of the house, triumphant in a silver throne made in figure of a [pyramid]. Her garments white and silver, the dressing of her head antique, and crowned with a luminary or sphere of light, which striking on the clouds, and heightened with silver, reflected as natural clouds do by the splendour of the moon. The heaven about her was vaulted with blue silk, and set with stars of silver which had in them their several lights burning. The sudden sight of which made Niger to interrupt Oceanus with this present passion.

NIGER: —O see, our silver star!
Whose pure auspicious light greets us thus far!
Great AEthiopia, goddess of our shore,
Since with particular worship we adore
Thy general brightness, let particular grace
Shine on my zealous daughters. Show the place
Which long their longings urged their eyes to see.
Beautify them, which long have deified thee.

AETHIOPIA: Niger, be glad; resume thy native cheer.
Thy daughters' labors have their period here,
And so thy errors. I was that bright face
Reflected by the lake in which thy race
Read mystic lines (which skill Pythagoras
First taught to men by a reverberate glass).
This blessed isle doth with that -*tania* end
Which there they saw inscribed, and shall extend
Wished satisfaction to their best desires.
Britannia, which the triple world admires,
This isle hath now recovered for her name;
Where reign those beauties that with so much fame
The sacred muses' sons have honoured
And from bright Hesperus to Eos spread.
With that great name, Britannia, this blest isle
Hath won her ancient dignity and style,
A world divided from the world, and tried
The abstract of it, in his general pride.
For were the world, with all his wealth, a ring,
Britannia (whose new name makes all tongues sing)
Might be a diamond worthy to enchase it,
Ruled by a sun that to this height doth grace it.
Whose beams shine day and night, and are of force
To blanch an Ethiop and revive a cor'se
His light sciental is and (past mere nature)
Can salve the rude defects of every creature
Call forth thy honored daughters, then,
And let them 'fore the Britain men
Indent the land with those pure traces
They flow with in their native graces.
Invite them boldly to the shore,
Their beauties shall be scorched no more,
This sun is temperate, and refines
All things on which his radiance shines.

TOPICS FOR WRITTEN AND ORAL DISCUSSION

1. In Shakespeare's Sonnet 18, the speaker compares his beloved to a summer's day. Considering the first twelve lines as three four-line sections, summarize what the speaker establishes through the comparison. Is his beloved like or unlike a summer's day? How? In what way does the speaker intend to ensure the lasting memory of his beloved?

2. Consider how the speaker in Sonnet 18 and the two lovers in *The Tempest* express attitudes of idealism. Find some examples from the play. Discuss how idealism fits with the romance of the courtly love tradition described in this chapter.

3. Try writing a sonnet for either Ferdinand or Miranda based on their love for each other. What kinds of metaphors or comparisons might fit with Miranda's experience of the island setting and Ferdinand's upbringing in the court of Naples?

4. In *A New Catechism*, what does Thomas Becon see as a maid's chief duty as an unmarried woman and what example does he supply to strengthen his point? What advice does he offer to young couples seeking marriage? Again, how does he reinforce his argument?

5. Discuss the marriage proposal between Miranda and Ferdinand. Does it seem conventional or untraditional? What view or views do you think Shakespeare is presenting about young people in love? How does his portrayal of the couple in *The Tempest* compare with the opinions expressed by Thomas Becon?

6. In *A Godly Form of Household Government*, what do John Dod and Robert Cleaver define as the primary condition of a legal and binding marriage? When might it not be binding? What rights do parents have and what are their limitations? How are the conditions Dod and Cleaver describe enacted in the marriage plans between Miranda and Ferdinand? What role does Caliban play in this situation?

7. Imagine a conversation between a conduct book writer such as Becon or Dod and Cleaver and Miranda and Ferdinand. What advice might be offered? How does Prospero serve as a sage giver of advice and/or a participant with a vested interest in the propriety and outcome of the situation?

8. Compare the marriage arrangement of Miranda to Ferdinand and King Alonso's daughter Claribel to the African king of Tunis. How are they alike? How might they seem different? Write a letter from Claribel to her father describing her newly married life. Alternatively, imagine a meeting between Claribel and Miranda after they become sisters-in-law. What might they share with each other?

9. What strikes you as the most spectacular aspects of the celebrations for the marriage between Princess Elizabeth and Prince Frederick V in 1613? Does the sea fight seem appropriate as a royal wedding festivity? Why or why not? What is the real focus of the celebration at the conclusion of the mock battle? Explain how patriotism fits with the arrangement for an international wedding.

10.   What seems noteworthy about the wedding ceremony for Elizabeth and Frederick? What marks it obviously as a royal wedding? What seems typical of many weddings even today?

11.   Imagine you are a writer for a tabloid newspaper. What headline will you splash across the front page about Elizabeth and Frederick's wedding and what will you write in your column?

12.   Compare the story of Elizabeth and Frederick's marriage preparations and wedding with the betrothal between Miranda and Ferdinand in *The Tempest*. What similarities and differences do you notice? Prospero has sometimes been compared with King James. Can you see any reasons why when you consider them as royal fathers?

13.   *The Tempest* was played during the festivities for Elizabeth and Frederick's wedding. Imagine you are a columnist for a daily newspaper and write a review of the performance, including observations about the court audience watching it and what you perceive as the play's appropriateness or suitability for the occasion.

14.   What visual display is described in the excerpt of Ben Jonson's *The Masque of Blackness*? What news does Æthiopia, the moon, bring to Niger concerning his daughters? How does Æthiopia's speech praise or glorify Britain? How is King James flattered?

15.   Summarize what happens in the masque in *The Tempest*. What is its purpose? How does it create a sense of wonder? Who does it celebrate?

16.   What other visual spectacles occur in *The Tempest* besides the masque? Why do you think Shakespeare includes them? What effect do they have on the atmosphere of the play?

17.   Consider the final scene of Miranda and Ferdinand playing a game of chess. What does this tableau suggest about their future relationship together? How do you perceive the balance between love and the tradition of patriarchy?

18.   Do some research and write an essay about the importance of marriage alliances in Renaissance Europe. Consider the relationship between religion and politics.

SUGGESTED READING

Dreher, Diane Elizabeth. *Domination and Defiance: Fathers and Daughters in Shakespeare.* Lexington: U of Kentucky P, 1986. See especially chapter 2, "The Renaissance Background."

Lewis, C. S. *The Allegory of Love: A Study in Medieval Tradition.* Oxford: Oxford UP, 1936. See chapter 1 on courtly love.

Orgel, Stephen. *The Jonsonian Masque.* New York: Columbia UP, 1981.

Parry, Graham. *The Golden Age Restor'd: The Culture of the Stuart Court, 1603–42.* New York: St. Martin's Press, 1981.

Peck, Linda Levy. *The Mental World of the Jacobean Court.* Cambridge: Cambridge UP, 1991.

Ross, Josephine. *The Winter Queen: The Story of Elizabeth Stuart.* London: Weidenfeld and Nicolson, 1979.

Valency, Maurice. *In Praise of Love: An Introduction to the Love-Poetry of the Renaissance.* New York: Octagon Books, 1975.

Welsford, Enid. *The Court Masque: A Study in the Relationship between Poetry and the Revels.* Cambridge: Cambridge UP, 1927.

6

Performance and Interpretation

This chapter traces the performance and interpretation of *The Tempest* over four centuries, examining ways in which cultural, social, and political influences have shaped the play on stage and in film and ways in which the play has supported and engaged in philosophies beyond the theater. *The Tempest* is unusual in being Shakespeare's shortest, most musical and spectacular play, and these characteristics have opened it up to a variety of interpretations as well as elaborations and adaptations. *The Tempest* is also unusual for the passions it has generated throughout the world because of ideas it seems to encourage about race, class, and colonialism, topics which have been addressed earlier in this book (see chapter 2) but which come to life in new ways in modern times. What a review of responses to the play indicates is that drama is a living art form in which each production remakes and renews the play according to the perspective of directors, producers, and actors of a particular time and place, as well as the technologies available to them. Furthermore, the values, expectations, and assumptions that change with the times dramatically influence the way the play is understood as a work of art and applied as a text to broader social concerns. Art speaks to the world and the world speaks back. The dialogue that develops is instructive of the way that we make culture and society relevant to one another. The relationship between Prospero and Caliban has become through history part of a very rich dialogue that continues to energize Shakespeare's text and exercise imaginations searching for ways to comprehend and reconcile some of the conflicts that have arisen as people attempt to empower themselves and assert dignity, often at the expense of other groups or individuals.

THE JACOBEAN STAGE

Shakespeare (1564–1616) can be identified by his place in history. He is known as a Renaissance dramatist because he wrote during the Renaissance or "rebirth" of humanism that began in Europe in the fourteenth century and took place in England in the sixteenth and seventeenth centuries. He is also identified as both an Elizabethan and a Jacobean playwright because his writing from 1590 to 1613 spanned the reigns of Queen Elizabeth I (1558–1603) and King James I (1603–1625). *The Tempest* (1611), recognized as the last play Shakespeare wrote alone (he wrote two others in collaboration), appears well into James's reign. Little is known about its early performances. On record is a production at the king's court on November 1, 1611, and a second production in 1612–1613 also at court as part of the marriage celebrations for James's daughter Elizabeth (see chapter 5). Shakespeare did not write solely for the court, however, and it can be assumed that *The Tempest* also appeared in public performances in London theaters, as well as possibly on tour outside the city. Compiling accounts and historical knowledge about acting companies, playhouses, and audiences in the early seventeenth century can help us imagine how *The Tempest* may have been performed and received in its early years.

Actors

Before Shakespeare's time, actors were sometimes identified as vagabonds because like other drifters they traveled from place to place as wandering minstrels did to perform their plays. Gradually, however, permanent theater buildings were established and acting companies became more socially acceptable as professional organizations. Their right to perform depended on the support or patronage of Elizabethan aristocrats and the approval of Elizabeth herself. Initially, Shakespeare wrote and acted for a company known as the Chamberlain's Men, which was supported by Lord Chamberlain. When James VI of Scotland became James I of England, he assumed patronage of the Chamberlain's Men and gave them a new title, the King's Men. As members of James's household, the King's Men not only became the leading company in London where they performed regularly, but were commissioned to entertain at court at various times during the year. All plays in Elizabeth's and James's time were subject to a degree of censorship, and acting companies had to register their plays with the Master of the Revels, a regulatory office that had the power to license plays or to forbid them if the content was deemed to be too politically sensitive. Playwrights such as Shakespeare often escaped censorship by choosing historical or imaginary settings for topics that, had they been set in contemporary times, would have been suppressed. One reason Shakespeare can address issues of power—its use and abuse—and treason in *The Tempest* is that he does so in an entirely imaginary context. Moreover, he concludes with a sense of order, even if some loose ends remain untied.

Playhouses

While the King's Men performed at court and possibly on tour, their main venues were playhouses in London. The Globe, a large outdoor theater on the south side of the Thames River in the theater district of London known as Bankside, was built in 1599 with the financial support of two men, Richard and Cuthbert Burbage. Other shareholders were also involved, and Shakespeare became one of them. He was in the unique position of being a theater businessman, as well as a playwright and actor. In 1608, the King's Men also acquired an indoor playhouse known as the Blackfriars Theatre, a venue where *The Tempest* was also likely performed.

The Globe was a polygonal building, three stories high, with an unroofed center open to the air. Spectators either stood in the central yard, crowded in shoulder to shoulder, or sat in tiers of covered benches in the three levels of roofed galleries. Wealthier patrons paid more for the privilege of being seated, while poorer audience members stood around the stage, which was an apron or thrust stage that extended out into the yard providing relatively intimate interaction with the audience whose numbers at full capacity are estimated to be between 2000 and 3000 people.

The stage had doorways on either side of the back wall with an opening or discovery space in the middle of the wall. It could serve as another entrance or could be used for interior action. Quite likely in *The Tempest,* the discovery space might have served as Prospero's cell and then in the final scene as the space in which Ferdinand and Miranda are revealed playing a game of chess. There was also a trapdoor in the floor of the stage for unexpected appearances or disappearances. Behind the back wall was a tiring room or dressing room, roofed as the galleries were, and supplied with a second story that could operate as a balcony for stage action. Again, it is difficult to know how the balcony might have served in *The Tempest,* but it may have provided the place from which Prospero surveyed the other characters without being a part of their interaction. The stage directions at 3.3.18 indicate that Prospero is "*on the top (invisible),*" which may place him on the balcony. For the masque scene in which Juno descends from above, the Globe was equipped with a machine that would have allowed her character to be lowered into the action as if from the sky.

Staging

Some aspects of the staging of a play such as *The Tempest* would have varied, depending on whether it was performed at the Globe or the Blackfriars, and there is strong evidence to suggest that Shakespeare had the smaller, indoor Blackfriars in mind when he wrote *The Tempest*. At the Globe, spectators and actors relied on natural daylight for stage productions, using a symbolic candle or simply speech description to indicate night scenes. At the Blackfriars, productions were illuminated by candlelight. Breaks between scenes were necessary to trim candlewicks to maintain the light. *The Tempest* has clearly demarcated act endings and beginnings, allowing pauses for candle maintenance. At the end of act 4, for example, Prospero and Ariel leave together, only to return again at the beginning of act 5. Their exit and reentrance would seem less unusual if there were a necessary pause in the action. At the Globe, they might simply exit and return immediately. A highly musical play, *The Tempest* includes nine songs and would likely also have included music by consort musicians during the pauses between acts. Spectacle is also an important part of the play; Shakespeare shows his interest in and influence by the masque, popular among seventeenth-century courtiers (see chapter 5). The Blackfriars was called a "private" theater; admissions were as much as five times higher than at the Globe and, therefore, plays tended to attract more upper-class spectators. The music, spectacle, and structural design of *The Tempest* all indicate that Shakespeare had this venue and the tastes of the social elite in mind. Undoubtedly, however, the Globe remained a relevant venue, too, for the King's Men tended to play at the Globe in the summer and at the Blackfriars in the winter after acquiring the second playhouse in 1608.

Two other important observations to make about Jacobean staging of Shakespeare's plays are that props were simple and costumes elaborate. Jacobean playwrights relied on language to set the scene and create the atmosphere rather than complicated sets, although stage backdrops began to appear at the Blackfriars while none existed at the Globe. The initial storm in *The Tempest* is conjured up by the violent, energetic reactions of those at sea, as well as by the description Miranda provides in her observations in the next scene:

> The sky, it seems, would pour down stinking pitch
> But that the sea, mounting to th' welkin's cheek
> Dashes the fire out....
> Had I been any god of power, I would
> Have sunk the sea within the earth or ere
> It should the good ship so have swallowed and
> The fraughting souls within her. (1.2.3–13)

The island also emerges in the minds of the audience through the word pictures offered by its inhabitants. Caliban speaks of "Sounds and sweet airs that give delight and hurt not" (3.2.141) that generate a dreamlike quality on the island, while Ariel describes harsher realities as he reports to Prospero that he has led the trio, Caliban, Trinculo, and Stephano, through "Toothed briers, sharp furzes, pricking goss, and thorns" and leaves them "I' th' filthy mantled pool beyond [Prospero's] cell, / There dancing up to th' chins" (4.1.179–183). The lines spoken by the characters establish the illusion of place that would otherwise not exist on the bare, simple Jacobean stage. Other props would be few, but significant, such as the bottle that Stephano shares with Trinculo and Caliban, the staff that Prospero uses, and the swords the others try to brandish defiantly. The rest would be left to imagination.

Costumes, on the other hand, were a major investment for acting companies and helped to identify the status of the characters within the play. Much is made of clothing in *The Tempest*. The shipwrecked party from Naples comment on how fresh and clean their garments appear in spite of the salt seawater. Prospero tells Ariel to costume himself as a sea nymph, while Caliban wears a large plain gabardine garment roomy enough that Trinculo can seek protection under it from the storm. Prospero himself mentions his magical robe which he takes off and puts on again. Trinculo and Stephano are distracted by a wardrobe of lavish garments that Ariel puts on display outside Prospero's cell, and Prospero transforms himself in the final scene when he takes off his magician's robe and puts on his duke's attire before the bewildered onlookers from Naples. The mythical figures in Prospero's betrothal masque create what Ferdinand describes as "a most majestic vision" (4.1.118), no doubt partly because of the way they were attired. Historical records indicate that acting companies owned clothing that came originally from aristocratic households. In *The Tempest,* the contrast between the garments of a butler or a mariner and that of the duke or prince would have been quite significant, demarcating the status of the individuals as well as adding to the sumptuous visual spectacle that is such an important part of this play.

Although virtually no specific information exists about early performances of *The Tempest,* what we know about actors, playhouses, and staging in general, besides clues picked up from words within the play allow us to make some valid speculations about what an English playgoer in 1611 might have seen and heard.

RESTORATION TO THE NINETEENTH CENTURY

At the outbreak of the Civil War in England in 1642, theatrical activity came to an end. Under Oliver Cromwell's Puritan government, theater buildings were destroyed and acting was deemed a prohibitive pastime, both idle and frivolous. When the monarchy was reestablished or restored under Charles II in 1660, acting began again but became a whole new experience. Playhouses were smaller and fewer, sets were more elaborate, and the stage had a curtained proscenium arch—the fourth invisible wall—as most modern theaters have. Prices for attending plays were higher, meaning that audiences were primarily from the upper and middle classes rather than from across the spectrum of society as they were in Shakespeare's time.

Many Shakespearean plays were revived for the new theaters, and *The Tempest* was one of them. However, like other Shakespearean revivals of the time, this one modified the text so significantly that the production became, practically speaking, a new play. William Davenant, with assistance from John Dryden, composed *The Tempest; or the Enchanted Island* for its first performance on November 7, 1667. They used less than a third of Shakespeare's original text, diminishing Prospero's role substantially, making him both less powerful and more repressive as the governor of the island. Other roles were added. Miranda was given a younger sister, Dorinda, while Caliban gained a twin sister Sycorax. Prospero maintained a young man under his protection, Hippolito. Ariel received a companion, a female spirit named Milcha. While young men or boys played female roles in Shakespeare's time, women became acceptable on stage in the Restoration period and all these additional characters provided parts for an emerging group of female actors. Even Hippolito was played by a woman, as was Ariel in most productions until the 1930s.

Prospero's reduced power meant that he was unable to prevent some dangers and misunderstandings from occurring and leading to potentially tragic outcomes. Ferdinand and Hippolito engage in a duel over jealousy of Miranda, and Hippolito is mortally wounded. Ariel, however, becomes the hero as he provides supernatural healing that restores the young man. Caliban and Sycorax offset the tragic possibilities by being portrayed comically as innocent rather than depraved individuals. Some of the radical changes to the play reflect the artistic tastes of the Restoration period that tended to favor balance and symmetry of one part against another. So, for example, as Miranda marries Ferdinand, Dorinda weds Hippolito. As Milcha pairs off with Ariel, Sycorax joins up with Trinculo. Other changes were both artistic and political. The sailors, for example, provide satiric humor popular in the late seventeenth and early eighteenth centuries with antics that overtly criticized the democratic impulses during Cromwell's Commonwealth before the restoration of the monarchy. In this way, Davenant and Dryden's play expressed explicitly royalist sentiments.

This version or revision of *The Tempest* was extremely popular, being played every year at a theater in London until the middle of the eighteenth century. Samuel Pepys, an ardent theater-goer, called it "the most innocent play that ever I saw." It became even more successful when Thomas Shadwell capitalized on its musical aspects in 1674, revising Davenant and Dryden's adaptation with even more changes, cutting lines to add new songs, dances, and instrumental music, turning *The Tempest* into an opera with elaborate scene designs and machinery that influenced the stage for nearly two centuries. In 1695, the opera was performed with music by Henry Purcell. One acclaimed eighteenth-century actor, David Garrick, attempted to return to Shakespeare's text in 1757, but although his rendition met with moderate acceptance the music and additional characters proved so popular that producers and performers kept returning to them. These post-Commonwealth versions of *The Tempest* represented one of the greatest theatrical spectacles of the time. Not until 1838 did actor William Charles Macready bring performances of *The Tempest* back fully to Shakespeare's text, playing Prospero very much as Shakespeare first created him. Still, the love of spectacle remained, and Macready's production, like many other nineteenth-century interpretations, involved a large ship, a realistic storm, golden sands on stage, as well as Ariel flying around above. On the whole, the approach to *The Tempest* in the eighteenth and nineteenth centuries was to produce a visual and musical extravaganza at the expense of Shakespearean text and simplicity dependent upon imagination.

Presentation of the main characters and their interaction is also noteworthy, for the relationship between Prospero and Caliban, for example, is crucial to any interpretation of the play. The comic Caliban of the eighteenth century was a burlesque creation who often appeared as a deformed character. In an age of moral certainties, Prospero was portrayed as right or justified in his authority and Caliban as deserving of his plight. Gradually, their relationship began to change, however, as outside influences affected an understanding of their roles. The radical theories of Charles Darwin in his *Origin of the Species* (1859) and *Descent of Man* (1871) saw races as separated according to evolutionary development, with "lower" or primitive races having lower mental and moral development. These scientific and social ideas affected artistic directors of the stage, and Caliban began to be seen as a creature between beast and man. Darwin believed that humans evolved from an aquatic animal, and so Shakespeare's fishlike references to Caliban only helped to confirm in the minds of stage producers that this strange creature of *The Tempest* was what one critic referred to as the "missing link" in human development from animal predecessors. One of the most famous players of Caliban, Frank Benson, spent hours in a zoo observing the movements of monkeys so as to imitate their behavior in his role, played in 1891.

At the same time, imperialist activity in the slave trade also influenced interpretations of Caliban. If he was portrayed as primitive or less than human, he was also associated with native slaves and presented as both more potentially harmful and more tragic. In physical appearance, he roamed the stage in some productions apelike on all fours or was decked out in fur and seaweed with pointed ears, fanglike teeth, and long nails. In other productions, he appeared as a noble "savage" in tune with nature and admirable because he attempted to resist a tyrannical oppressor who sought to curtail his freedom. As Caliban grew more sympathetic although less "human," Prospero lost some of his eighteenth-century dignity and moral rectitude. Portrayed as less stately and benevolent and more flawed in his actions and reactions, Prospero shared some of the blame for Caliban's circumstances and for the plight of other characters. In an early twentieth-century production by Herbert Beerbohm Tree (1904) very much in keeping with nineteenth-century traditions, Caliban's role is expanded, overshadowing Prospero, and drawing the most sympathy. At the end of the play, Caliban gestures in despair as the ship leaves the island, placing him at the emotional center of the play.

THE TWENTIETH CENTURY AND BEYOND

If the eighteenth- and nineteenth-century tradition relied on elaborate, realistic stage sets and extravagant music and spectacle for its interpretation of *The Tempest,* the twentieth century began to return to the simplicity of staging more in keeping with original Shakespearean playhouses, as directors and actors continued to explore relationships in the play, most especially the connection between Prospero and Caliban.

While at the turn of the twentieth century, Caliban became the character actors preferred to play, Prospero gained some ground as the century progressed. The powerful actor John Gielgud played Prospero a record number of four times in his career, from 1930 until 1973. Each time, his rendition of the part changed according to the designs of the director as well as his own experience and the shifting views of society. In 1930, he appeared as a turbaned eastern conjurer, in 1940 as a colder individual, in 1957 as a harsh, resentful banished duke whose decision to forgive his enemies was not a foregone conclusion, and in 1974 as a detached, understated but calculating man. The variations show not only Gielgud's versatility as an actor, but the range of interpretations possible for *The Tempest*'s main character. As a general trend in the twentieth century, in noteworthy productions Prospero became less and less the benevolent gentleman and more the powerful controller of everyone around him, especially Caliban.

Caliban's part has been subject to changing perspectives too, and the balance between him and Prospero has become the chief dynamic in the play. Until the First World War, Caliban was seen as an emblem of fallen humanity who desired to rise from ignorance and corruption. After the war and with the influence of Sigmund Freud (1856–1939), Austrian physician who invented psychoanalysis and promoted belief in an interior unconscious, Caliban came to be perceived as the evil that exists within the human psyche.

Increasingly in the second half of the twentieth century, actors and directors interpreted Caliban as an oppressed native suffering under Prospero's exploitation. This perspective grew out of more acute awareness of the plight of minorities such as African and Native Americans. In 1970, director Jonathan Miller explicitly staged *The Tempest* as a colonial play, casting Caliban and Ariel as black characters; one reviewer commented that "It will be hard...ever again to see *The Tempest* as a fairy tale" (Hilary Spurling, *Spectator,* 27 June 1970, in Vaughan and Vaughan, *Critical Essays* 148). Since the 1980s, however, conflicting visions of Caliban as monstrous or as oppressed seem to have coalesced into a single identity in which the character is both brutish and victimized. Such complexity understandably makes the part an appealing challenge for actors, however small the role is in the context of the entire play.

Film and television versions of *The Tempest,* unlike many of Shakespeare's other plays, have been few and far between with no acclaimed production yet marking modern film history. Television tends to lend itself to psychological exploration with close-up shots that do not fit the nature of the play while potential special effects are often undermined by the small screen. What have been more memorable have been several adaptations of the play into contemporary movies. The first is an early science fiction film of the 1950s called *The Forbidden Planet.* This is a story set in 2257 on a planet known as Altair IV. The main character is a philologist, Dr. Morbius, who lives on the planet with his daughter Altaira and their robot, Robby, who serves as an all-purpose Ariel. Men from earth land on Altair IV intent on taking an uncooperative Morbius and his daughter back to earth. What emerges in the action is an awareness of a powerful negative force on Altair IV—a Caliban-like "thing of darkness"—that begins to threaten everyone. As the plot unfolds the invisible monster turns out to be a projection of Morbius's mind attempting to destroy him until in sacrificing his own life, he effectively annihilates the powerful id within. The movie is a study of the Freudian inner psyche as well as an exploration into technology as a valuable but potentially harmful development of science. While *The Forbidden Planet* is one of the best science fiction movies of its time, its acting and special effects are dated enough to provoke amusement from twenty-first-century movie viewers bred on the effects of improved film technology.

The second movie adaptation of Shakespeare's play is simply called *Tempest* (1982). This film, by Paul Mazursky, depicts the life of a Manhattan architect, Phil, who in a midlife crisis flees his job and his wife, taking his daughter Miranda to a Greek island where a goatherd Kalibanos dwells. Miranda is a brooding teenager; Kalibanos lusts after her. The tempest that occurs washes a yacht onto the shores of the island with Phil's wife and her lover, Phil's enemy Alonso. Forgiveness is offered: the family becomes reconciled and returns to New York.

If *Forbidden Planet* turned Shakespeare's plot into a larger-than-life story, Mazursky reduces the parameters of the Renaissance plot of ducal rights, treason, and royal alliances into a simple family conflict without any broad, sweeping ramifications.

Prospero's Books (1991) by Peter Greenaway is yet another adaptation of *The Tempest*, although this one stays much closer to the original drama and uses Shakespeare's language. Greenaway plays with the age-old idea of artistic parallels between Prospero and Shakespeare, having his Prospero engaged in the act of writing the drama as it unfolds. John Gielgud plays this role, as he played Prospero many times before, but this time speaks virtually all the lines of the other characters as he writes their parts while they act out scenes before him. Water is an important image throughout, and at the end Prospero drowns all his books. Significantly, Caliban manages to salvage two: the First Folio edition of all Shakespeare's plays (missing *The Tempest*) and *The Tempest*, which Prospero has just written and that becomes the first play in the First Folio edition of 1623. One critic responds negatively to the film, saying,

> Greenaway isn't so much a storyteller as he is a philosophical enemy of the very storytelling process that Shakespeare perfected. Perhaps that explains why he and Jarman [another film adapter of *The Tempest*], as antinarrative artists, so relish any opportunity to adapt the Bard. Rather than merely making a nonstory film, they can puckishly poke fun at the greatest storyteller who ever lived, undermining rather than servicing his key aim. (Brode 230)

Another reviewer is much more positive, saying,

> The marriage of Greenaway's always extravagant vision with one of Shakespeare's most mature plays is a remarkable union. . . . *The Tempest* benefits from a potent and original retelling. (Burgin)

It is difficult to know why *The Tempest* has not generated more memorable and more current films. That is a topic that bears thoughtful discussion. What is significant, however, are the interpretations and uses of the play in sociopolitical discourse beyond dramatic performances. *The Tempest* has become a cultural symbol representing international conflict generated by colonialism and postcolonial identity. This development began as early as the 1890s in Central and South America but has persisted especially since the 1950s in the Caribbean and Africa where the play is identified as a drama about imperialist oppressors. Leonard Barnes's *Caliban in Africa* (1930) attacks Dutch Afrikaners as creators and enforcers of apartheid. Interestingly, Caliban appears for him as a symbol of cruelty, stupidity, and sloth identified with the

Afrikaners. Twenty years later, Octave Mannoni switches Caliban's identification, portraying Caliban as a symbol of oppressed people in his description of French colonialism in Madagascar. Prospero is competitive and power hungry, turning from a benefactor to an exploiter as he occupies Caliban's homeland. In most recent sociopolitical discourse, Prospero is viewed as totalitarian, while Caliban is perceived as a hero and a rebel demonstrating dignity, intelligence, and sensitivity. There is a strong symbolic Third World association with Caliban. Beyond the stage, then, *The Tempest* has become a highly political document reflecting moral and social concerns of the twentieth and twenty-first centuries. Such uses and readings of *The Tempest* indicate that the play's contexts are multiple rather than narrow and that its meanings are highly sensitive to changing times and varied cultures.

CALIBAN AND EVOLUTION

In the late nineteenth century, Daniel Wilson drew upon Charles Darwin's recent theory of evolution to provide a reading of Shakespeare's Caliban as "the missing link" between apes and human beings. While the ship's crew and Stephano and Trinculo are simply coarse or debased human beings, Wilson sees Caliban as different. He does not have human reasoning powers but he does have an innate affinity with nature and its other creatures, allowing him to be poetic about the world around him. According to Wilson's reading, Caliban inspires the sympathy of a caged animal rather than the contempt that a "savage" human being might evoke. The freedom Caliban receives at the end of the play is something to celebrate. As you read this passage, consider how Wilson might be a product of his own time and how his views strike you as a reader in the twenty-first century.

FROM DANIEL WILSON, *CALIBAN: THE MISSING LINK*

(London: Macmillan, 1873)

...Caliban is...to all appearance in his twenty-fifth year, as we catch a first glimpse of this pre-Darwinian realisation of the intermediate link between brute and man. It seems moreover to be implied that he has already passed his maturity. At an earlier age than that at which man is capable of self-support, the creature had been abandoned to the solitude of his island-home, and learned with his long claws to dig for pig-nuts; and now, says Prospero, "as with age his body uglier grows, so his mind cankers." We may conceive of the huge canine teeth and the prognathous jaws which in old age assume such prominence in the higher quadrumana. Darwin claims for the bonnet-monkey "the forehead which gives to man his noble and intellectual appearance;" and it is obvious that it was not wanting in Caliban: for when he discovers the true quality of the drunken fools he has mistaken for gods, his remonstrance is, "we shall all be turned to apes with foreheads villainous low." Here then is the highest developement of "the beast that wants discourse of reason." He has attained to all the maturity his nature admits of, and so is perfect as the study of a living creature distinct from, yet next in order below the level of humanity. (78)

If we can conceive of a baboon endowed with speech, and moved by gratitude, have we not here the very ideas to which its nature would prompt it. It is a creature native to the rocks and the woods, at home in the haunts of the jay and marmoset: a fellow-creature of like nature and sympathies with themselves. The talk of the ship's crew is not only coarse, but even what it is customary to call brutal; while that of Stephano and Trinculo accords with their debased and besotted humanity. Their language never assumes a rhythmical structure, or rises to poetic thought. But Caliban is in perfect harmony with the rhythm of the breezes and the tides. His thoughts are essentially poetical, within the range of his lower nature; and so his speech is for the most part, in verse. He has that poetry of the senses which seems natural to his companionship with the creatures of the forest and the seashore. Even his growl, as he retorts impotent curses on the power that has enslaved him, is rhythmical. Bogs, fens, and the infectious exhalations that the sun sucks up, embody his ideas of evil; and his acute senses are chiefly at home with the dew, and the fresh springs, the clustering filberts, the jay in his leafy nest, or the blind mole in its burrow.

No being of all that people the Shakespearean drama more thoroughly suggests the idea of a pure creation of the poetic fancy than Caliban. He has a nature of his own essentially distinct from the human beings with whom he is brought in contact. He seems indeed the half-human link between the brute and man; and realises, as no degraded Bushman or Australian savage can do, a conceivable intermediate stage of the anthropomorphous existence, as far above the most highly organised ape as it falls short of rational humanity. He excites a sympathy such as no degraded savage could. We feel for the poor monster, so helplessly in the power of the stern Prospero, as for some caged wild beast pining in cruel captivity, and rejoice to think of him at last free to range in harmless mastery over his island solitude. He provokes no more jealousy as the inheritor of Prospero's usurped lordship over his island home than the caged bird which has escaped to the free forest again. His is a type of development essentially non-human,—though, for the purposes of the drama, endued to an extent altogether beyond the highest attainments of the civilised, domesticated animal, with the exercise of reason and the use of language;—a conceivable civilisation such as would, to a certain extent, run parallel to that of man, but could never converge to a common centre. (90–91)

A COLONIAL *TEMPEST*

In 1970, in a production at the Mermaid Theatre in London, Jonathan Miller directed the first explicitly colonial version of *The Tempest*. Miller wanted to get away from a sentimental or romantic interpretation of the play. He was influenced by anthropologist Octave Mannoni, who used *The Tempest* as a metaphor for the racial unrest in Madagascar. In Miller's production of Shakespeare's play, Caliban becomes a black field hand and Ariel—rather than a fairylike spirit—becomes an opportunistic black house slave. At the end of the play, Caliban shakes his angry fist at the departing ship and Ariel retrieves Prospero's abandoned staff, hoping that it might serve him. The following excerpt is from an interview with Jonathan Miller as he describes some of the ideas that influenced his colonialist production of the play. In Miller's view Prospero achieves maturity by the end of the play. Notice what Miller feels Prospero has to give up in order to achieve that maturity.

FROM RALPH BERRY, *ON DIRECTING SHAKESPEARE: INTERVIEWS WITH CONTEMPORARY DIRECTORS*

(New York: Hamish Hamilton Ltd., 1989) 33–35

Jonathan Miller: Yes, I think that some of the notions of colonialism . . . have only become available to us since we have seen the break-up of the colonial system and of the colonial mind. . . . I think that we can actually now by hindsight understand a great deal more of the relationship of white Europe to the black world. . . . Now once again I wasn't using *The Tempest* as a political cartoon to illustrate the Nigerian dilemma, nor, as it were, to castigate modern colonialism or to expose the wickedness of Rhodesia, but to use the images of Rhodesia, Nigeria and indeed the whole colonial theme as knowledge which the audience brought to bear on Shakespeare's play. . . . Now by doing it in this way I hoped to bring them into a closer relationship with the whole notion of subordination and mastery which I think is one of the things which Shakespeare is talking about with great eloquence in that play.

So often you get rather immature personalities flourishing in the colonial situation because it has in it people who cannot resist the superior technology of advanced society and Prospero achieves his maturity in surrendering his power over his slaves, in leaving the island and returning to the world in which he must actually face his peers and equals, in a society where everyone has access to the same skills. . . .

He surrenders three things: he surrenders the power over his own children, he surrenders the power over subordinates, or at least over helpless subordinates, and he surrenders this impractical desire for power over the forces of nature. By breaking his staff he is doing what the child really does after the age of five—he realises that his rage will not call down the tempest but only produce contempt.

PETER HALL DIRECTS *THE TEMPEST*

In 1973, Peter Hall directed *The Tempest* at the National Theatre in London. John Gielgud was playing Prospero for the third time in his career. The following short excerpt provides insight into the director's mind as he creates his own interpretation of Prospero's role and wrestles with the issue of getting his main actor, Gielgud, to play the part as he envisions it. Hall feared Gielgud might be "too gentle and too nice" when what the director wanted was "a man of power, of intelligence, as shrewd and cunning and egocentric as [Winston] Churchill"—wartime prime minister of England (*Peter Hall's Diaries* 12).

FROM JOHN GOODWIN, ED. *PETER HALL'S DIARIES: THE STORY OF A DRAMATIC BATTLE*

(London: Hamish Hamilton, 1983) 76–77

Friday 11 January [1974]

A run-through rehearsal of *The Tempest*. A shambles with nothing precise, nothing fixed. But it gave me the possibility of seeing how the play was working, or could work, and gave everybody concerned with it the opportunity of getting to know it.

The play is monstrously difficult and I realise with a shudder that five weeks from now we are actually out of the rehearsal room and on the stage.

Gielgud worries me. Prospero is a man who is contained and careful. He does not reveal himself to the audience. He can hardly reveal himself to himself. He is controlled. His passion for revenge is not emotional but puritanical. John shows the agony that Prospero is going through from the very beginning of the play. He should wait until the end. Macbeth has to be played by an actor who is content to act dangerously little for the first half of the play. The technique is the same with Prospero. Except that Prospero must wait until three-quarters of the play is over until he gets emotional—in the masque.

But I am very hopeful.

Thursday 15 January

A wonderful afternoon's rehearsal. We went from Prospero's first scene through to the end of the meeting of Ferdinand and Miranda: the great arc of exposition. Gielgud is becoming contained and strong.... I am happy and free. One of those afternoons when the scene comes into one's head without any beating of the brains.

GIELGUD AS PROSPERO

John Gielgud, a renowned twentieth-century actor, played Prospero's role on stage four times during his career. In the following observations, he comments on two of those performances, in 1957 with director Peter Brook and in 1974 with Peter Hall. Notice the main distinction between Gielgud's understanding of his presentation in those two productions. Also read the previous excerpt, which gives Hall's perspective on Gielgud's Prospero to see how the director's and the actor's views reflect one another. Gielgud also offers his opinion of Caliban's role, which he acknowledges is extremely difficult to play, although he has strong views about what he identifies as a poor interpretation of the part.

FROM JOHN GIELGUD, *AN ACTOR AND HIS TIME*

(London: Sidgwick and Jackson, 1979) 202–204

In all four productions of the play I have acted over the years...I never looked at Ariel. He was always behind me or above me, never in front of me. I tried to see him in my mind's eye, never looking at him physically. It heightened the impression of Ariel as a spirit....

In directing the play in 1957 for Stratford, and afterwards for Drury Lane, Peter Brook conceived the last scene in the play as the great triumph for Prospero returning home to accept the dukedom; I had a beautiful blue robe with a coronet which I placed on my head as Ariel dressed me. At the end, as I moved to the back of the stage, some ropes fell from above, the other characters turned their backs to the audience and the scene changed and became a ship sailing away, then I turned and came down to the front to speak the Epilogue. But in 1974 Peter Hall wanted me to play Prospero as a disillusioned man who had kept his old court suit in his cave for twenty years and got it out very reluctantly. He felt that Prospero did not want his dukedom back and resented having to leave his island. My reading of the Epilogue thus became quite different, more humble and not as grandiloquent as in the Peter Brook version....

Caliban is always a difficult part to cast in *The Tempest*. He must be a tragic figure as well as providing comic relief. In 1930, Ralph Richardson contrived to combine both these qualities to perfection. I remember seeing one production with an actor called Louis Calvert, who wore an animal skin and walked about on all fours like a pantomime bear and was perfectly ridiculous.

INTERPRETATIONS OF CALIBAN

David L. Hirst's study of *The Tempest* includes the following observations about two different interpretations of Caliban. The first appeared in Giorgio Strehler's Piccolo Teatro production in Milan in 1978—done in translation. Strehler, like Peter Hall in 1974, gave Caliban two faces by varying the makeup from one half of his face to the other. This feature was designed to help audiences recognize the complex nature of Caliban's character, as potentially both brutal and dignified or noble. Derek Jarman's film version of Caliban in 1980 is somewhat less complex. Notice in both instances how the interpretation of Caliban is dependent on the understanding of Prospero and vice versa. It is the dynamic between the two characters that continues to give the play its most fascinating appeal.

FROM DAVID L. HIRST, *THE TEMPEST: TEXT AND PERFORMANCE*

(London: Macmillan, 1984) 48–49

Strehler, in his Milan (1978) production, worked in a somewhat different manner [than Hall's 1974 production]. Again, the make-up of Caliban—at a certain stage in the play—was divided. One side of his face became covered in war-paint after the first confrontation with Prospero while the other remained clear. He was portrayed as a black native by a white actor whose physicality was powerfully emphasised. On his first appearance (from the trap in the stage floor) his cursing was complemented by a crouching animal posture which further stressed his brute nature. But when Prospero ordered him to work, Caliban raised himself to his full height, stepped back and looked his master straight in the eye. He immediately became a handsome boy with a beautiful figure and, as he glared at Prospero with wide open eyes, the impression was of a noble innocent cruelly oppressed by a tyrannical overseer. As he turned and slowly walked off-stage his majestic bearing made Prospero, his belt raised threateningly, seem the true savage.

Derek Jarman's Caliban in his 1980 film production is…Jack Birkett.… He is in every sense a grotesque figure: bald, shambling, displaying in grisly close-up his ugly teeth set in a permanent grimace of hatred. Yet his Caliban is irresistibly pathetic despite his ugly appearance, though it would be counter to Jarman's emphasis on the benign and all-powerful magic of Prospero to present the slave in such a way as to discredit the master. A striking shot early in the film establishes his repulsive bestial nature which at the same time retains an intense fascination. We see him breaking a raw egg with his teeth and sucking out the contents with noisy relish. His danger is very considerably toned down. Instead of being afraid of him, Miranda sees him as a figure of fun.

PROSPERO ABJURES HIS MAGIC

The following description from Roger Warren's study of Shakespeare's late plays focuses on the significant moment in the last act of *The Tempest* when Prospero, alone on stage, gives the speech in which he vows his intention to give up his "rough magic" (5.1.33–57). The description comes from a 1988 production at the National Theatre in London, directed by Peter Hall, with Michael Bryant playing Prospero. Warren's account provides insight into the way a play takes shape as actors and directors work with the text and discover new ways of understanding it. In the interpretation that emerges from this production, Prospero turns the speech into a plea for God's forgiveness as he comes to a fuller recognition of what wrongs he has committed in using his magic. Read the description carefully and notice what new understanding Prospero comes to and why he should sense relief or freedom in breaking his staff.

FROM ROGER WARREN, *STAGING SHAKESPEARE'S LATE PLAYS*

(Oxford: Clarendon, 1990) 200–201

But at the second rehearsal of this scene, Hall suddenly suggested that when Prospero says he needs "heavenly" music, he is being very specific: "he prays, asks forgiveness of God" for his indulging in "rough magic"; he promises to break his staff and drown his book, then "waits for the music which will signal God's forgiveness, and eventually receives it" in the following stage direction, "*solemn music.*" The suggestion that the music is literally from heaven transforms the scene. It is also, I think, quite original....

Having hit on the point, Hall then worked on the scene with Michael Bryant in order to explore its implications to the full, with regard both to the gravity of the "rough" magic and to the contrasting connotations of the "heavenly music." At first, Bryant simply delivered "graves at my command" sombrely; but as he realized the full implications of this revelation, he paused in mid-line before "graves" and turned away, his hand across his mouth, unable to pronounce the word, shutting out the awful spectacle. The phrase began to express a major crisis for Prospero: he thus acknowledged his extreme act of *hubris* in "playing God" in this way, and asked for forgiveness. To match the gravity of the fault, the forgiveness was slow in coming. After "I'll drown my book" (5.1.57), he knelt in prayer, a penitent. In the long silence that followed, Bryant assumed that his fault was not to be pardoned...and bowed his head in despair. Then, very quietly, music sounded. Bryant slowly raised his head, hardly daring to believe it, relief flooding his face; and, keeping his contract with God to renounce his magic, he snapped his staff in two and threw the two pieces into the sand.

THE TEMPEST AS POLITICAL SYMBOL

Octave Mannoni is an anthropologist who uses the relationship between Prospero and Caliban as a political symbol as he explores in detail the inter-relationship of colonizer and colonized in twentieth-century Africa. Mada-gascar, a tribal culture, had been colonized by France. Then in 1947, there was a revolt by the Malagasy people. Mannoni attempts to understand the revolt in psychological terms by looking at the nature of Malagasy dependence and identifying in the French an inferiority complex. He sees the combination of a dependence complex and an inferiority complex as the source of the deep-rooted problems in colonial relationships. The following excerpt relies on Cal-iban's accusations against Prospero to suggest that the colonial predicament is one in which the colonized is first made dependent and then abandoned be-fore being taught or allowed to become an equal. This abandonment leads to hatred and violence in response because the culture of the colonials has been destroyed without being fully replaced by another. Consider whether your reading of the passage below gives you any insight into Caliban's role in the play or whether it helps you see colonization differently.

FROM OCTAVE MANNONI, *PROSPERO AND CALIBAN: THE PSYCHOLOGY OF COLONIZATION* (1950), TRANS. PAMELA POWESLAND

(1950; New York: Frederick A. Praeger, 1964)

It is worthy of note that disturbances broke out at the very time when a number of Europeanized Malagasies were returning to Madagascar. Some of them—those who had been truly assimilated—broke with their compatriots, and thereafter had no in-fluence on them. Others, whose assimilation had been incomplete, fomented and led the revolts, for they are the people most likely to develop a real hatred of Europeans. Caliban's dictum:

> You taught me language; and my profit on't
> Is, I know how to curse...,

though over-simplifies the situation, is true in essence. It is not that Caliban has savage and uneducable instincts or that he is such [sic] poor so that even good seed would bring forth bad plants, as Prospero believes. The real reason is given by Caliban himself:

> ...When thou camest first,
> Thou strok'dst me, and mad'st much of me...
> ...and then I lov'd thee

—and then you abandoned me before I had time to become your equal.... In other words: you taught me to be dependent, and I was happy; then you betrayed me and plunged me into inferiority. It is indeed in some such situation as this that we must look for the origin of the fierce hatred sometimes shown by 'evolved' natives; in them the process of civilization has come to a halt and been left incomplete. (76–77)

.... Caliban has fallen prey to the resentment which succeeds the breakdown of dependence. Prospero seeks to justify himself: did Caliban not attempt to violate the honour of his child?...There is no logic in this argument. Prospero could have removed Caliban to a safe distance or he could have continued to civilize and correct him. But the argument: you tried to violate Miranda, *therefore* you shall chop wood, belongs to a non-rational mode of thinking. (106)

TOPICS FOR WRITTEN AND ORAL DISCUSSION

1.   Design a poster of *The Tempest* to be put up in public places in London announcing the play as a coming attraction at the Globe or Blackfriars in Shakespeare's time. Would you make the poster different according to which one of the theaters it will be performed at—the "public" Globe or the "private" Blackfriars?

2.   Music is an integral part of *The Tempest*. Select musical compositions that you think would be appropriate for a version of the play, compiling them on a cassette or CD and explaining where they are to occur in the action. What overall effect are you hoping to achieve: something magical, powerful, delicate, ominous?

3.   Draw a series of costume designs for characters in *The Tempest*. Will you choose a simple or elaborate approach? Will it be modern or Renaissance? How will you distinguish the various groups or classes in the play?

4.   Imagine you are an eighteenth-century theater buff and that you have seen the Davenant-Dryden rendition of *The Tempest; or The Enchanted Island* and then go to one of David Garrick's more purely Shakespearean renditions. Write a letter to a friend in which you advise him or her about which production to see and why.

5.   What does Daniel Wilson mean by the term "missing link" as he applies it to Caliban? How does Wilson see Caliban as different from other characters in the play or from other races or groups of people? Why or how does he find Caliban sympathetic?

6.   How does Wilson's nineteenth-century Darwinian interpretation of Caliban appeal to your twenty-first-century sensibilities? How might you see Wilson as a product of his own time? Does his view of Caliban still have relevance for you? Explain.

7.   What does director Jonathan Miller see as one of the key notions active in *The Tempest*? Do you agree or not? Explain your position.

8.   How does Miller view Prospero as maturing through the course of the play? What does Prospero have to surrender as steps toward maturity? Do you agree that Prospero matures? Explain why or why not.

9.   Miller suggests that he was not "using *The Tempest* as a political cartoon." Imagine you are a newspaper cartoonist and draw several cartoons of Shakespeare's play that might portray it as a political satire. Explain what effect this interpretation of the play could have. What audience do you have in mind?

Alternatively, write a serious analysis of *The Tempest* as a colonialist play. What colonial context might you imagine for the setting? Assume an audience made up of the colonizer and the colonized. How would their reactions be different?

10.   Imagine Caliban as a modern North American aboriginal or black man and Prospero as a white North American of European background. What impact does this have on your understanding of the play and of race relations in North America? (Refer to chapter 2 for background information.) How would you portray the relationship

between Caliban and Prospero? How does Ariel fit into the picture? What would be politically or culturally significant about the end of the play?

11.   Hold a class debate about whether *The Tempest* seems like a colonialist play or a fairy tale to you. Choose sides and draw on material from the play to support your opposing positions. At the end, discuss which seemed to be the easiest position to defend and why.

12.   Read Peter Hall's view of Prospero's role and how it should be played. Do you agree with Hall that Prospero should remain unemotional until his outburst in 4.1.139 when he remembers Caliban's conspiracy? Looking back on Prospero's role prior to that, can you find places where Prospero might potentially display any emotion, positive or negative?

13.   Would you portray Prospero as a "shrewd and cunning" man, as Hall suggests, or as one who agonizes over his moves, or as someone who is in any way "gentle" or "nice"? Offer support from the play for your interpretation.

14.   According to actor John Gielgud, what were the significant differences in his portrayal of Prospero in 1957 and 1974? Find a partner and try reading Prospero's epilogue in different ways according to the varied interpretations Gielgud describes. Do the differences seem subtle or obvious to you? Is it easy or difficult to render the distinctions?

15.   Why does Gielgud suggest Caliban is such a difficult role to play? Do you agree with him or not? Explain why, providing examples from the text.

16.   How did director Giorgio Strehler attempt to convey Caliban's complexity? In what ways was Derek Jarman's film production quite different? Discuss the fine balance in the relationship between Prospero and Caliban. How does the interpretation of one necessarily affect the interpretation of the other and what range of possibilities do you see?

17.   Roger Warren offers a detailed description from Peter Hall's 1988 production of Prospero's soliloquy in 5.1.33–57 in which Prospero gives up his magic. How would you describe Prospero's attitude and behavior as actor Michael Bryant interprets them? Why does Prospero seem relieved at the end? Discuss with a partner whether you think this is a valid interpretation. Can you imagine the scene being played another way, and, if so, how?

18.   Octave Mannoni sees the relationship between Prospero and Caliban as a political symbol. What does the symbol represent to him? According to Mannoni, what is the central issue that creates tension in any colonial relationship? Does reading Mannoni make you more sympathetic to Caliban? Why or why not? Do you agree with Mannoni that Prospero's logic is faulty in his argument about Caliban's attempt to violate Miranda? Why or why not? Study that dialogue carefully as you make your decision. Do you think Mannoni might be too easy on Caliban? Why or why not?

19.   Imagine you are hired as a set designer for a production of *The Tempest*. Draw small-scale versions of the various sets and props you will use and indicate where the sets will change. Use your imagination. What would you do if you wanted to make the stage sets appear as simple as possible? Or how might you envision a more elaborate design?

20.   Choose a scene from *The Tempest* and act it out, filming it with a video camera. Afterward, discuss what challenges you faced, what interpretation you intended, and what effect you hoped to achieve.

21.   Watch a movie or TV version of *The Tempest* and write a review. Or, if you can, watch two versions and compare them, sharing your observations and personal preferences.

22.   Watch one of the modern adaptations of *The Tempest* such as *The Forbidden Planet* or *Prospero's Books* and write your response to it. If you see *Prospero's Books,* refer to the two critics' perspectives offered in this chapter and decide which one you agree with.

23.   Based on the discussion provided in this chapter, do you think stage and film interpretations of *The Tempest* have focused too much on Caliban and Prospero at the expense of other characters and dynamics in the play? If so, why, and if not, why not? Refer to a production of *The Tempest* you have seen or your own imaginative assessment of the play.

24.   Read one of the novels or poems listed at the end of this chapter and review it, discussing how it uses *The Tempest* as a means for further creative exploration and indicating whether you like the work or not.

SUGGESTED READING

Brode, Douglas. *Shakespeare at the Movies: From the Silent Era to* Shakespeare in Love. Oxford: Oxford UP, 2000.

Burgin, Michael. "Prospero's Books." *Pif Magazine* (1991). Mar. 2003 <http.www. pifmagazine.com/2000/07/v_prosperos_books.php3>.

Dorsinville, Max. *Caliban without Prospero: Essays on Quebec and Black Literature.* Erin, ON: Press Porcepic, 1974.

Dymkowski, Christine. Introduction. *The Tempest: Shakespeare in Production.* Cambridge: Cambridge UP, 2000. 1–93.

Hirst, David L. *The Tempest: Text and Performance.* London: Macmillan, 1984.

Hulme, Peter, and William H. Sherman. The Tempest *and Its Travels.* Philadelphia: U of Pennsylvania P, 2000.

Orgel, Stephen. Introduction. *The Tempest.* Oxford: Clarendon, 1987. 1–87.

Vaughan, Alden T., and Virginia Mason Vaughan. *Shakespeare's Caliban: A Cultural History.* Cambridge: Cambridge UP, 1991.

Vaughan, Virginia Mason, and Alden T. Vaughan. *Critical Essays in Shakespeare's* The Tempest. New York: G. K. Hall and Company, 1998.

Warren, Roger. *Staging Shakespeare's Late Plays.* Oxford: Clarendon, 1990.

The following novels and poems represent some fictional adaptations of *The Tempest:*

Auden, W. H. *The Sea and the Mirror* (1944). (poem)

Browning, Robert. "Caliban upon Setebos" (1864). (poem)

Buechner, Frederick. *The Storm: A Novel* (1998). (American novel)

Lamming, George. *Water with Berries* (1971). (West Indies novel)

Roberts, Charles G. D. *The Heart of the Ancient Wood* (1906). (Canadian novel)

7

Contemporary
Applications

While previous chapters in this casebook have explored dramatic and historical contexts of *The Tempest,* including seventeenth-century political concerns, the relevance of magic, and the changing interpretation and appropriation of the play through the centuries, this final chapter turns to more modern issues that share threads of connection with matters in the play. Suggested parallels are based on the assumption that our appreciation of Shakespeare's play can be broadened as we try to see it in relation to the world around us. Topics that are presented here emerge from the concerns in preceding chapters and encompass both political and nonpolitical material.

The first two topics are political. An exploration of the postcolonial tensions in Zimbabwe points to popular contemporary readings of *The Tempest* which see in it a colonial relationship between Prospero, the white European dominant power holder, and Caliban, the "native" dependent slave. This discussion links today's international news stories with colonial aspects of the play addressed in chapter 2 and in the last section of chapter 6. The second political topic centers on the anticorporate globalization movement that has come to international attention at the turn of the twenty-first century. Just as Prospero may be seen as a figure of the political elites in the play, transnational economic and financial corporations appear as the strongest and most influential world elites today. A protest movement has grown up around this transnational power, with a history-making demonstration at the World Trade Organization meeting in Seattle in 1999 to which corporations have since reacted and from which new protests have drawn energy. Again, one can see the Prospero-Caliban tension as a model for this current conflict of interests.

The final two topics stem from more traditional readings of the play as a comedy and a romance in which magic and enchantment frame the drama. A look at what today defies understanding in seemingly "magical" ways—paranormal phenomena—takes us back to the discussion of seventeenth-century magic in chapter 3 and asks us to consider how we respond to the element of the unknown or the mysterious when we live in a scientific age in which so many details of our world can be explained into neat compartments. If a rare individual can bend metal with sheer mental strength, what do we call such a feat? What do we do with phenomena we cannot explain? Finally, this chapter enters the literary genre of fantasy, recognizing that in many ways, *The Tempest,* defined by literary scholars as romance, comedy, or tragicomedy, relates in its hopeful vision of humanity and its enchantment to the magical worlds of works such as J. R. R. Tolkien's *The Hobbit* and *The Lord of the Rings* or J. K. Rowling's popular phenomenon, the Harry Potter series. Although common sense tells us there is no such thing as magic, we embrace these literary worlds because our imaginations love to revel in the realm of possibility rather than being confined to necessity. This last chapter, then, invites us to consider the themes and issues of *The Tempest* broadly beyond the scope of the play as we confront political controversy, marvel at "magical" incongruity, and enter the realm of hopeful possibility.

ZIMBABWE AND THE WHITE FARMERS

> Caliban: This island's mine by Sycorax my mother,
> Which thou tak'st from me. (1.2.331–332)

The Republic of Zimbabwe is a central South African country with a racial mix including a majority of black Africans and a white minority of British descent. The country has been a site of racial strife for over a century since 1890 when white settlers moved in searching for gold and claiming land as their own. The two main African tribes who inhabited the area rebelled against white settler occupation but by 1923 the country became a colony of the British Empire. It was named Southern Rhodesia after its white founder Cecil Rhodes. As one of the last states to break away from Britain's long history of colonization beginning in Shakespeare's time (see chapter 2), Southern Rhodesia claimed independence in 1979 as newly named Zimbabwe and held its first elections in 1980. Independence has not brought peace and prosperity, however. At the center of ongoing tensions has been the issue of land settlement and who has the right to own farm property: black Africans whose ancestors lived in the area before British settlers came or white Zimbabweans whose fore-bears have toiled to make the land fertile and productive, passing on their farm-ing expertise through generations.

This story, which continues to unfold, recalls the issue of colonization as critics have perceived it in *The Tempest*. References to the New World in the play invite one to weigh Prospero's governing disposition against the views of the island inhabitants, Caliban and Ariel, whom Prospero treats as his slave and servant although they lived on the island long before Prospero arrived. The questions of rightful ownership and rightful authority in the play have become such compelling concerns in the context of twentieth and twenty-first century postcolonial times that Prospero and Caliban have come to represent white and indigenous sides of the struggle for postcolonial independence (see chapter 6). The island in *The Tempest*, like Zimbabwe, can be seen as the site of colonial dispute, and the conflict especially between Prospero and Caliban invites one to reflect on a power struggle that involves race, class, and justice. Shakespeare seems to raise colonial questions and leave them unanswered by having Prospero depart from the island at the end of the play without any rec-onciliation between him and Caliban. By contrast, the conflict in Zimbabwe that has continued since independence is indicative of just how complicated attempts to restore justice can be when fallible human beings and international economic repercussions are part of the process.

Prior to independence, the white land grab in Southern Rhodesia was quite blatant. Following the initial colonization, a Land Apportionment Act initi-ated in 1930 extended the white area of Rhodesia, including some of the coun-try's most fertile land, and stipulated that no black African could hold land in white areas. In quantifiable terms, the Act of 1930 gave whites 50.8 percent of the entire land area in the country, while blacks whose population was twenty times the white population, were allocated only 29.4 percent (Cheney 92–93). Blacks were forced off their land so that whites could develop bigger commercial farms. Opposition momentum to the land distribution grew into rising black nationalism, and by the 1960s protest movements and national-ist parties sprang up. Violent conflict also began. By the 1970s an all-out civil war raged, marked by significant casualties on both sides. With no end to the violence in sight, Britain reached a compromise with the nationalists in 1979 in which for 10 years the new independence government could purchase and redistribute land only on a "willing seller–willing buyer" basis. Under these terms, Robert Mugabe was elected as Zimbabwe's first prime minister in 1980.

Mugabe had a difficult task before him. He campaigned on land redistri-bution, which even Britain accepted as necessary and was willing to help sup-port with some financial assistance. However, the small white minority who owned and ran Zimbabwe's large commercial farms contributed enormously to the nation's supply of wealth and food. They also employed vast numbers of black farm laborers and ran schools for their children. Inexperienced black Africans without the proper equipment and training could not be assumed to take over small apportioned sections of farmland and keep it equally viable. The greater problem was how to administer such an enormous redistribution plan and what could be termed a fair agreement for both the black landless majority and the white landed minority whom many—including blacks—believed deserved some compensation for their contribution to Zimbabwe's productivity.

Mugabe seemed to deal with the problem partly by backing down from the issue and partly by presiding over a government that grew increasingly corrupt in its practices. While a small percentage of black families were allocated farmland in Mugabe's first 10 years in power, much of the land that was initially taken from whites ended up in the hands of government ministers and loyal party followers rather than given to the poor. With little to show for his campaign promise, Mugabe brought it back to the spotlight prior to elections in 1990, saying, "It makes absolute nonsense of our history as an African country that most of our arable and ranching land is still in the hands of our erstwhile colonisers" (Meredith 121). In 1992, a Land Acquisition Bill passed in parliament prevented the courts from intervening to challenge what the government determined to be the value of white farmlands, in effect overturning the justice system and robbing white farmers of their property rights. When political action seemed slow, pressure from angry war veterans turned Mugabe's attention back to the land issue prior to elections in 2000 when he promised to fast-track land legislation and appeared to revise his views of fairness even further. He no longer insisted that white farmers be financially compensated at all for their loss and seemed to approve of some black war veterans seizing white-owned farms for themselves. Gangs of blacks invaded white-owned farms and occupied them. They called themselves war veterans although many were too young to have fought in Zimbabwe's war of independence. Many farms were taken by force, and the violence that erupted killed both blacks and whites.

In the June 2000 elections Mugabe's party achieved a narrow victory but an opposition party, the Movement for Democratic Change (MDC), garnered strong support. As Mugabe began preparing for the presidential election in 2002, he turned up the temperature of his rhetoric in his campaign, blaming Britain for the land distribution problem, painting the MDC as a conspiracy of white national and international power, and referring to white farmers as "enemies of Zimbabwe." Mugabe won the 2002 election, giving him another six years in power, but the land issue remains far from settled, and Zimbabwe continues to suffer from unemployment, inflation, and a growing economic crisis, as well as lawlessness, disorder, and political corruption. The problems indicate just how difficult it is to rectify the injustices of colonization without incurring new injustices, especially if those in power have a narrow agenda.

What is happening in Zimbabwe is also a reminder of similar issues needing attention in North America where colonizers once took away the land and rights of aboriginals and built nations in which Native Americans have shared little of the prosperity. Governments now face the challenge of finding equitable solutions for the injustices suffered by generations of First Nations people. Entire government departments have been involved for decades seeking to address calls for native self-government and land and treaty claims. An occasional roadblock or protest reminds those who are not directly involved in the issues that solutions are not easily obtained and require much political fortitude. Shakespeare's Caliban says to Prospero, "I am all the subjects that you have, / Which first was mine own king" (1.2.341–342), a comment that suggests the central colonial problem of unjust subjugation which has wide-sweeping implications for the parties involved in recent times, whether in North America or Africa. The rest of this section includes a brief chronology of important dates in Zimbabwe's history, as well as excerpted quotations that illuminate some of the perspectives and concerns shaping the ongoing land issue in that African country.

Brief Chronology of Zimbabwe's History

1894	Followers of Cecil Rhodes establish a small state in south-central Africa
1896	African Ndebele and Shona tribes are defeated after rebelling
1923	Rhodesia becomes a British colony
1930	Land Apportionment Act passed, giving whites 50.8 percent of country's land
1940s–1950s	Black Africans are forced off their land to allow for larger farms for white settlers
1965	Prime Minister Ian Smith makes unilateral declaration of independence from Britain; Britain refuses to recognize decision; UN imposes trade sanctions
1972	Zimbabwe African National Union (ZANU) begins guerilla war
1979	Republic of Zimbabwe created
1980	Robert Mugabe, leader of ZANU, is elected prime minister of Zimbabwe
1992	Land Acquisition Bill denies courts the right to overturn parliamentary assessment of white-owned farmland
1999	Movement for Democratic Change (MDC) is created
2000	Mugabe's party wins election but MDC wins over 47 percent of vote, 1 percent more than Mugabe's ZANU
1999–2000	Mugabe encourages black farmers to seize white-owned farmlands

March, 2002   Mugabe wins another six-year term as president of Zimbabwe

May, 2002   All white commercial farmers in Zimbabwe served eviction notices by
                Mugabe's government

Aug. 8, 2002   Deadline for eviction notices for all commercial white farmers

Aug. 18, 2002   Dozens of white commercial farmers arrested for failing to comply with
                eviction notices

LAND INVASIONS

The following two passages offer contrasting perspectives on the fast-track land redistribution process that the Mugabe government initiated in 2000. The first quotation, from David Blair's book *Degrees in Violence,* describes joy, celebration, and promise for black Zimbabweans granted farmland taken from white farmers in the redistribution policy. The governor of the province sees the move as a small step toward rectifying an historical injustice. The second passage, from Martin Meredith's book *Our Votes, Our Guns,* describes the experience of land invasions from the perspective of one of the white farmers, Cathy Buckle. She and her husband bought their farm after Zimbabwe's independence in 1980 and had received a certificate indicating that the government was not interested in their property (Meredith 167). Suddenly, in 2000, they were faced with violence and the prospect of losing their farm which they had spent 10 years developing. Notice the contrast in the two perspectives. Consider also the contrast between Prospero's and Caliban's perspectives of ownership, rights, and authority in *The Tempest.*

FROM DAVID BLAIR, *DEGREES IN VIOLENCE: ROBERT MUGABE AND THE STRUGGLE FOR POWER IN ZIMBABWE*

(London: Continuum, 2002) 169–170

The joyful gathering in the midst of an endless plain burst into song....

As Cephas Msipa, Governor of the Midlands province, put aside the hat, he appeared as delighted as the new owners of this expanse of Zimbabwe's soil. A genial kindly figure in his late sixties, ... Msipa had quiet, affable words for everybody. He was even conciliatory about the neighbouring white farmers, whom he felt sure would help the new owners of Vlakfontein. When Msipa spoke to me, ... I found the absence of hectoring aggression, so wearily familiar from the Big Men of Zanu-PF, quite disconcerting. 'We want to live as Zimbabweans together. There is enough land for everyone, all we want is fair distribution. We have begun bringing about that fairness today,' he said. Msipa then gravely told the gathering that he would do 'everything possible' to help them farm successfully and give them, as he put it: 'clinics, roads, schools, proper houses and a good life'.

Vlakfontein ranch was the first white-owned farm to be seized in Midlands province and handed over to blacks under the 'Fast Track' resettlement scheme. On 15 July [2000], barely three weeks after Zanu-PF's narrow election victory, this programme had been launched. As Mugabe never ceased to proclaim, the whole purpose of his government (and presumably of the violence and terror that sustained it) was to allow ceremonies of this sort to take place. What I had just witnessed was, so the propaganda went, the *raison d'être* of the Mugabe regime, the defining testament of what Zanu-PF stood for. Land, the white man's land, was at the heart of everything. Mugabe's passionate crusade was designed to correct a monstrous injustice bequeathed by colonial history. What I had seen, so Msipa told me, was one small step towards putting that right.

FROM MARTIN MEREDITH, *OUR VOTES, OUR GUNS: ROBERT MUGABE AND THE TRAGEDY OF ZIMBABWE*

(New York: PublicAffairs, 2002) 168

Rumours that Stow Farm was to be invaded left Cathy Buckle shaking and sobbing in disbelief. Her initial reaction was to flee, but after taking precautions to send her seven-year-old son away from home, she decided to stay, waiting in fear and trepidation.

The first she knew of their arrival on March 4 [2000] was when her storekeeper, Jane, came running through the gum trees screaming: "They're coming, they're coming. Hide yourself, they're coming." Cathy ran to the house, locking the gates. In the distance she could hear the invaders singing war songs and whistling, one voice shouting above the rest: "Hondo! Hondo! Hondo!"—chiShona for war.

A group of men wearing dark blue overalls came to the gate, calling for Cathy to come out. In the fields below, others began to peg out plots of land. They left later that day, but returned a week later to build a permanent camp, hacking down trees and bringing cattle with them. The police refused to intervene. A large blue tent was pitched a hundred yards from the farmhouse, enabling the invaders to watch every move the Buckles made.

In a dispatch to the local newspaper, Cathy Buckle wrote: "Two small earth dams are now in 'liberated land' and I can no longer water my livestock. I have had to move all my cattle and probably only have enough grazing for another three or four weeks.... When is enough, enough? Can any of us, town and country alike, ever feel safe again when the police refuse to act? I don't know about you, but I'm ashamed to be a Zimbabwean at the moment."

EFFECTS OF ZIMBABWEAN LAND REFORM

The following newspaper article documents the economic and political situation in Zimbabwe at the end of 2002, after Prime Minister Mugabe became more aggressive about redistributing farmlands from white farmers to the black landless majority. Prior to the land revolution, Zimbabwe had a relatively prosperous economy, dependent on the productivity of white-owned farms. As you read about the growing crisis in Zimbabwe in this article, pay attention to the two different sides of the issue, from the perspective of the new black farmer, Makosana, and the former white farmer, Southey, who lost his land. Consider whether the reporter has offered a fair assessment of the issues or whether her perspective seems biased in any way.

FROM SUSAN RAGHAVAN, "ZIMBABWE'S LAND-REFORM POLICIES ADD TO HUNGER CRISIS"

By Susan Raghavan, Knight Ridder Newspapers, Sunday, November 24, 2002

NYAMANDHLOVU, Zimbabwe—Joseph Makosana, 48, is a black war veteran who fought to free his country from white colonial rule. He recently took over a white-owned farm, one of the thousands that once helped to feed southern Africa. Now, he's struggling to grow corn.

Gerry Southey, 40, is a white farmer. Prime Minister Robert Mugabe's government seized his farm two years ago and gave it to poor blacks. Now, it's a wasteland.

The man-made roots of southern Africa's hunger crisis are visible in the lives of these two men at opposite ends of Zimbabwe's controversial land-reform policies.

Although they were born into different worlds, both their lives are imploding from the combustible mixture of long dry spells, political turmoil, colonial wounds and shoddy economic policies. In a resource-rich nation that once was self-sufficient, half the population of 12 million is facing chronic food shortages. This also could worsen the crisis in neighboring nations that traditionally buy food from Zimbabwe, aid workers say.

An estimated 60 percent of Zimbabwe's commercial farms have stopped producing because of government evictions, threats from militant war veterans or fear of arrest, according to the Commercial Farmers Union of Zimbabwe. The production of corn and other cereals has plummeted 70 percent this year, the United Nations says. The winter wheat harvest, the United Nations estimates, will fall as much as 45 percent.

As a result, exports have plunged, bringing in very little of the foreign exchange the country needs to import food, aid workers say.

Zimbabwe "would not be facing food shortages now if they had left the commercial sector to function as it had been before," said Andrew Natsios, the head of the U.S. Agency for International Development. "The disastrous decision to confiscate these farms tore up the one insurance policy the people had to get food."

"Here they are on the edge even in the best of times," said Roger Winter, the deputy head of USAID. "So you get the dry spell and you go over the edge."

Zimbabwe has been on the edge since 2000, when Mugabe, now 78, ordered the seizure of white-owned farms that were on property taken from blacks during British colonial rule. It was widely seen as a move to bolster his sinking popularity.

White farmers, aid officials and Western diplomats agree that land reform is needed to undo colonialism's legacy in Zimbabwe, where whites make up 1 percent of the population but own 70 percent of the most fertile land. But they say the program's fast pace and Mugabe's hardball tactics have spawned violence and aggravated the food crisis.

A dozen white farmers have been killed since the land-reform campaign began in 2000, and nearly 3,000 have been evicted without compensation. At least 300 have been arrested, and Zimbabwe's parliament passed laws in October that make it even easier to seize white farmers' land.

"Time is not on their side," Mugabe said on state radio.

The United States and Europe have responded with economic sanctions and sharp condemnation. In October, Secretary of State Colin Powell blasted Mugabe for "the lack of respect for human rights and the rule of law" that has helped "push millions of people toward the brink of starvation."

"It is absolute nonsense," Mugabe said, defending his land redistribution. "If anything, it's the only way to empower people to produce, not just enough for subsistence, but more. To enable them to enjoy life."

But an estimated 150,000 black farm workers have lost their jobs, and although most of them are skilled farmers, they haven't received any of the seized land.

Nor has Mugabe's government kept its promises to provide tractors, fertilizer, seeds, cattle and training, and Zimbabwe's 140 percent inflation has tripled the black-market prices of fertilizer, seeds and other goods.

Makosana, the former anti-colonial fighter, is proud to have a piece of the land that once belonged to his ancestors, but as he gazes at his untilled soil he sees a bleak future. The soft, red earth that surrounds his kraal, or homestead, in Matabeleland province is peppered with thin, mangled cornstalks. His granary is empty.

On good days, he and his six children survive on black tea and one meal.

Makosana's $7-a-month government pension doesn't go far in these days of soaring corn prices. He and other war veterans who've settled on seized land nearby travel 100 miles south to Bulawayo to wait in long lines for food handouts.

"Help us. We can learn how to get better," Makosana said in a tired voice dulled by months of hunger and dashed expectations. "The white farmers are necessary. They've got expertise."

In a normal year, Southey, the white commercial farmer, would be harvesting his crop of winter wheat now. He also used to grow corn, cotton, soybeans and sorghum.

He exported flower seeds to the United States, Denmark and France. He had 120 head of cattle and 200 sheep.

The cattle, sheep and flowerbeds are gone. On his 4,450-acre farm in Concession, north of Harare, tall, overgrown weeds sway in the wind. Goats are munching on the yellow grass, which used to be emerald green this time of year. Southey dismantled the irrigation pipes and sprinkler system and put them in storage.

"It's a terrible feeling coming to your farm and seeing these people ruining it," said Southey, a trim man with sun-leathered skin.

The farm, which was in Southey's family for four generations, has been carved into 14 plots. Businessmen and government officials loyal to Mugabe own some of them. War veterans occupy the remainder.

Southey's black farm workers, now unemployed, want him to return because the war veterans have no money to pay them. Some militants have threatened them for accepting food, blankets and school fees from Southey, who wants his workers to stay on his farm and safeguard it.

"This is where I was born. I have a right to live here," Southey said. "We've had a good 20 years here. We've built our farm up nicely. We've kept a lot of people employed. And we've contributed to the economy."

In the last growing season, commercial farmers earned $800 million, 52 percent of Zimbabwe's export earnings. This season, that's expected to plunge to $390 million as the farmers' share of gross domestic product drops to 6 percent from 14 percent, according to the Commercial Farmers Union.

Price controls and foreign restrictions have made matters worse, raising food prices and creating a thriving underground economy. The government has a monopoly on trading corn and other grains, which prevents private traders from importing grain.

"Even people who have the money cannot go to the shop and buy food," said Robinah Mulenga, the head of the World Food Program office in Bulawayo. "It's not there."

Malnutrition rates among Zimbabwean children are rising, and hunger is taking a toll on education. Children are dropping out of school to help their parents work in the fields, look after younger siblings or take care of sick relatives.

"Some of the kids are falling asleep in the class because they are not getting enough food at home," said Abednegho Sapuka, the headmaster of the Mbuhulu primary school in the province of Matabeleland. "They are too weak to learn."

In some parts of the country, food has become a political weapon, human rights groups and the opposition Movement for Democratic Change charge.

In Binga, a sleepy MDC stronghold on the shores of Lake Kariba, armed war veterans shut down for two months a Roman Catholic Church project to feed 40,000 children, claiming that the people who ran it supported the MDC. In other areas, Mugabe's ruling ZANU-PF party is accused of doling out government-bought food aid only to people with party identification cards.

"In some areas, many people are in desperate need of food, but they don't get it because they're thought to be affiliated to an opposition party," said Sylvester Phiri, the head of the Zimbabwe Peace Project, a nonpartisan human rights group in Bulawayo.

Mugabe has publicly denied using food to gain political leverage. However, his deputy foreign minister, Adbenic Ncube, was quoted by the nation's independent *Standard* newspaper as telling starving villagers in June: "You cannot vote for the MDC and expect ZANU-PF to help you."

It's no surprise that scores of white farmers—many of whom backed the MDC—have moved to neighboring Zambia and Mozambique, which have welcomed them. Southey, who is thinking about moving to Australia, has appealed his eviction from his farm and is awaiting a court date.

"Things can turn around quickly if law and order is restored and people are given a viable farming option," he said. "Give it another six months. . . . I don't know how quickly we can recover. The whole thing is collapsing quickly."

TOPICS FOR WRITTEN AND ORAL DISCUSSION

1. In David Blair's account of Zimbabwean land redistribution in *Degrees of Violence*, what celebration is taking place? In what way is the event seen as a moment of justice? Try to determine Blair's tone in the excerpt. Is he convinced, skeptical, or antagonistic to the changes taking place? How can you tell?

2. In Martin Meredith's *Our Votes, Our Guns*, what is the central event taking place? Does it seem like a tragedy, an act of justice, or neither? Explain.

3. Discuss how reading both excerpts, by Blair and Meredith, shapes your perspective on the land redistribution policy in Zimbabwe. What is the effect of putting a human face on the conflict?

4. Consider Cathy Buckle's question, "When is enough, enough?" in terms of the whole history of land and race issues in Zimbabwe. Is it possible to see this question from the standpoint of both the black and the white sides of the story? Explain how?

5. In Susan Raghavan's article, "Zimbabwe's Land-Reform Policies Add to Hunger Crisis," we learn much about the impact of the land policy formulated by Robert Mugabe's government. List some of the problems that have resulted. How has the international community responded? Does their response seem appropriate? Why or why not?

6. What specific political actions would you label as corrupt on the part of the Mugabe government?

7. Raghavan's article provides the perspective of two farmers, a black war veteran, Joseph Makosana, and a white farmer, Gerry Southey. What are each of their circumstances? What are their responses? Are they hopeless or hopeful? Angry or discouraged? Do you identify with one more than the other? Why or why not?

8. Reviewing the various perspectives in the excerpted documents, can you name the justice or the injustice of the Zimbabwean story? Is the issue one in which there is a clear right or wrong? Explain your position.

9. Pretend to be a lawyer for one of the farmers identified in these documents. What sort of defense would you prepare? Find a partner who is willing to defend the opposite party in the struggle. After you have written your defenses, present them to the class and open up the floor for discussion of the issue.

10. Go on-line and look on the Internet for recent articles about the political and economic development in Zimbabwe. Prepare a report about what has changed since 2002. Has the situation improved or worsened? Who is in political power and how is the leader responding?

11. Review discussion in this book about colonial perspectives on *The Tempest* (in chapter 2 and 6). Describe how the relationship between Prospero and Caliban can be seen as a colonial relationship based on power and subjugation. Explain how this relationship might offer a parallel to the situation in Zimbabwe. Where does the comparison break down?

12.   Seeing the relationship between Prospero and Caliban as power-based, do you identify more with Prospero or Caliban? Explain why. Do you think the relationship between the two ends satisfactorily? Why or why not?

13.   Imagine a conversation between Prospero and Robert Mugabe. Would one of them have advice for the other or harsh words of criticism or a hint of admiration? What role would class, race, or power play in their dialogue?

14.   Imagine a conversation between Caliban and either a landless black Zimbabwean or a landed white farmer. What would they have to say about their sense of entitlement or injustice, their hopes and expectations?

15.   Consider the aboriginal call for self-government and land claim settlements in North America. Do some research. What are the issues at stake? You may want to focus on one story or generalize more broadly. Can you see the need for change or not? Explain your position on the justice or injustice of the situation.

16.   Compare North America's land settlement problem with Zimbabwe's. How are they alike? How do they differ? Does either one seem more hopeful than the other? Why or why not?

17.   Review the discussion about the genre of *The Tempest* in chapter 1. It can be considered as a comedy, a tragicomedy, or a romance, but has never been described as a tragedy. Consider the real-life stories of land settlement issues in Zimbabwe or North America, and discuss whether they could be seen as tragic or not. How do your conclusions affect the way you may or may not see *The Tempest* as parallel to these unfolding modern stories?

SUGGESTED READING

Blair, David. *Degrees in Violence: Robert Mugabe and the Struggle for Power in Zimbabwe.* London: Continuum, 2002.

Cheney, Patricia. *The Land and People of Zimbabwe.* New York: J. B. Lippincott, 1990.

Meredith, Martin. *Our Votes, Our Guns: Robert Mugabe and the Tragedy of Zimbabwe.* New York: PublicAffairs, 2002.

Rogers, Barbara Radcliffe, and Stillman D. Rogers. *Zimbabwe.* New York: Children's Press, 2002.

ANTICORPORATE GLOBALIZATION

Caliban: You taught me language, and my profit on't
                    Is, I know how to curse. (1.2.363–364)

Gonzalo: I' th' commonwealth I would by contraries
                    Execute all things. For no kind of traffic
                    Would I admit...
                                        riches, poverty,
                    And use of service, none. (2.1.152–156)

From November 29 to December 3, 1999, the World Trade Organization (WTO) met in Seattle for regular discussion of international trade issues. The meetings were interrupted, however, by a mass protest of between fifty and sixty thousand people from across the world representing a broad spectrum of interests from environmental concerns to labor laws to rights of indigenous peoples. There was a strong anticorporate or anti-big-business tone to the protest, as its participants endeavored to promote a message of fair trade rather than free trade (Tabb 4). The protest shocked not only the WTO but the Western world, in general, because never before had so many predominantly Western demonstrators come together against what was an essentially Western phenomenon: free trade and corporate global mobility and power. The demonstration also had an impact beyond Seattle, as it set the tone for a subsequent protest in Washington, D.C., in April 2000 against the World Bank and the International Monetary Fund (IMF). Another protest occurred in Quebec, Canada, in the spring of 2001 against those meeting to negotiate a Free Trade Area for the Americas. The corporate sector reacted, too: the WTO planned its next meeting in Qatar, a Middle-Eastern country with closed borders to shut out protesters; and other international trade and financial groups called for much tighter security at the places throughout the world where they scheduled meetings (Tabb 5). These recent developments in world politics have served notice that there is a new perception about the pursuits of global corporate organizations and new energy for activism against international corporate agendas.

Such issues may seem far removed from Shakespeare's play about an enchanted island and its inhabitants. And yet, as earlier chapters have indicated, *The Tempest* is very much a political play in both its context and its content. Prospero represents the political elite: a duke in his past and future life and lord of the island in the present tense of the play. Caliban represents those who serve the interests of the political elite against their own wishes and with power to complain but not to change their circumstances. In many ways, what the recent protests against global corporate power indicate is that the political elites of our time have gradually shifted from nations and national governments to nongovernment organizations of finance and commerce who are removed from the due process of government laws and regulations and whose influence spreads beyond national borders. In short, if one identifies Prospero as an overly powerful, potentially oppressive ruler, one could say that the Prosperos of modern times are no longer dukes or presidents, prime ministers or kings, but the CEOs of transnational companies and financial groups whose budgets and global influence surpass the power of most heads of state. Demonstrators are protesting decisions being made behind closed doors and corporate hidden agendas that can evade the eye of public scrutiny in ways that government policies in democratic countries never can. Demonstrators are also protesting because they believe strongly in an alternative system of global organization, one that puts people before commodities and the environment before profits. In their voices we can perhaps hear some of the utopian language of *The Tempest* where Gonzalo in particular muses about a society that does not have to engage in the tainted business of politics and trade (2.1.150–172). His dream of a world of innocence and equality where there would be an abundance without riches or poverty reflects the idealism of a political counselor who has seen the corruption of treason and usurpation and desires a new way of doing things that would return to the mythical perfection of the Golden Age. Today's protestors share a measure of idealism, too, or they would not be trying to effect change through raising public awareness and trying to hinder activities of the giant organizations they oppose.

Seattle marked a key moment in the history of protest movements at an international economic and political level. One of the aspects that differentiated it from previous protest movements is that it drew support neither solely from the political right nor from the political left but from across the spectrum. Another distinguishing feature was its reliance on the Internet and the World Wide Web to organize, communicate, and disseminate information. This dependence on modern communications technology marked the protest as a movement of its own time, operating on global terms even as it rejected not globalization itself but corporate power that has been burgeoning in a global market. A third related characteristic of the Seattle demonstrations is that they were largely democratic and inclusive. Multiple groups came together and each of those groups consisted of smaller groups. The Internet organization allowed individuals to link together in a participatory fashion without a ruling hierarchy. Consequently, structurally as well as topically, the protest stood in opposition to the WTO, for the WTO functions on a rigid hierarchy of elites. Finally, what characterized the protest was the predominance of young people. This was the work and the energy of a new generation who had been raised in an era of growing corporate strength and declining government autonomy. They seemed to sense that the way to be heard was to bypass government officials and go to the source of the power they saw as the root of their frustration and indignation: the organization that represented a global corporate agenda.

Criticism of the WTO, the World Bank, and the International Monetary Fund (IMF) before and since Seattle's meetings in 1999 ranges widely across many concerns apart from the central complaint that these bodies operate without any democratic openness. Animal rights activists protest tourist development that threatens the survival of sea turtles. Labor groups protest the employment policies of companies such as Wal-Mart and McDonald's who offer low wages, discourage unions, and hire part-timers to avoid paying benefits. Human rights activists condemn the working conditions and safety issues created by transnational companies who set up so-called "sweatshops" with children and women employees in countries that have few regulations. Peace activists deplore the selling of arms for profit and war. Environmentalists demonstrate against the destruction of redwood forests or the shameful record of oil companies drilling in third world countries. Health lobbies protest genetically modified foods and farm products. Other civil rights groups speak out against racism, sexism, and ageism. Some groups speak out against the lending policies of the World Bank and the IMF who impose conditions on money they give to developing countries that compel these countries to open their borders to foreign corporations, freeze or lower wages, and withdraw funds from health and education spending. The list of advocacy groups is long. What they share is a belief that corporations have wrongly been empowered to exploit and oppress people. What they share in their voice against corporate globalization is indignation that people have become significant only as consumers and not as citizens of a civil society. What they desire in protesting is to shock, anger, educate, and change. They want corporations to become accountable to populations and governments, not simply to wealthy elites.

The preponderance of youth in recent demonstrations raises questions about where this relatively new protest movement will go, for protest is only one part of activism. To effect significant change, activists may need to move beyond placard-carrying demonstrations, although such activities have already yielded some results. A few questions that activism generates are the following: how and where will the young channel their energies as they become the leaders of the next generation? Will the corporate agenda still matter to them? How will they live out their convictions? Shakespeare's *The Tempest* ends with an awareness that a new generation is soon to assume power. It belongs to Ferdinand and Miranda to shape a future that does not repeat the corruption of the past.

Shakespeare leaves us with a sense of hope but also with a sense of uncertainty. Can the young couple handle the likes of Antonio and Sebastian? Will they avoid Prospero's former delinquency of public duties? How will they treat their subjects—as Prospero treated Caliban and Ariel? What brave new world will be born?

The following excerpted quotations present some of the various perspectives on anticorporate globalization. In *On Globalization,* George Soros, who is actually a proponent of corporate globalization, establishes the need for balance between markets and political institutions because they serve different functions. Notice what those functions are. William K. Tabb, in *Unequal Partners,* then defines the two different visions that are in opposition: corporate globalization and what he refers to as the global civil society. From his perspective, globalization is not the contentious issue but rather corporate dominance on the global playing field. Naomi Klein's *No Logo* describes some of the reasons for the development of a strong anticorporate protest movement, pointing out what the profit motive of corporations costs in human and global terms. Finally, Amory Starr offers specific examples of the impact of the WTO on national autonomy and civil and human rights. Reading these excerpts together will provide a broad context for what sparked the mass protest in Seattle in 1999 and the demonstrations that continue in corporate meeting places throughout the world.

FROM GEORGE SOROS, *ON GLOBALIZATION*

(New York: PublicAffairs, 2003) 4–7

Globalization is indeed a desirable development in many ways. Private enterprise is better at wealth creation than the state. Moreover, states have a tendency to abuse their power; globalization offers a degree of individual freedom that no individual state could ensure. Free competition on a global scale has liberated inventive and entrepreneurial talents and accelerated technological innovations.

But globalization also has a negative side. First, many people, particularly in less-developed countries, have been hurt by globalization without being supported by a social safety net; many others have been marginalized by global markets. Second, globalization has caused a misallocation of resources between private goods and public goods. Markets are good at creating wealth but are not designed to take care of other social needs. The heedless pursuit of profit can hurt the environment and conflict with other social values. . . .

Political processes generally speaking are less efficient than the market mechanism, but we cannot do without them. Markets are amoral: They allow people to act in accordance with their interests, and they impose some rules on how those interests are expressed, but they pass no moral judgment on the interests themselves.... It is difficult to decide what is right and wrong; by leaving it out of account, markets allow people to pursue their interests without let or hindrance.

But society cannot function without some distinction between right and wrong. The task of making collective decisions about what is allowed and what is forbidden is left to politics—and politics suffers from the difficulties of reaching collective decisions in a world that lacks a strong moral code....What is less well recognized is that the globalization of markets without a corresponding strengthening of our international political and social arrangements has led to a very lopsided social development.

FROM WILLIAM K. TABB, *UNEQUAL PARTNERS: A PRIMER ON GLOBALIZATION*

(New York: The New Press, 2002) 1–3

The clash is between advocates of free-market neoliberalism who espouse deregulation of the political economy, open borders for increasingly mobile investment, trade, and money flows with minimal government intervention, and worldwide acceptance of Western-style democracy and those who privilege social justice and call for an alternative globalization from below which regulates capital, respects local cultural preferences, and builds a shared international sense of how best to meet global societal needs.

The first vision is called *corporate globalization,* or globalization from above. It is encouraged by transnational capital and international finance and by politicians who stress the efficiency of markets in promoting more rapid growth....The era of globalization captures an awareness that at a certain point in the last third of the twentieth century large corporations became more single-mindedly transnational in focus, seeing their home country as only one among many profit centers and reorganizing their operations to coincide with this vision of a globalized world economy. The large transnational corporations...used their considerable power to influence governments to accept rules favorable to their views of how trade and investment should be focused. [They]...expanded their influence through the creation of new rules that restrict what governments can and cannot do in terms of interfering with globalized corporate interests.

The opposition to this expanding power of transnational corporations is more diffuse and made up of many coalitions. In general, the groups include those who on a visceral level feel their lives becoming more insecure and their future uncertain because of the nature of the changes in the global political economy. These are the organizations of global civil society that offer an alternative vision of globalization from below: environmentalists, labor rights activists, and advocates of the good global society that is inclusive and caring in its policies of distribution and regulation.

FROM NAOMI KLEIN, *NO LOGO: TAKING AIM AT THE BRAND BULLIES*

(Toronto: Knopf Canada, 2000) 338–340

Until the mid-eighties foreign corporate investment in the Third World was seen in the mainstream development community as the key to alleviating poverty and misery. By 1996, however, that concept was being openly questioned, and it was recognized that many governments in the developing world were protecting lucrative investments—mines, dams, oil fields, power plants and export processing zones—by deliberately turning a blind eye to egregious rights violations by foreign corporations against their people. And in their enthusiasm for increased trade, the Western nations where most of these offending corporations were based also chose to look the other way, unwilling to risk their own global competitiveness for some other country's problems. (338)

At the heart of this convergence of anticorporate activism and research is the recognition that corporations are much more than purveyors of the products we all want; they are also the most powerful political forces of our time. By now we've all heard the statistics: how corporations like Shell and Wal-Mart bask in budgets bigger than the gross domestic product of most nations; how, of the top hundred economies, fifty-one are multinationals and only forty-nine are countries. We have read (or heard about) how a handful of powerful CEOs are writing the new rules for the global economy. . . . [Author] Tony Clark . . . argues that citizens must go after corporations not because we don't like their products, but because corporations have become the ruling political bodies of our era, setting the agenda of globalization. We must confront them, in other words, because that is where the power is. (339–340)

FROM AMORY STARR, NAMING THE ENEMY: ANTI-CORPORATE MOVEMENTS CONFRONT GLOBALIZATION

(London and New York: Zed Books, 2000) vii–viii

The 1994 Uruguay Round of GATT (the General Agreement on Tariffs and Trade) institutionalized 'the right to free trade' as having precedence over human, civil, environmental, workers' and governmental rights. GATT's new standing enforcement body, the World Trade Organization (WTO), unelected and meeting in secret, can demand repeal of member nations' laws. Corporations are now protected by binding and enforceable international agreements whose powers far outstrip (while contradicting) the United Nations' International Declaration of Human Rights, which celebrated its fiftieth birthday in 1998, still non-binding and unenforced. Corporations now have global rights. People still do not.

An example: the French government had imposed an import ban on US beef because it contains residues of drugs and growth hormones. Recently the US government took the French government to the WTO, complaining that the French ban was a 'barrier to free trade'. The court agreed, warning France to repeal the ban or face trade sanctions in an amount equivalent to lost sales claimed by the US beef industry. France conformed....

The US state of Massachusetts' ban on products made in Myanmar/ Burma, like other legislation against products made with child, slave or prison labour, can be challenged on the basis that it makes an illegal 'process distinction', a distinction based on an aspect of production that cannot be discerned in the quality of the end product. The continuation of such challenges will make it impossible to use economic pressure to deal with countries committing human rights violations....

... Existing laws must be rescinded if they are shown to be 'barriers', and member nations have agreed not to implement any new legislation that could conflict with free trade. Under this logic, civil and human rights (which often conflict with market freedoms) are not defensible.

TOPICS FOR WRITTEN AND ORAL DISCUSSION

1. According to George Soros in *On Globalization,* why is globalization desirable? What are its pitfalls? What role do political processes have to play?

2. In *Unequal Partners,* William K. Tabb talks about a clash in global visions. What are the two opposing perspectives and how do their goals differ? What is a transnational corporation?

3. In *No Logo,* what does Naomi Klein point to as the perspective that has changed support for foreign corporate investment in the Third World? Why should consumers speak out against corporations?

4. Read the excerpt from Amory Starr's *Naming the Enemy.* How did the World Trade Organization (WTO) begin? What is the power balance between corporations and people? What examples does Starr offer about the negative effects of WTO policies and why does Starr find these examples so unethical?

5. Soros says markets are amoral: they are neither moral nor immoral. Are there ways, however, in which corporations, if not markets, can act morally or immorally? Explain why or how. Provide an example or two.

6. The most recent anticorporate globalization has been represented by a large number of youth. Discuss whether you can identify with any of the causes listed in this section or whether there are other causes that matter to you and that corporate giants seem to exploit. Would you ever be willing to march in a demonstration or have you already done so? For what cause?

7. One complaint against the WTO and other transnational corporate bodies is that they are not accountable to governments or the common people. They are undemocratic elites and operate apart from the participatory process of democracy. Discuss what you perceive as the relationship between democratic government and the global results of the corporate open market system. Do they seem contradictory to you or complementary? Explain.

8. Prospero can be seen as a political elite with enormous power. Do you feel he uses his power justly or unjustly, appropriately or inappropriately, for good or for harm? Explain.

9. Most of the main characters in *The Tempest* come from an elite class of rulers, although Caliban certainly does not, nor do Stephano and Trinculo. What sort of options do the underclass have? Does it seem appropriate to describe Caliban as an oppressed or exploited individual? Why or why not?

10. Imagine setting *The Tempest* in the twenty-first century. Script Prospero as the CEO of a powerful transnational company. How does that change the story? What parts might the other characters play in relation to him? How would their ambitions be modified? What would Caliban's cause and complaint be? Is this exercise helpful to you? Does it allow you to see the play in a new more modern light or does it seem to take too many liberties with Shakespeare's original text?

11.   Gonzalo imagines an ideal world in 2.1.150–173. Why do you suppose that such a society is appealing to him? What are its characteristics? Do you think a decision to protest a global corporate agenda also requires some idealism? Why or why not? Do you consider idealism a positive or a negative quality?

12.   Miranda and Ferdinand are the new generation in *The Tempest* on whom Prospero and the others place all their hopes and expectations. What challenges do you think the couple will face as they take over power of the combined states of Naples and Milan? Is youth in their favor or to their disadvantage? Explain.

13.   Do you feel that youth is to your advantage or disadvantage in any desires you might have to generate change in the political, economic, or social world around you? Discuss this issue as a class and determine whether you can reach any consensus.

14.   Go on-line and research on the Internet some of the recent developments in the WTO, the World Bank, or the International Monetary Fund (IMF) and see if there is still momentum and energy opposing their operations. Have any of their policies changed because of opposition? Have the demonstrations had an effect? What other ways might there be to effect change besides marching in a demonstration?

SUGGESTED READING

Klein, Naomi. *Fences and Windows: Dispatches from the Front Lines of the Globalization Debate.* Ed. Debra Ann Levy. Toronto: Vintage Canada, 2002.

———. *No Logo: Taking Aim at the Brand Bullies.* Toronto: Knopf Canada, 2000.

Soros, George. *On Globalization.* New York: PublicAffairs, 2003.

Starr, Amory. *Naming the Enemy: Anti-Corporate Movements Confront Globalization.* New York: Zed Books, 2000.

Tabb, William K. *Unequal Partners: A Primer on Globalization.* New York: The New Press, 2002.

Welton, Neva, and Linda Wolf. *Global Uprising: Confronting the Tyrannies of the 21st Century: Stories from a New Generation of Activists.* Gabriola Island, BC: New Society Publishers, 2001.

THE PARANORMAL AND FANTASY

If the political and economic concerns of Zimbabwean land rights and anticorporate globalization draw connections to political, almost anti-comic and antiromantic readings of *The Tempest,* attention to contemporary paranormal phenomena and the modern literary genre of fantasy reintroduces the magical world of enchantment and mystery that provides the romantic and comedic impulses in the play. Because of such widely varying interpretations of Shakespeare's play, there is broad scope to consider contemporary applications.

The Paranormal

Prospero: We are such stuff

As dreams are made on, and our little life

Is rounded with a sleep. (4.1.156–158)

Prospero: I have bedimmed

The noontide sun, called forth the mutinous winds,

And t'wixt the green sea and the azured vault

Set roaring war. (5.1.41–44)

In Shakespeare's time, the supernatural represented that which could not be explained in the natural world. Magicians were artists. People displayed great fascination with spells, astrology, numerology, alchemy, prophecy, and divination (see chapter 3). Common supernatural beliefs also centered on spirits, witches, and monsters. Although skeptics existed and a new scientific method of understanding the world was beginning to take shape, much of the Renaissance population accepted without question the reality of magic that bred superstitious ways of thinking. In our age, we have lived through several centuries of strong scientific influences that have caused us to discount many occurrences that cannot be proven by natural laws and through scientific experiment and explanation. Yet phenomena still exist that defy explanation according to natural laws, and there are people in our scientifically advanced Western world who accept, study, or practice "arts" related to these mysterious phenomena which fall under the broad category of the "paranormal," referring to what lies beyond normal experience as an unseen and unseeable reality.

The paranormal can take a number of forms, addressing many behaviors or outcomes that defy common sense or scientific explanation, including ESP (extra sensory perception) which encompasses clairvoyance, the ability to see distant objects or concealed events without any known senses; telepathy, the ability to read minds; precognition, foretelling the future; and retrocognition, awareness of past events. Along with ESP, another element of paranormal experience is known as psychokinesis, in which the mind does not simply sense something directly but has the ability to cause objects to move. An example of psychokinesis is levitation or the ability of material bodies to fly or hover in the air. Larry Kettelkamp's account below about the Russian psychic Nelya Mikhailova describes an incidence of psychokinesis in which the psychic exercises "mind over matter." Gary L. Blackwood's quotation that follows offers a whole series of bizarre occurrences that seem incredible although they have been documented in recent history.

FROM LARRY KETTELKAMP, *INVESTIGATING PSYCHICS: FIVE LIFE HISTORIES*

(New York: William Morrow and Co., 1977) 16–17

At the Utomskii Institute in Leningrad an unusual Russian psychic named Nelya Mikhailova was studied by Dr. Genady Sergeyf. Mikhailova had the remarkable ability to cause certain distant objects to move just by looking at them and concentrating. In one test a large aquarium was positioned six feet from Mikhailova. It was filled with salt water into which a raw egg was broken. She was asked to perform the impossible-sounding task of causing the egg white and egg yolk to separate and move apart. During the test, cameras photographed the activity, and she was wired with electronic devices to monitor her brain waves, heartbeat, and the electromagnetic field around her body. Although human beings are known to have weak magnetic fields, Mikhailova's in even her resting state was surprisingly powerful, being one tenth as strong as that of the earth itself.

As Mikhailova strained to affect the distant egg, her heartbeat first increased to four times its normal rate. Then, just as the egg began to separate, her electromagnetic field began to vary in intensity, or pulsate, at four cycles per second. Her heartbeat and brain waves also changed to the same four cycles per second. Though dizzy and exhausted, Mikhailova succeeded in causing the egg white and the egg yolk to move apart under the watchful eye of the camera.

FROM GARY L. BLACKWOOD, *SECRETS OF THE UNEXPLAINED: PARANORMAL POWERS*

(New York: Benchmark Books, 1999) 43–46

It might be useful to be a "human cork" like Angelo Faticoni, who could float in the water even with a twenty-pound cannonball lashed to his legs; of course, it would be unhandy if you wanted to go scuba diving....

But chances are you wouldn't be so happy to have some of the other strange pow-ers that people have been blessed—or plagued—with. It would be inconvenient, to say the least, to be Jacqueline Priestman; she has so much static electricity in her body that she burns out electrical appliances, and her TV set changes channels whenever she gets near it.

Or imagine being Jennie Morgan, whose handshake delivered an electric shock that knocked people unconscious. Or Peter Strickland, whose presence makes computers and calculators go haywire. Or physicist Wolfgang Pauli who, when he walked into a laboratory, caused pieces of lab equipment to tumble off shelves and shatter.

Even worse, you could be like Bendetto Supino, the nine-year-old Italian boy whose bedclothes and furniture and comic books burst into flame when he stared at them.

And then there are the folks with "magnetic personalities." In the wake of the ac-cident at the Soviet nuclear power plant at Chernobyl, a disturbing number of Rus-sians have reported a newfound ability to make frying pans and irons and silverware stick to their bodies. Some even attract glass and plastic as well as metal. American Frank McKinstry was reportedly so magnetic that if he stood still, his feet stuck to the earth and had to be pried loose.

It's hard to imagine anyone wanting to duplicate the feats of Mirin Dajo. The Dutch mystic regularly allowed a sword to be driven through his body, with no lasting in-jury....He repeated his daring demonstration some five hundred times before he died.

Although the above examples have appeared in recent history, the paranormal is not a modern phenomenon; psychic or mystical experiences have been reported for thousands of years. However, perhaps we find such strange encounters especially fas-cinating and simultaneously doubtful because we live in an era when so much within our awareness—from distant stars and galaxies to minute particles of energy—can be explained or known through physics, mathematics, and other scientific methods. Within our model of understanding, where do we put seemingly "magical" occur-rences such as a report about someone who can bend spoons or other metal objects without touching them? How do we respond to the story of someone who can find an underground water or oil well, or even missing objects or bodies, simply by using a forked stick, a penny, or a bent coat hanger? What kind of response can we offer to the clairvoyance of someone who can describe or draw a map of a location simply by being given its latitude and longitude coordinates? Do we need to see with our own eyes even to begin believing that these accounts are real or can we accept the reports as possible and acknowledge that not every experience can be explained or understood? There may indeed be elements of reality that are unknown and entirely unknowable.

Science, of course, will continue to seek explanations, and society will continue to turn to psychic sources for occasional enlightenment. Detectives and police depart-ments, for example, have relied on psychics to help solve crimes, and organizations such as the CIA have explored the possibility of using ESP as a spying tool. But as one expert, Brian Inglis, acknowledges,

[I]t is safest to regard psi [paranormal phenomena] as the equivalent of the force which prompts people to fall in love: that is, something which happens to and through people, but cannot be laid on in the way that a piece of steel can be magnetized. Some people are more susceptible than others, and become the channel for psi; a few—mediums, or psychics—can sometimes switch on the current, as it were, at will. But nobody has ever been able to switch it on, and keep it on, sufficiently consistently to convert sceptics. (18–19)

Inglis's comment insists that we must dwell with a sense of mystery about certain phenomena that are a part of life. Love, like the romance immediately sparked between Shakespeare's Miranda and Ferdinand, defies logical explanation. Similarly, what falls into the realm of the paranormal—what we might be tempted to call "magic"— remains inexplicable. In spite of scientific advances, our world still cannot be defined in entirely black and white terms. This is part of the reason *The Tempest* continues its captivating appeal centuries after the first audiences were delighted by its spectacle of improbabilities.

FANTASY

Ferdinand:

I will resist such entertainment till

Mine enemy has more pow'r.

He draws, and is charmed from moving.

Prospero:

[*To Ferdinand*] Put up thy sword, traitor—

Who mak'st a show but dar'st not strike, thy conscience

Is so possessed with guilt! Come, from they ward!

For I can here disarm thee with this stick

And make thy weapon drop. (1.2.466–474)

Fantasy is a genre of literature in which the story takes place in an imaginary world set apart from the one we know. Like our world, it contains good and evil and requires that characters make choices, but the setting or the geography of the place is make-believe and is filled with a sense of enchantment. Part of this enchantment comes from the beauty or strangeness of the natural world that is portrayed, and part of it comes from creatures portrayed that are unlike any in the human and animal kingdoms we know. In fantasy, animals can talk, trees can move, and fairies, dwarves, and elves dwell together. None of this seems surprising to us as we read a tale of fantasy because we suspend our disbelief in the same way that we do when we watch a play that includes magicians and spirits or a play about love. Fantasy may not be factual but neither do we expect it to be. We expect, rather, that it is in some sense true, that the plot or the adventure and the outcome are experiences we can understand and identify with as parallel to our own world of conflict and decision, cause and effect, struggle and hope.

Fantasy usually features a character on a journey or quest for something that may not always be clear. The outcome of the quest matters urgently not only for the individual who seeks but for the imaginary world in which he or she dwells where some situation must be corrected or set right for the good of everyone. The character on the quest is like us in that he or she has shortcomings or limitations as well as a desire to do good. That character or hero's strength and endurance are tested in the course of the story and although other creatures or helpers happen along the way, the hero must ultimately rely on personal intelligence and human imagination to pass the tests and fulfill the demands of the quest. Fantasy always includes within the quest pattern elements of magic and the supernatural. Sometimes the greatest delight for readers is being able to participate in this magic simply by following the adventures of the main characters and seeing through imagination the mystery or enchantment of the story unfold. The ultimate satisfaction comes in seeing "the world put right"—the world of love or survival, and life itself.

J. R. R. Tolkien is one of the most renowned crafters of fantasy in modern times. His story *The Hobbit* and his trilogy *The Lord of the Rings* established many of the patterns and archetypes for the imaginary world of the quest story that many subsequent authors would recreate in their own plots. Tolkien invents a place called Middle-earth where creatures called hobbits or halflings dwell in homes dug into the sides of hills in a region known as the Shire. They are simple creatures with simple desires for the small comforts of life: hearty food, a good pipe, and a warm hearth. They hardly seem like the type to seek adventures or willingly face dangers, and yet for Bilbo Baggins in *The Hobbit* and his nephew Frodo in *The Lord of the Rings,* adventure seems to choose them. They find themselves on a quest and encounter many obstacles and magical beings along the way. Chosen to help a band of dwarves regain their Kingdom under the Mountain, Bilbo also has to destroy the dragon Smaug who dwells there guarding mountains of dwarf treasure. Frodo, in *The Lord of the Rings,* has an even greater task than Bilbo had. He must take a powerful ring that allows its wearer to become invisible and journey to the dark land of the evil ruler Sauron where he must throw the ring into the fires of a mountain and destroy it before its evil powers destroy all the creatures of Middle-earth. Although the primary task belongs to Frodo, a supporting company of others travels with him and partakes of his adventures. This fellowship includes elves, dwarves, other hobbits, Gandalf the wizard, and two men, one of whom is destined to become a king.

The three excerpts below, one from *The Hobbit,* one from the first part of *The Lord of the Rings, The Fellowship of the Ring,* and one from the second part of the trilogy, *The Two Towers,* capture some of the magic and enchantment of the world Tolkien has created and the sense of power and mystery that causes the hobbits to respond with uncertainty and sometimes with wonder. In the first excerpt from *The Hobbit,* Bilbo and the dwarves, his fellow companions, have been captured by goblins. Suddenly, out of nowhere, someone comes to the rescue. That somebody is Gandalf the great wizard who uses his magic and his wisdom to lead the captives, hands still tied, to a place of greater safety. Notice how his power allows him great stature and composure in the midst of danger and how he uses his magic for good. Think of how Prospero compares. In the second excerpt, from *The Fellowship of the Ring,* Frodo discovers early in his adventures the power of the ring that has been placed in his keeping. Pay attention to his reaction and the reactions of others when the ring makes him invisible during an otherwise lighthearted song and dance at the inn where he and his friends, Pippin, Merry, and Sam, are staying. In the third excerpt, from *The Two Towers,* Gandalf and the powerful wizard Saruman confront each other. Saruman had been a white wizard and an ally against the forces of evil, but he betrayed Gandalf and the cause for good. Now Gandalf, who has risen to greater heights than Saruman, offers Saruman freedom if he chooses to leave the cause of evil behind, but Saruman mocks Gandalf and remains unrepentant, as well as unprepared for Gandalf's power over him. Consider how Gandalf's response to his friend-turned-enemy compares with Prospero's treatment of his betrayers in *The Tempest.*

FROM J. R. R. TOLKIEN, *THE HOBBIT*

(1937; London: HarperCollins, 1999) 62–63

Suddenly a sword flashed in its own light. Bilbo saw it go right through the Great Goblin as he stood dumbfounded in the middle of his rage....

The sword went back into its sheath. "Follow me quick!" said a voice fierce and quiet; and before Bilbo understood what had happened he was trotting along again, as fast as he could trot, at the end of the line, down more dark passages with the yells of the goblin-hall growing fainter behind him. A pale light was leading them on.

"Quicker, quicker!" said the voice. "The torches will soon be relit."...

Then Gandalf lit up his wand. Of course it was Gandalf; but just then they were too busy to ask how he got there. He took out his sword again, and again it flashed in the dark by itself. It burned with a rage that made it gleam if goblins were about; now it was bright as blue flame for delight in the killing of the great lord of the cave. It made no trouble whatever of cutting through the goblin-chains and setting all the prisoners free as quickly as possible. This sword's name was Glamdring the Foe-hammer, if you remember. The goblins just called it Beater, and hated it worse than Biter if possible. Orcrist, too had been saved; for Gandalf had brought it along as well, snatching it from one of the terrified guards. Gandalf thought of most things; and though he could not do everything, he could do a great deal for friends in a tight corner.

"Are we all here?" said he handing his sword back to Thorin with a bow.

FROM J. R. R. TOLKIEN, *THE LORD OF THE RINGS; PART ONE: THE FELLOWSHIP OF THE RING*

(1954–55; London: Unwin Paperbacks, 1966) 172–173

They made Frodo have another drink, and then begin his song again, while many of them joined in; for the tune was well known, and they were quick at picking up words. It was now Frodo's turn to feel pleased with himself. He capered about on the table...he leaped in the air. Much too vigorously; for he came down, bang, into a tray full of mugs, and slipped, and rolled off the table with a crash, clatter, and bump! The audience all opened their mouths wide for laughter, and stopped short in gaping silence; for the singer disappeared. He simply vanished, as if he had gone slap through the floor without leaving a hole!

.... All the company drew away from Pippin and Sam, who found themselves left alone in a corner, and eyed darkly and doubtfully from a distance. It was plain that many people regarded them now as the companions of a travelling magician of unknown powers and purpose....

Frodo felt a fool. Not knowing what else to do, he crawled away under the tables to the dark corner by Strider, who sat unmoved, giving no sign of his thoughts. Frodo leaned back against the wall and took off the Ring. How it came to be on his finger he could not tell. He could only suppose that he had been handling it in his pocket while he sang, and that somehow it had slipped on when he stuck out his hand with a jerk to save his fall. For a moment he wondered if the Ring itself had not played him a trick; perhaps it had tried to reveal itself in response to some wish or command that was felt in the room.

FROM J. R. R. TOLKIEN, *THE LORD OF THE RINGS; PART TWO: THE TWO TOWERS*

(1954–55; London: Unwin Paperbacks, 1966) 188–189

"The treacherous are ever distrustful," answered Gandalf wearily. "But you need not fear for your skin. I do not wish to kill you, or hurt you, as you would know, if you really understood me. And I have the power to protect you. I am giving you a last chance. You can leave Orthanc, free—if you choose."...

[Saruman] laughed wildly....He turned and left the balcony.

"Come back, Saruman!" said Gandalf in a commanding voice. To the amazement of the others, Saruman turned again, and as if dragged against his will, he came slowly back to the iron rail, leaning on it, breathing hard. His face was lined and shrunken. His hand clutched his heavy black staff like a claw.

"I did not give you leave to go," said Gandalf sternly. "I have not finished. You have become a fool, Saruman, and yet pitiable. You might still have turned away from folly and evil, and have been of service. But you choose to stay and gnaw the ends of your old plots. Stay then! But I warn you, you will not easily come out again. Not unless the dark hands of the East stretch out to take you. Saruman!" he cried, and his voice grew in power and authority. "Behold, I am not Gandalf the Grey, whom you betrayed. I am Gandalf the White, who has returned from death. You have no colour now, and I cast you from the order and from the Council!"

He raised his hand, and spoke slowly in a clear cold voice. "Saruman, your staff is broken." There was a crack, and the staff split asunder in Saruman's hand, and the head of it fell down at Gandalf's feet. "Go!" said Gandalf. With a cry Saruman fell back and crawled away.

Since Tolkien, one of the most recent and highly popular writers of fantasy is J. K. Rowling. In her series, Harry Potter discovers on his eleventh birthday that he is a wizard, that the jagged scar on his forehead marks him as a gifted wizard because, as an infant, he escaped the curse of the dark lord, Voldemort, and that he is about to enter Hogwarts School of Witchcraft and Wizardry. Like Tolkien's Middle-earth, the imaginary world Rowling creates portrays a conflict between good and evil. Harry, like Tolkien's Bilbo and Frodo Baggins, is chosen to struggle against evil perpetuated by Voldemort and his followers. In each book in the series, Harry's courage is tested as he encounters the dark forces in new forms and must act against them. In the first book, *Harry Potter and the Sorcerer's Stone* (published in the United Kingdom as *Harry Potter and the Philosopher's Stone*), Harry and his friends, Ron and Hermione, head out on a night mission to retrieve the powerful, magical philosopher's stone from a hidden place at Hogwarts School of Witchcraft and Wizardry. They believe someone is after it to use its life-giving properties in support of the dark purposes of the evil Lord Voldemort. When another friend, Neville, tries to stop them, unaware of their purpose, Hermione "freezes" him with a spell. Consider how such a spell parallels some of the magic art practiced by Prospero in *The Tempest*.

FROM J. K. ROWLING, *HARRY POTTER AND THE PHILOSOPHER'S STONE*

(London: Bloomsbury, 1997) 197–199

"What are you doing?" said a voice from the corner of the room. Neville appeared from behind an armchair, clutching Trevor the toad, who looked as though he'd been making another bid for freedom.

"Nothing, Neville, nothing," said Harry, hurriedly putting the cloak behind his back.

Neville stared at their guilty faces.

"You're going out again," he said.

"No, no, no," said Hermione. "No we're not. Why don't you go to bed, Neville?"

Harry looked at the grandfather clock by the door. They couldn't afford to waste any more time. . . .

"You can't go out," said Neville, "you'll be caught again. Gryffindor will be in even more trouble."

"You don't understand," said Harry, "this is important."

But Neville was clearly steeling himself to do something desperate.

"I won't let you do it," he said, hurrying to stand in front of the portrait hole. "I'll— I'll fight you!"

"*Neville*," Ron exploded, "get away from that hole and don't be an idiot—"

. . . .

Harry turned to Hermione.

"*Do something*," he said desperately.

Hermione stepped forward.

"Neville," she said, "I'm really, really sorry about this."

She raised her wand.

"*Petrificus Totalus!*" she cried, pointing it at Neville.

Neville's arms snapped to his sides. His legs sprang together. His whole body rigid, he swayed where he stood and then fell flat on his face, stiff as a board.

Hermione ran to turn him over. Neville's jaws were jammed together so he couldn't speak. Only his eyes were moving, looking at them in horror.

"What've you done to him?" Harry whispered.

"It's the full Body-Bind," said Hermione miserably. "Oh, Neville, I'm so sorry."

"We had to, Neville, no time to explain," said Harry.

"You'll understand later, Neville," said Ron, as they stepped over him and pulled on the invisibility cloak.

TOPICS FOR WRITTEN AND ORAL DISCUSSION

1.   Reading Larry Kettelkamp's account of the Russian clairvoyant and Gary L. Blackwood's list of bizarre powers manifested by different people, explain your reaction to these anecdotes. Are you a skeptic? Are you amazed and intrigued? Do you know of anyone with unusual powers?

2.   In the Renaissance, belief in magic and the supernatural stimulated many superstitions. Do you have any superstitions? What are they, what are their origins, or with what do you associate them?

3.   In this scientific age, how far do you let yourself believe in the unseeable or unknowable? Where do you draw your line between belief and disbelief? How would you compare the terms "magic" and "science"?

4.   Why do you think we encourage children to believe in the tooth fairy or Santa Claus or other magical figures when we know they are not true? Do you think we lose our imaginations when we grow up or simply become more aware and realistic? How was Shakespeare, writing about a magician for an adult audience, encouraging his viewers to think about imagination?

5.   What kind of special powers does Gandalf the magician demonstrate in the excerpt from *The Hobbit*? What can you imagine would have happened to Bilbo and his friends if Gandalf had not appeared? In the excerpt from *The Lord of the Rings: The Two Towers*, what other powers does Gandalf possess? What gives him the authority to speak as he does?

6.   Gandalf is a good wizard. Saruman becomes a traitor. How does Gandalf treat his friend-turned-foe? What is your response to the choice Gandalf makes and the choice Saruman makes? Would any other options seem reasonable? Compare Gandalf in this passage to Prospero. How are their responses to their betrayers similar or different? Do you think Gandalf and Prospero would approve of each other? Why or why not?

7.   What happens to Frodo in the passage from *The Lord of the Rings: The Fellowship of the Ring*? How does Tolkien seem to portray magic in this episode? How does Frodo react to the magic and how do others react to him? How do these reactions compare with some of the varied responses to magic in *The Tempest*? Try to think of several examples.

8.   How is magic portrayed in the passage from *Harry Potter and the Philosopher's Stone*? Compare how Hermione uses a magic spell with the way Prospero uses similar spells in *The Tempest*. What are their purposes? How do the old wizard and the young witch feel about their magical powers?

9.   Imagine Prospero meeting with the young magicians in the Harry Potter story: Harry Potter, Hermione Granger, and Ron Weasley. What words of advice or encouragement would he offer? Or, considering that he gives up magic himself at the end of the play, might he have words of caution instead?

10.   What does Prospero rely on to carry out his magic in *The Tempest?* What powers does he gain through his devices or supports? If you are familiar with Tolkien's novels or the Harry Potter series through reading or watching the films, discuss what magical devices appear in Tolkien's or Rowling's stories, how they are identified with the various characters and whether the devices seem good, evil, or neutral and why.

11.   If you are familiar with Rowling's *Harry Potter and the Philosopher's Stone,* refer to chapter 3 on magic in this book and research beyond it to find out more about the philosopher's stone. How does your historical investigation affect your appreciation of Rowling's plot?

12.   Consider what defines the genre of modern fantasy. Are there ways in which you can think of *The Tempest* as fantasy? Discuss how the term may appear useful and how it may seem limited or inappropriate.

SUGGESTED READING

Becker, Alida, ed. *A Tolkien Treasury.* Philadelphia: Running Press, 1989.

Blackwood, Gary L. *Secrets of the Unexplained: Paranormal Powers.* New York: Benchmark Books, 1999.

Inglis, Brian. *The Paranormal: An Encyclopedia of Psychic Phenomena.* New York: Granada, 1985.

Kettelkamp, Larry. *Investigating Psychics: Five Life Histories.* New York: William Morrow and Company, 1977.

Kronzek, Allan Zola, and Elizabeth Kronzek. *The Sorcerer's Companion: A Guide to the Magical World of Harry Potter.* New York: Broadway Books, 2001.

Timmerman, John H. *Other Worlds: The Fantasy Genre.* Bowling Green: Bowling Green UP, 1983.

Index

About the Author

FAITH NOSTBAKKEN is the author of four other casebooks in the Literature in Context series including *Understanding Othello* and *Understanding A Midsummer Night's Dream.*

Lightning Source UK Ltd.
Milton Keynes UK
UKOW06n1016130915

258526UK00011B/111/P